Praise for Uncaged

"Katia is a brilliant teacher and a transformational healer. *Uncaged* is a powerful road map for the emotional reset and rebirth we all have longed for. Katia's journey is our journey, and the deep insights contained in each page help us navigate our own constrictions and blockages as she guides us to our most authentic and magnificent expression. In the process, this very personal story lovingly guides us and inspires us to step into our own power."

davidji, author of *Sacred Powers*

"*Uncaged* is a firestorm of truth—a call to arms for any woman who has ever felt trapped by her own life. This book isn't just her story; it's a manifesto for all of us who've built our own cages through the expectations we swallowed without questioning. Katia's unapologetic narrative teaches us that reinvention isn't about changing who we are; it's about stripping away the nonsense until all that's left is our pure, unbridled, magnificent self. *Uncaged* is not for the faint of heart—it's for the brave of spirit. For anyone ready to stop pleasing and start living, this is THE guide."

Shivangi Walke, founder of Thrive with Mentoring and coauthor of *Unstoppable: Inspiring Stories of Growth*

"Using her own experience, Katia presents a vivid picture of the dilemmas so many women face when we look to pivot a career and relaunch back into the workforce, and regain control over our lives in the process. She dives deep into the connection between breadwinning and power in a marriage and her emotional journey navigating through a harrowing divorce to success on her own terms. *Uncaged* provides hard lessons learned and inspiration for those who find themselves similarly situated. If that's you, *Uncaged* is a must-read."

Carol Fishman Cohen, CEO and cofounder, iRelaunch

"An absolute must-read for every woman! In her poignant narrative, Katia beautifully captures the universal experience of grappling with self-doubt and the nagging sensation of inadequacy. With grace and warmth, she invites readers to confront the cozy confines of their golden cages—where life appears perfect but stifles the soul. This book serves as a compelling reminder to embrace growth and self-discovery, and to seek and integrate the most authentic parts of ourselves."

Pragati Siddhanti, tech leader, lecturer, community builder, and founder of My Swiss Story

"Captivating! *Uncaged* feels like an intimate conversation with a dear friend. Every woman will find pieces of her own story reflected in this memoir, making it a profoundly relatable and empowering read."

Anna Stando, DEI trainer and consultant, and co-leader of Lean In Network Switzerland

"A delightful and engaging read! Katia's story of a 'caged' life vividly illustrates the bars we've built around ourselves, while also revealing the path to breaking free. Both captivating and liberating!"

Karin Kollenz-Quétard, professor of strategy, EDHEC Business School

"Katia's journey from conformity to liberation is a testament to the resilience of the human spirit and the universal quest for authenticity. In a world often defined by conformity and conventionality, Katia's story serves as a beacon of hope for anyone who has ever dared to question the status quo. Her journey reminds us that true freedom lies in embracing the fullness of our identities, that the path to liberation begins with the courage to embrace our authentic selves. *Uncaged* is a heartfelt and transformative read that speaks to the deepest aspirations of the human soul."

Meera Remani, executive leadership coach

"I thought I was about to read the memoir of someone with a fascinating story. Instead, I immediately got sucked deep into reflecting on my own journey. While providing a captivating and beautiful story, this memoir subtly uncovers the imposed, and the self-inflicted, invisible mechanisms that lead many women to feel trapped in an unfulfilled life. This is the book that will give you the inspiration and the courage to break free from what holds you back, make bold choices, and get uncaged yourself!"

Amel Derragui, business and marketing coach, founder and host of *The Time is Now* podcast

"In *Uncaged*, Katia illustrates with power and depth the courage it takes to claim one's true self and live a life of fulfillment. In her compelling memoir, we are swept along by story, identifying with and rooting for the heroine she embodies. In sharing her journey, Katia invites the reader to tap into their own longing and dreams. The fact that her life's work is empowering people to manifest these dreams is icing on the cake. Bravo Katia!"

Mary Jeanne "MJ" Cabanel, MBA, PCC, CPCC, executive coach, facilitator, and senior faculty at The Co-Active Training Institute (CTI)

www.amplifypublishinggroup.com

Uncaged: A Good Girl's Journey to Reinvention

For more information, please contact:
Amplify Publishing, an imprint of Amplify Publishing Group
620 Herndon Parkway, Suite 220
Herndon, VA 20170
info@amplifypublishing.com

Library of Congress Control Number: 2024907023

CPSIA Code: PRV0624A

ISBN-13: 979-8-89138-284-8

Printed in the United States

To my children, my life.
To Michael, my one true love.

A MEMOIR

Uncaged

A Good Girl's Journey to Reinvention

KATIA VLACHOS

an imprint of Amplify Publishing Group

CONTENTS

PART THREE

Preface

I WROTE THIS BOOK because I wanted you to know that there is a way out.

I wanted to reassure you that what you're going through is real, even if others in your life may tell you it's not.

I see you.

You are not alone. There are many of us in similar situations, experiencing the same emotions.

So many of us—talented, capable, ambitious, hard-working, responsible, brilliant women—find ourselves stuck at one point or another, feeling trapped, disconnected from our desires, our needs, ourselves; overwhelmed by all the demands and expectations placed on us (or that we place on ourselves); perpetually overcome by guilt; left aimless, frustrated, and, often, resentful.

We find ourselves caged.

While we may not know quite how we got here, it wasn't always this way. When we first arrived in the world, we were pure, unconstrained, magnificent. That was our essence.

Even so, most of us entered our cages early in life, through no fault of our own. It happened because of the way we were raised and the messages we received over and over around what we needed to do (put others' needs first, achieve, check all the "right" boxes) and who we needed to be ("good") to be worthy of appreciation. To be worthy of love.

1

Whether those messages were loud or subtle, explicit or implied, the outcome was always the same: they lodged themselves deeply within our souls. They became second nature and part of our identity. They were the lens through which we came to see ourselves and the world. And they kept us small, quiet, working constantly, harder and harder, to achieve something that should have been our birthright: being worthy of love, worthy of realizing our true selves.

Because it is your birthright to be loved unconditionally, simply for who you are, and to realize your potential. You weren't born magnificent just to be stuck in a cage.

Of course, our cages are often comfortable, sometimes even golden—and I suspect that you, like myself, are grateful for what life has given you—but they are cages, nevertheless.

Perhaps you've caught yourself too often, in the midst of your daily activities, wondering, *Is this all there is? Is this really my life?* And maybe you've felt guilty for even asking those questions.

Maybe you had big dreams and aspirations to make a difference in the world, and now you're wondering what happened to them, asking yourself, *Is it too late for me?*

Or there may be times when you feel like you don't recognize who you are anymore or whose life you're living.

You probably know, deep down (or not-so-deep-down), that something needs to change, that you're ready for things to be different in your life, but you have no idea how or where to start—and just thinking about that fills you with overwhelm.

And then there's the ever-present fear, obligation, and guilt. You wonder if wanting to change things will harm your loved ones or if you're being selfish for wanting more.

On those days, it may feel like you have no control over your life, that you're powerless and will stay in the cage forever, so you might as well make yourself comfortable. But there are also days when you can't ignore the fire growing inside you, that inner voice telling you there is more—you just need to reach for it.

If any of this resonates, then this book is for you.

I see you.

I was you.

I was caged.

And I got out.

This is the story of how I did that. I had to reclaim myself before I could reinvent myself. Why? Because the only way to find out what you truly want and how to get it is to know who you truly are, at your core, beneath all the layers you've accumulated over the years (and I'm not talking about those around the hips). Reconnecting to the essence of who I was—who I am—allowed me to take down the bars of my cage (my "good girl" conditioning), one by one, in order to leave it behind. When you remember and reclaim your true essence, magic happens. It happened for me, and it can happen for you.

My hope for this book is that it offers you both an inside view and a promise: that we can overcome the Saboteurs—the ones in our own minds and those outside us—who judge and limit us (even if they claim it's an act of love). We can risk, change, forgive, and grow. We can find genuine meaning and purpose. We can carve out a life on our own terms. We can create home and belonging and even love, no matter where in the world we find ourselves.

My path—from my beautiful, promising beginnings, to my years in the cage, to life on the other side—doesn't have to be yours. You will find your own path. How do I know? Because you are magnificent and worthy of everything you desire, simply because you are (no qualifier necessary). I hope my story inspires you to step out of the cage and fly free.

I'm rooting for you.

Prologue

"It's one of the inescapable truisms of life.
You have to lose yourself to find yourself, give
yourself away to get everything back."
— David Brooks, *The Second Mountain:
The Quest for a Moral Life*

"The biggest concentration camp is in your
mind, and the key is in your pocket."
— Dr. Edith Eger, Auschwitz survivor

IT'S JUST MY DAD AND ME in the small chapel of the cemetery where the service will take place.

The cemetery is built on a hill overlooking the whole of Athens. Even though it's a five-minute drive from my parents' place, I've never visited and it takes me by surprise. *What a breathtaking view—for no one to enjoy*, I think.

I arrive early and ask the man from the funeral home to open the casket for me. "I wasn't here when he passed away," I say. "I live abroad, you know. I didn't get the chance to say goodbye."

The man's eyes are kind. He nods and motions me to follow him into the chapel. Together with one of his colleagues, they gently lift the cover. "Call us when you're done," he says, and they leave.

My father looks sharp in his suit and tie. His hands are clasped just below his chest and there's an arrangement of tiny white flowers—baby's breath?—that look as if they're sprouting from between his fingers. He's not wearing his wedding ring; my mother must have removed it to keep. Babás* looks fresh, almost youthful, the skin on his face shiny and smooth, as if it were made of wax, not grey and tired like it was the last time I saw him. When I place my palm to his cheek it feels cold, slippery. Somehow, this startles me and I pull back.

But his expression is peaceful, calm, no longer strained. I swear, I even detect a hint of his mischievous smile—the one he wore when he had done something he knew would set off my mom or me—or maybe I'm making it up because this is how I want to remember him. My dad could tease me all he wanted; I knew he had my back. Still, his rebellious nature ticked me off, perhaps because I was trying so hard to suppress my own.

I dare to stretch out my hand again and place it on his crossed hands. I've never touched a dead person before. I sit here for a while, silent, like I used to do in the afternoons when I visited him. I'd sit on a folding chair next to him while he dozed, too weak to have a conversation. I'd hold my book or type out emails with one hand, always holding his hand with the other.

I lean toward my father's ear. "I miss you," I whisper, glancing around me to make sure I'm still alone. My eyes fill with tears and the knot in my throat becomes so tight it threatens to choke. I close my eyes and try to slow my breathing.

In my mind, I can hear my father's voice. "It's ok. You'll be ok. I won't let anything happen to you."

---

*   In Greek, *Babás* is a familial nickname for "Dad."

PART
ONE

CHAPTER 1

Broken Glass

"Such silence has an actual sound,
the sound of disappearance."
— Suzanne Finnamore, *Split: A Memoir of Divorce*

I BECOME AWARE OF MY LACK OF AGENCY over my own life on a grey November Sunday afternoon in the kitchen of our home in Zollikon, an affluent suburb of Zurich. I'm making spaghetti Bolognese— comfort food. Our two teens are in their rooms, doors closed, and our four-year-old is watching his favorite cartoon. I have a twenty-minute opening to prepare the meat sauce.

I grab a deep frying pan from below the stove, pour in the olive oil, and turn the heat to medium-high. I'm wearing single-use latex gloves as I chop the onion and garlic—a trick my best friend, who's a passionate cook, taught me after I complained my fingertips smelled like food for days after cooking. By the time I'm done chopping, the oil is hot enough; the onion sizzles as I toss it in the pan. Stirring, I watch as the onion becomes translucent, an almost meditative task.

I don't hear my husband walk in.

"Where's the little guy?" he asks.

"Watching a cartoon," I say, and then quickly add, "I was just about to go get him."

"Should he be watching so much TV?" My body tenses. I don't answer.

We're going through another rough patch in our marriage, which feels more and more like a series of rough patches punctuated by a few redeeming moments. Parenting is one of our points of contention. I'm either overprotective, like my mother, or too soft, not directive enough, a pushover. Letting our youngest watch television is yet another example of my subpar parenting.

Despite the tension, we manage to keep the peace at home—for the kids, the nanny, in the presence of our friends. No public arguments, no raised voices, no sulking. But behind the closed doors of our bedroom, that peace is heavy; it wraps itself around my shoulders and chest like an iron blanket, and I find myself gasping for air.

We've talked about separation. We go back and forth, agreeing it's best and then deciding to give the marriage another try. Like the definition of insanity, we keep hoping the situation will improve if we keep doing the same things. When all of it gets to be too much, we use stopgap measures like going away—spending time apart—for a few days. Viktor goes on business trips, and I take off to see friends or family.

I look up from the frying pan to catch the last rays of winter sun—softer and cooler than the lush summer sunsets I'm used to at home in Greece. We moved here from our house down the road a few months ago, in the summer of 2014. I searched for a space where I could create a home for the children and myself; this renovated old stone house felt like home the minute I entered. It was the light flooding the living area through the floor-to-ceiling windows; the spacious dining room where I imagined Sunday lunches around a massive rustic wooden table we hadn't bought yet; the generous, sunlit attic with the light wooden floors, where I had a vision of myself sitting at my desk overlooking the lake, writing again.

I always missed the light. I needed more of it in my life. I longed to get back to my writing and was excited to have a space that was exclusively my own, not also the guest room, as in our last house in Vienna.

"Enough cartoons." Viktor's voice is sharp. "I'll go get him." He turns to go, then hesitates. "Did you see my email about the girls?"

He sent it while I was in Vienna over the weekend, visiting a friend. In it, he asked if it's okay for his two nieces, his older brother's young adult twin daughters, to come live with us for three months starting in the new year. *"Lizi and Astrid are doing a gap year and would love to get to know Switzerland. They'll help with the household and can even take care of the little guy so we can save on the nanny, and you can do your work. It's a win-win."*

"Yes, I saw it."

"And?" He bounces from one foot to the other.

"I don't know, Viktor." He stops moving and looks at me. "It's just not a good time for me," I say softly. "I'm committed to finishing my book by the summer. I can't care for six at the same time. I'm sorry, but I can't do this right now."

I know from experience that the burden of running the household will fall to me, despite good intentions from all parties involved. My husband is gone most of the time, either traveling or at evening work events. I worked hard to make sure everyone was settled in the new house. It took much longer than the three months I had budgeted. I should have known—I've done the research. After all, I'm writing a book about how to make successful moves.

Things are good. We've unpacked all the boxes, and all three kids are feeling settled in their rooms. I've set up my home office and begun to get back into the flow; I'm finally making progress. My goal is to finish the manuscript by summer and pitch it to publishers.

Now, my husband is asking me to run a household of six for the next three months: plan meals, go shopping, do laundry, all while doing the "usual" stuff with the kids—homework, playdates, doctors' appointments. I'm not willing. After giving up my career as a defense analyst and taking a step back for almost a decade to raise our children, I'm done being the one to make all the professional sacrifices. I want to focus on my future, on what's important to me.

I feel at peace with my position on this. I expect him to understand. He prides himself on being so supportive of my career.

Not tonight.

"It's selfish of you to prioritize your book project over family." His voice is cold and a bit shaky. His lips are pressed tightly as he waits for my response.

Did he just say, book "project"?!

Viktor considers my work a hobby, a "project" that keeps me occupied.

"So, it wasn't really a question, was it?" My throat feels tight. "You just want my consent for something that you've already decided is happening."

It's not the first time. In the past, I've chaffed but accommodated.

"Family means that you're always welcome," he throws me a familiar line, "not just when it's convenient. How can you be so selfish?"

There's that word again.

"Am I selfish for wanting to create something for myself? For wanting a new career after I gave up the one I had to follow you to Vienna? How will that ever happen if I keep putting myself last?"

"Well, that's disappointing, Katia." There's contempt in his voice. "But I won't back down, not this time. The girls are coming to stay with us, whether you like it or not." He storms out of the kitchen.

I'm used to his attacks on my character, but this is the first time he flat-out overrules me. Or perhaps it's the first time he *needs* to overrule me.

The smell of burning onions wafts through the kitchen. I pour the contents of the frying pan into the garbage. My hands tremble as I pull another pair of rubber gloves from the drawer and set to chopping another onion. Suddenly, I feel cold. My body is shaking, and I can't stop it.

CHAPTER 2

My Father's Daughter

"If you look deeply into the palm of your hand,
you will see your parents and all generations
of your ancestors. All of them are alive in this
moment. Each is present in your body. You are
the continuation of each of these people."
— Thich Nhat Hanh, *Present Moment Wonderful
Moment: Mindfulness Verses for Daily Living*

MY FATHER WAS THE PROVERBIAL GREEK MAN. He
was large, exuberant, a patriarch, a free spirit; his presence filled any room
he entered. He was also a notorious charmer. Babá loved women—or, as
he liked to say, he "appreciated beauty." The ways in which he appreciated
beauty didn't always sit well with my mother—or later, with me. My father
had a way of homing in on the most attractive woman in any room. He
could then be counted on to stare or walk over and start flirting. Age was
immaterial. And his charms were boundless and unfailing; no woman
seemed capable of resisting. When faced with my mother's (justified) indignation, his defense was to disarm her: he was simply an admirer of beauty.

If my dad's behavior ever got to my mother, she never let it show. Most
women would have been enraged, regularly. I once asked her how she'd
kept her cool all those years. It was simply a matter of confidence, she said,

and of knowing her own worth. Or perhaps it was a survival mechanism.

Always caring and generous, my dad made it hard for anyone to stay angry at him. He felt it was his sacred responsibility to take care of my mother and us children. And he could always be counted on to help family and friends in their time of need. Babás was the one everyone turned to when they needed to borrow money. A man of considerable charisma, you could think of him like the Godfather, though thankfully without the mafioso's penchant for violence.

My father was a teenager when the Second World War broke out, and he experienced the brutal German occupation of Greece. I remember once discovering an old notebook from 1942 or 1943 that he'd written in, the only one my grandmother managed to save. Its pages were yellowed and so thin you could almost see through them. There, in an essay that began, "How do I manage with so little bread?" my twelve-year-old father described how devastated he felt to see his parents go to bed hungry so he could have the single piece of bread they had available for dinner. No wonder then that, when he later had his own children, he did not tolerate us leaving food on our plates at mealtimes. To this day, I find the same thing quite wasteful and disrespectful, almost insulting. Perhaps we're destined to live out certain family patterns.

When my father was sixteen, the World War was replaced by a bloody civil war in Greece. My grandmother, a widow by then, was extremely worried that her son—who was constantly getting into trouble—would be recruited by one of the factions. In a preemptive strike, she sent my dad to her brother who had emigrated to Douala, Cameroon, the country's largest city and commercial center. My father would remain there another thirty-five years, eventually building a fortune from nothing.

My mother was born in Istanbul in 1941. Her mother was a Turkish citizen, but both her parents were Greek minority in Turkey. My grandfather came from a small town in Greek Macedonia and moved to Istanbul in the late 1930s to find work in construction. When my grandmother was pregnant with my mother, he volunteered to fight for the Allies in Africa, leaving his wife behind. By the time he returned home, my mother was three years old. She never forgave him.

Their relational rigidity went both ways. My grandfather was tough on my mother, never allowing her much freedom. Despite being a star student, my mother never received praise from her father.

"Why should I praise you?" he'd say. "You're doing this for yourself, not for me." (Later, when I brought home my own grades, my mother would repeat her father's words to me.)

My mother never experienced closeness or tenderness from her father. All her life, she spoke to him only in the polite form, holding him always at a distance. Still, in the years before my grandfather passed away, my mother personally cared for him, attending to his every need and consistently ensuring his comfort.

By then, her mother was already gone. She died the same way she lived: putting her own needs last. My grandmother was the family martyr, the model of self-sacrifice and service to others, so for my mother, this was the image of what a woman should be.

My grandmother began experiencing irregular menstrual bleeding in her forties but was too embarrassed to see a gynecologist "at [her] age." My mom was already living in Cameroon when she got the call: her mother was very ill and deteriorating quickly. As Mamá boarded the plane to Greece, she had a vision of herself dressed in black. When the plane landed in Athens, my grandmother had already passed.

Mamá studied chemistry at the American College of Istanbul in the mid-1960s, the only woman in her cohort, and just one of nine women among 1,200 men at the entire college. She didn't speak a word of English when she arrived but learned it during her first year.

While she was studying in Istanbul, her father was deported from Turkey—along with all other Greek citizens. My mother stayed to finish college. After graduation, she left for Athens. As if being a woman in a man's world wasn't enough, in Greece, she felt treated like an immigrant, an unwelcome foreigner in a place that was supposed to be her home.

A year later, she met my father, who was in Greece visiting his widowed mother. Their whirlwind romance lasted ten days before my dad had to return to Cameroon. A few months and many passionate letters later, he proposed and asked my mother to follow him to Africa. Scrapping a Fulbright scholarship to pursue her master's degree in chemistry at the University of Kansas, she said "yes."

When my mother became pregnant, she and my father—true romantics—decided she would stay and give birth to me in Douala so they could be together. They weren't expecting complications.

The story goes that my very pregnant mother was at a party, dancing to rock 'n' roll, when her water broke. The entire gathering accompanied her to the hospital and stayed to wait for my arrival with my father. (At the time, men were not allowed in the delivery room, nor did they want to be there, I suspect.)

Then, in a bit of cosmic foreshadowing, a storm blew up and power to the hospital was cut. My mother's gynecologist, upset that he'd had to cut short a hunting trip, smoked a cigar—*in the operating room*. (My mom nearly passed out from the smell.) Nature's *coup de grâce*: I was breech.

In the smoke-filled darkness, the medical team finally managed to turn me around. Then, the cigar-smoking doctor took two long metal spoon-like instruments, inserted them into my mother's body, and pulled me out. (I'm told my temples were bruised for days.) As everyone focused their attention on ensuring my survival, my mother began rapidly losing blood. No one noticed when she fell unconscious.

Perhaps a well-timed jolt of lightning brightened the space just long enough for the nurse to see that Mamá's blood pressure had plummeted to almost zero. She rallied the troops, thereby saving my mother's life. A party broke out in the darkened waiting room, where the revelers hugged and kissed and congratulated my father.

From the beginning, my parents were physical in their love; I was hugged and kissed and cuddled. I was kept safe. And I was very much my father's daughter; I quickly became the apple of his eye. Babás was playful and funny. He loved to tease me. As a toddler, we had a game: he would let me walk ahead of him, then kick me gently in the behind with the side of his foot and pretend it wasn't him. I would turn around and glare at him, pretending to be annoyed, but then turn my back so he could do it again.

Sadly, Mamá never felt at home in Cameroon. What began as an exciting adventure eventually soured. Douala's endless days of rain, the musky smell of the continent, the dust and mold that penetrated every corner of her household—all of it weighed on her, as did other things. The culture felt foreign. It was very French, like the majority of my father's social circle. Even though she spoke the language, Mamá was an introvert. Amidst endless invitations to dinner parties, she preferred to spend time at home or with her sister and the few other Greek women she was close to there.

After the traumatic experience of my birth, my mother swore she'd never have another baby in Cameroon. When she became pregnant with my brother, she kept her word. Besides, I was nearly four and would soon be starting kindergarten, and she wanted me to be schooled in our native language. Some of my parents' Greek friends had put their children in the local French-speaking school system and watched dismayed as they gradually lost their native Greek language skills. My mother was horrified by this; she didn't want her child to turn into a "foreigner."

After being in Cameroon with my father for ten years, she told him she was leaving for Greece. My dad couldn't follow us. He had built a business in Cameroon; it was his life's work. He was torn apart by my mother's decision, but he never challenged it.

After our move, we were separated by four thousand kilometers of land and sea. Tropical monsoons were replaced by temperate Mediterranean breezes; lush greenery and towering palms gave way to dry rolling hills and olive groves; French voices and customs returned to the soon familiar colors and sounds and smells of Greece. But my father was far away.

It took him another seven years to decide to sell his business and return home.

CHAPTER 3

Into the Cage

"Perfectionism is based on the obsessive belief that if
you run carefully enough, hitting each stepping-stone
just right, you won't have to die. The truth is that you
will die anyway and that a lot of people who aren't even
looking at their feet are going to do a whole lot better
than you, and have a lot more fun while they're doing it."
— Anne Lamott, *Bird by Bird:
Some Instructions on Writing and Life*

IN ATHENS, WE STAY WITH my paternal grandmother. It's
November and my father has come. One afternoon, my parents return
from the hospital with an infant and a small gift for me "from the baby"—a
plastic sewing machine.

My new brother is quiet and uncomplicated. They name him Michalis,
for my father's father. Michalis has a large head, tight curls, and prominent ears that will be the cause of much teasing as he grows. He'll keep
his easygoing, low-maintenance disposition, and will be happiest while
playing any kind of ball sports, especially football and basketball. Like
many boys, he'll be prone to accidents, frequently sporting bumps and
bruises, sometimes even stitches. While still very young, he'll become suddenly ill with a high fever and my mother will rush him to the emergency

room more than once, until his tonsils are finally removed. Unlike me, Michalis will be known for his altruism and laid-back nature. He will be my mother's favorite.

It is the first day of fourth grade; I'm ten years old, and I have been called to the school counselor's office. Three of my friends are there. I take a seat beside them in the tiny office and the counselor addresses me directly.

"Katia, I want to speak to you on behalf of the other girls." I shuffle in my seat, confused. "They tell me they have been feeling intimidated by you in class. You are very smart, perhaps *too smart*," Ms. Kyriakou says. Her glasses are several times too large for her pointy, narrow face. "The girls say your teachers favor you, that they always call on you for answers. And the others feel they don't get a chance to contribute to the lessons."

My confusion grows. Is it my fault teachers call on me? Why don't the others raise their hands? As my dilemma sets in, so does shame. And it paralyzes me. I want to disappear.

I also want everyone to like me. I look down at my lap. "I'm sorry," I mutter.

Ms. Kyriakou smiles, satisfied. "Good!" she says. "Now, everyone, please give Katia a nice hug." The girls all stand and line up awkwardly for a hug.

"After all," says Ms. Kyriakou, cloyingly, "we're still friends."

School had been a place of security, comfort, and confidence, but in a single afternoon, everything changes. I stop speaking up. I become quiet and learn to keep a low profile. *If I manage to stay invisible,* I think, *others will like me.* I start to use my talents for the benefit of others. I let other students copy my homework and look over my shoulder during tests. *It's okay to be smart,* I think, *as long as I'm not seen as threatening.*

I still get the best grades in class. I can't quite compromise my standards and my desire to excel runs deep. But I learn to hide it. Teachers comment on my "weak class participation," but I refuse to raise my hand, even when it might hurt my grade. Everyone—including me—attributes this to my being "shy," though it has nothing to do with shyness.

At school, I wear a mask, an invisibility cloak. The ruse is suffocating. But after school, I head to dance class, where I feel free, uncaged. Myself.

Ballet feels natural, as if I've done it before in another life. I and a dozen other ten-year-old ballerinas warm up at the barre along the wall, then move to our places on the floor. Our teacher, Ms. Anita, calls out the steps to us in French: we do the *pas de chat* ("cat's step") and *grand battement* ("big beating"). Ms. Anita is beautiful, tall, and thin with long blond hair neatly tucked into a ballet bun. She's kind but commands our respect, as any true ballet teacher should.

I love going to class every week, which I've done since the first grade. I take quickly to the tall neck, open chest, and proud back—the ballerina's posture—and it becomes part of my DNA. I learn to feel graceful, strong, joyous.

For our end-of-year performance, we dance to Vivaldi's *Four Seasons*, and I perform as Spring. It's my first solo and my first performance danced *on pointe*, with beautiful pink satin ribbons wrapped around my ankles. I'm even allowed to wear makeup! My solo is only a couple of minutes long, but I feel ecstatic. My parents are there to watch, along with everyone at school. Afterwards, a boy I like tells me how impressed he was with my dancing; I'm over the moon.

I dance at parties, for my friends, and at home, by myself. Babás buys me an LP with highlights from Tchaikovsky's *Swan Lake* on one side and *Sleeping Beauty* on the other. I pull the sliding doors to our living room closed and pretend I'm a waltzing Princess Aurora, or Odette the Swan Princess dancing a *pas de deux* with Prince Siegfried.

After sixth grade, my school no longer offers ballet classes. To continue, I'll need to find a private studio. Ms. Anita tells my parents it would be a real shame if I stopped, yet I convince myself I no longer have time for ballet; schoolwork demands are increasing. In truth, I am too intimidated to leave my well-oiled comfort zone and join a new studio with a new teacher and new fellow dancers. As the years unfold, I regret it.

For now, my thoughts are occupied with my father's return; he's come home!

Quickly, he sets out to reestablish himself as a successful businessman. My father's standards of professionalism and his eye for quality are matched only by his enthusiasm. He's unstoppable, fully immersed in each new venture. Whether a promising business idea or the prospect of learning to play bridge, Babás is obsessive, devoting all his time and energy to the task and making use of every resource he can get his hands on. He has no fear and seems to revel in risk.

None of this sits well with my mother, of course. Her levelheadedness and innate risk aversion serve as the saner voice of reason, a reality check against my father's hell for leather urges. And she is often right, though he hates being held back. This dynamic becomes an unremitting source of tension between them.

But Babás is having a hard time readjusting to Greece—the mentality, the people, the business conditions. Having lived most of his adult life and some of his youth in Cameroon, he's used to the French way of doing things, especially in business. Greece is very different. In Greece, you must be constantly on guard, he says. "People will often take advantage or even cheat you, if you let them."

Apparently, my father learns this the hard way—repeatedly.

My dad feels like a foreigner in his own country; he doesn't fit in. Ever the entrepreneur, he tries several times to start a new business in Greece, but each one fails. He opens a café in the center of Athens; he launches an import business, bringing over I'm not sure what from Madagascar. And there are others. Every time, his associates prove to be "untrustworthy" and "take advantage" of him, or the Greek market "isn't interested" in the high-quality products and services he offers. He starts to resemble a caged animal, pacing the perimeter.

Babás's entrepreneurial philosophy to "start first, perfect later" is based in his belief that you can never predict everything that will happen, so why try? But after each failure in Greece and my mother's inevitable "I told you so" look, my father changes, growing gloomier and more depressed in turns. Reckless charm and unstoppable will to generate new and bigger things have always belonged to him, part of his wild, internal spark, the same fire that has always served as a kind of pilot light for my father's creative furnace. Finally together again as a family, we watch as that light gets extinguished.

Perhaps as an unconscious counterweight to my father, I double down on my efforts at school. I excel especially in languages, as I've been exposed to more than one from an early age. For an advanced English class, I take part in a Forensics competition, a public speaking and debate event more common in American schools. With my mother's help, I choose a topic, research it, and write my speech, then practice it diligently. Our families are all present in the school auditorium one evening when the winner is announced, and my name is called. Shocked, I take my trophy and perform my speech under the big stage lights. I feel proud and happy.

The next year (1983), I compete again, this time on the subject of George Orwell's famous novel, *1984*, and its significance. The topic is my mother's idea but as I read from her yellowed, dog-eared copy kept from college, I find the book fascinating. I am eleven years old.

There is a silent pressure—indirect, but always present. I am expected to do well. No one is impressed when I achieve, but what if I don't? What would happen if I stopped winning awards or getting the best grades in class? I don't know. I feel on a knife-edge most of the time, terrified of making a mistake. What if I fail? What if I forget something? What if I run out of talent? What will everyone think? The walls start to close in. I begin avoiding any perceived challenge or risk—to protect myself from failure at all costs.

I must be perfect. I must be perfect at everything.

I'm always on; I have to keep up. I must get the best grades in every class, on every exam. I must achieve the highest grade point average at the end of the year, the most academic awards. And I must do all of this quietly, shyly, without appearing to *want* to do so.

Being "the best" becomes my secret identity, which only amplifies the pressure I feel to excel. I must check the next box and the next and then the next. It never stops. I never pause to consider what I might actually enjoy, or even what I really want; the idea of stopping is unimaginable to me.

Everyone is gathered in the school auditorium, where members of the current student government present on why it's important to take part in it. They make student government sound fun, so when they ask for candidates, I raise my hand. I hadn't planned to do so and certainly wasn't prepared for what came next.

"Katia!" The student body president was a senior with long, skinny legs and confident eyes. "Why don't you come tell everyone your agenda?"

My agenda? He must have sensed my confusion. "Come tell us what you'll do for everyone if you're elected."

I instantly regret raising my hand. I have no idea what sort of "agenda" is expected, no one's example to follow. I stand to walk to the microphone as instructed and consider running from the room. Too late. I'm standing at the podium, facing my *entire* high school student population.

I stare into the sea of bodies and try to speak. A half-squeak, half-cough comes out.

"*Speak up!*" A hand reaches out from nowhere and positions the mic closer to my face.

I clear my throat and manage to utter a few words, something about organizing more excursions if I'm elected. I step down quickly and turn to flee, suddenly confused about the location of the exits. The nearest door feels a thousand kilometers away. As I dash to reach it, my face blazes with humiliation. I want to disappear.

Before I crest the door, I hear another classmate, Stephanos, take the stage and perfectly articulate his "agenda." He's convincing, a natural politician, as if he were born for student government. By the end of that meeting, Stephanos is elected—of course he is—and I crawl into a little cage and lock the door. *So what if I won awards for public speaking two years in a row? That was before. I'm not good at it anymore. Besides, I'm not a leader. I shouldn't be in the spotlight; I can't handle it. I don't have the talent. This is why I have to stay quiet, hidden.*

(Spoiler: I'll be in my mid-forties before I dare to attempt public speaking again and will avoid any association with leadership for nearly as long.)

After the election, I return my focus to checking boxes and set about getting into a good college and a prestigious graduate program. I stick to familiar areas where I'm already skilled or knowledgeable and can reliably rise to the occasion. I follow the map without question: avoiding risks and never, ever venturing into new terrain. This is how I stay in control and cope with my overwhelming fear of failure (for now).

On the surface, perfection seems rewarding, but mostly it takes the joy out of things. I apply myself to piano lessons and the study of French, i.e., standard regulation Good Girl curriculum. Each morning, I affix my mask and cloak and set off about my days in perfect numbness, perfectly dissociated, perfectly disconnected.

CHAPTER 4

Lightning Strike

"Do you want me to tell you something really subversive?
Love is everything it's cracked up to be. That's why people
are so cynical about it. It really is worth fighting for,
being brave for, risking everything for. And the trouble
is, if you don't risk anything, you risk even more."
— Erica Jong, *Fear of Flying*

NATURALLY, I CHOOSE THE SAFEST, straightest line, the path of least resistance. I make the "good," respectable choice: I pick a business studies major. I can pull it off easily and it will land me a good job coming out of university. I ace the national entrance exams, get into the university of my choice, and am among the top twenty admissions nationwide. Check, check, check.

For my second semester, I switch to the American College of Greece, a private institution that follows the American system, and opt for an Accounting and Finance major because I'm good in math; I can do it in my sleep. I never consider whether this path will bring me joy or what I might in fact be passionate about. I adjust my mask, I tick all the boxes, I fly safely under the radar.

Somewhere along the way, I meet a nice young man (check) who falls madly in love with me (check?). I care about him. His family adores me.

We were friends first. He takes me to the senior dance in college and buys me a lovely corsage made with white baby's breath and a red rose to match my dress. "Perfect." His parents meet my parents (check).

I graduate university with honors and move my game piece forward on the board, the next logical step toward my prescribed career. I take a job at a bank—a well-respected bank, where I spend the next year and a half slowly succumbing to the abyss of boredom-induced despair. I convince myself that all first jobs are a huge disappointment, but some mornings, I feel so down on my walk to work that I detour into a small, nearby chapel dedicated to the Virgin Mary, where I light a candle and pray for strength to make it through the day. (May the miserable always possess a flair for the dramatic. Amen.)

Good boy that he is, the boyfriend wants to go to graduate school overseas. His words take the shape of an emergency parachute; I strap myself to them and leap. We make plans to go away to grad school together.

We choose New York. Good Boy accepts an offer from a modest but decent university, with plans to start in January. I'm accepted into a program at Columbia and will follow in September. Then another offer arrives from the Harvard Kennedy School, and who can say no to Harvard? I move to Boston instead of New York.

Even though he's barely started his first year of graduate school, Good Boy—desperate and in love—manages a transfer to another university in Boston, "So we can be together." By this time, I've a) become panicky at the thought of commitment and b) been introduced by a friend to Bad Boy. Greek playboy, charmer, scoundrel, Lothario. In other words, I cheat on my boyfriend—the first crack in my perfect, good girl mask.

But it's summer in Greece and I'm having too much fun.

The new guy is older, over thirty, and hangs out with an interesting crowd. He's only ever seen with models and refuses to settle down, which makes him an irresistible challenge. I'm neither tall, blond, nor a model, but I throw caution to the Aegean and dive in. How can I refuse? He's so different from the conventional "nice guys" I've always gone out with.

Bad Boy takes me out to cool places—clubs and restaurants where I've previously never managed to get past the bouncers. They all know him, so he cuts the line and they let him right in. We escape for weekends to his family's summer house on a nearby cosmopolitan (of course) island, or to London, where he did his studies (of course). The sex is bitterly disappointing, but nevertheless, I become engrossed, totally consumed in my experience with this man. I forget to eat, skipping most meals when I'm not at home (I'm almost never at home). I forget my checkboxes, my perfect plans. I make no effort to hide what I'm doing, which surprises even me.

It's this carelessness that gets me caught. My boyfriend's sister sees me and tells him. He's devastated.

When he comes back to Athens later that summer, Good Boy breaks up with me. My family, having been informed of my behavior, is appalled. They know my boyfriend's parents and, caring what they think, feel humiliated by my actions. More proof of my selfishness.

When I end things with Bad Boy, he promises to wait for me.

"That's up to you," I say. "But I probably wouldn't."

I'm dejected. I was only just flying—so free and full of firelight—and now here I am again, trapped. The walls of my cage are closing in.

I catch myself in a mirror and notice how thin I've become. Something new I can control.

Still on summer break in Greece, my parents host a small dinner party one evening. The son of a family friend joins his mother for the evening and gives me something new to study. In his mid-twenties, he has dreamy hazel eyes and light brown hair. He's solid, not skinny, and when he speaks, it's with a low, soft voice that almost has a bedroom quality.

I'm instantly enraptured by his wit. Every sentence he utters glitters with a note of humor, at times sarcastic and often self-deprecating. He's an only child, I learn, who calls his mother by her first name. An unusual relationship, I think—complicated.

Alexis is a journalist but also an artist. In his spare time, he creates jewelry. And he writes poetry. I'm not sure how it all fits together exactly; he's a complex personality and I'm intrigued.

From the way he carries himself, it's clear he knows he's attractive. There's no hint of self-consciousness. I find him charming. Incredibly sexy.

And he's good with parents—mine seem to like him a lot, so they offer no objection when he asks me out after dinner. His Harley is parked outside my parents' place—he asks me if I want to go for a ride. It's big and shiny with a bright turquoise gas tank and details. I've never been on a Harley. I'm thrilled.

By the end of the evening, we've been struck by lightning. *Coup de foudre*, as the French say. A clap of thunder. Love at first sight.

My Harley rider is in the army, stationed on a Greek island off the coast of Turkey, quite a hike from Athens. He's on a weeklong leave when we meet, so we have only a few days together before he goes back. In that week, I essentially move into his place, an apartment he keeps near the center of the city. He takes me there on our first date and we make love. Lightning strikes again; I come undone.

We spend the days that follow in bed with few breaks. When I finally pull away and dash home for a shower and fresh clothes, my parents confront me, horrified. It is only weeks before I leave to go to Harvard and this man threatens to derail everything. I must have completely lost my mind.

But what is new love if not losing one's mind completely?

He is all I can think about, all I *want* to think about. I'm blind to everything and everyone else—my friends, my family, my upcoming transatlantic move, my future plans. This is my first *coup de foudre* experience and I'm lost on Planet Love. Alexis leaves little love notes for me everywhere—in my purse, inside the book I'm reading, on the bathroom mirror. "Good morning, beautiful. Know that I'm thinking of you." He writes stories and poetry for me. His writing is simple and raw, poetic. Like a Greek Hemingway-turned-Cyrano de Bergerac, he writes in short, beautifully crafted sentences in my native language and it captivates me. He speaks directly to my soul.

Again, I lose myself in love and forget to eat. I become rail thin and stop getting my periods. I'll later be horrified by how thin I look in photographs from that time, but my lover doesn't seem to mind. He reassures me there's nothing to worry about. Unbeknownst to me, he has a plan.

Everything we do has an intense sensory quality to it. We bake bread, plunging our hands together into the bowl of fluffy, sticky dough. He makes homemade peanut butter for me, to go with the bread. We bake a cake for my birthday (it's in a few weeks, but we decide to celebrate early)—chocolate frosting and all—and eat it in bed. (To this day, I can't taste Betty Crocker's box cake without thinking of him.) His plan works: my appetite comes back and I start to look healthy again.

On a couple of occasions—very few, given how little time we have together—I get a glimpse into his vulnerable side and sense the trauma he carries with him. One night after we've both had too much to drink, he starts to cry. I'm unsure what to do or how to handle it. He's suddenly a little boy who desperately misses his dad, just like I must have missed mine.

"Why did he have to go away?" my lover mumbles through his tears.

I learn that his parents divorced when he was young and he never got over his father leaving. His mother wasn't the nurturing type, so she never really mothered him. She came and went out of his life, and he was raised mainly by his grandmother and aunt. *Here is the tender source of that wry sarcasm*, I think. *Here is the origin of a man who calls his mother by her first name. Here is a little boy who misses his father and just wants to be loved.* And I fall even harder for him.

Before he leaves to return for duty, he gives me a ring—one he made himself. It's silver with a large tiger's eye stone attached by tiny silver claws. As he places the ring on my finger, he asks me to marry him. "Yes," I say. I'm in love.

My parents hardly knew each other when my father proposed and neither do we. But I don't think of that now. I'm under a spell. My friends are all stunned when I share my news.

When my lover leaves, my world collapses. I spend my time either at home waiting for him to call (no mobile phones yet) or at his place, for which he's given me the keys. I feel closer to him there. I don't have an answering machine, but he does, so we exchange messages through it. He's left me little notes and poems all over his apartment, and I set about finding them one by one. For my birthday, he sends a stunning bouquet of thirty red roses. He plans to come back to Athens to see me before I leave for Boston.

Alexis and I make plans for him to join me in Boston when he's finished with the army. Our dream: He'll land a journalism job with Voice of America and we'll live happily ever after in the US.

The evening before my early morning flight to Boston, Alexis shows up. My parents are hosting a small gathering of friends who come to say goodbye, but I ride off with my lover.

I don't return home until shortly before my mother and I must leave to make our flight (she's flying with me). My parents must be apoplectic, but I am in my own world, utterly distraught to have to leave the love of my life.

For the duration of a nine-hour transatlantic flight, I sob, inconsolable.

CHAPTER 5

Eyes Wide Open

"I wanted to punch him and understand
him at the same time."
— Shannon A. Thompson, *Take Me Tomorrow*

THE FIRST WEEKS ARE ROUGH. We're an ocean and seven
hours apart, and the army doesn't offer access to phones that make long-
distance calls.

My mom and I stay with a friend of the family in Walpole, a suburb of
Boston. We visit prospective flats for rent around Cambridge and shop for
the basics I'll need wherever I land—bedlinens, towels, kitchen utensils,
etc. I was here the year before, but this will be my first time experiencing
it all on my own.

Foods taste different here. Vegetables come in unfamiliar shapes.
Carrots come in a bag, already peeled clean, smooth and perfectly formed
into identical miniature sizes. I try celery sticks for the first time. My
eyes are wide when we enter the vast outdoor shopping malls. They have
massive stores with names like "Bed Bath & Beyond" and "Home Depot,"
where I find anything I could possibly want for my new apartment. The
size of the shopping carts alone is astonishing.

Despite the abundance and newness all around me, I feel completely
cut off from the world—which is to say, from my fiancé. I spend every

moment agonizing about how and when I'll next communicate with him. I search desperately for a payphone, where I could use my credit card and a special code for cheaper international rates. I'm too embarrassed to ask our hosts for help. Whenever we venture out, I feel like I'm coming out of prison, scanning everywhere for a phone I might slip out discreetly later to use.

We finally find an acceptable flat. It's small, on the ground floor, part of a condo. It certainly isn't bright or charming and doesn't feel terribly safe; my only entrance is through a sliding glass door accessed through the garden (or as Americans say, the lawn). I write a check to my new landlady, Brianna, from my newly opened Bank of Boston account, and my mother sets off in a frenzy, attempting to turn my new apartment into a home.

(This will be the first of many homes, through many moves, my mother will help set up for me. She'll unpack, clean the kitchen cabinets, buy new furniture or bath towels to replace the ones that are worn out—whatever needs doing, she'll do.)

My mom stays in Boston with me for three weeks, but as soon as classes start, we hardly see each other. I leave early on my new bike and don't return until evening. We have a bite to eat together and then I sit at my desk to study until the early morning hours. My mother sits on the bed solving her crossword puzzles until she falls asleep. She will forever joke that all she ever saw of me in Boston was my back. Perhaps it reveals a hint of sadness (or was it resentment?).

After she leaves, I dread going back to my lonely studio in the evenings, so I delay as much as possible. I walk around Cambridge, buying stuff I don't need or hanging out in bookstores till late. Finally, I grab something for dinner and take it home to eat. Adjusting to the loneliness is rough.

I buy a desktop computer for school and install on it an answering machine that connects to the phone line. I leave the computer on all day so it can receive messages while I'm gone. When Alexis is awake, I'm at school; when I'm home, it's the middle of the night for him—so we communicate through voice messages like before. The few times we're able to speak—I, from a payphone near Harvard Square and he, from the cafeteria

34

of his army barrack—are intense and heartbreaking. It feels wrong to be so far away from each other.

At orientation, I meet a girl from Sri Lanka, Sam (short for Samadhi). She's slightly older than me and very protective; we become best friends. She watches over me. In the beginning, I rely on Sam entirely, but slowly I make other friends. One of those is another Business School student, a Greek girl who invites me to drive down to New York City with her for a weekend to visit friends. I love New York City, so I jump at the opportunity.

When I tell Alexis about my plans, we argue.

"Should I only spend my time being miserable and missing you?" I'm defiant.

"Who is this guy you're visiting in New York? Is he interested in you?"

It's the first time I see this side of him—the jealousy, the possessiveness. I'm not sure I like it. He hangs up on me. I call him back, but he doesn't answer. I try a few more times. No answer. For the next few hours, I don't know what to do with myself. I go to the library and try to work but can't focus.

After I'm back from school that evening, I call his home number and leave a few voice messages. He retrieves them remotely every day, so I'm hoping he'll have heard them by the next morning and that he'll have cooled down by then. After all, he loves me, and this is not a serious reason to be upset with me.

I get no response from my fiancé the next day or the next. So, I leave for NYC, thinking surely it will blow over.

But I don't hear from him—for weeks.

Initially, I'm desperate and depressed. How can the love of my life end things like this? How can anyone who professed such love for me only weeks ago want me to suffer like this? I leave a string of forlorn messages on his machine. Silence.

Then one morning, three weeks after our fight, something shifts. I wake up and decide I need to love myself a little bit more; I don't deserve this kind of treatment. I decide that it's over. The following day, I arrive home to find a message on my answering machine. He talks into the recording as if nothing has happened.

I never call him back. I feel light. I feel like, finally, I can be here, in Cambridge—at *Harvard University*—present in my new life.

(A year later, he calls to wish me happy birthday. It's August and I'm at my parents' home in Greece. Viktor and his daughter are playing in the garden.)

I love being around smart people, perhaps even "too smart" people. I raise my hand in class without worrying about attracting attention to myself or making someone else resentful toward me. I don't have to hide how good I am.

I jump straight into the next relationship: another Harvard student, one year ahead of me. He's in his midtwenties with dark curly hair, a slowly receding hairline, and glasses—not the type I usually fall for. But then, I don't really fall for him. He doesn't try to charm me. We're friends, so Dan, who's American, is sort of hanging around when my (imminent) breakup happens. He's quick to console me.

I'm attracted to Dan's wit and intellect. He's bright, ambitious. I become part of his inner circle of (mostly American) friends. We spend our time discussing politics and current events, and I'm learning a lot about American culture. Dan reads a lot. He's interested in economics, finance, and politics. His plan after grad school is to land a high-powered job in investment banking, have a successful career earning good money, and then switch tracks to "do something in the public sector." He's got it all sorted out.

Dan thinks I'm smart. In our discussions, he often challenges me—on current events, especially politics—which I love. It feels nice to have a man appreciate me for my brains, rather than just my appearance. He doesn't write me poetry or hide love notes in my books, but he treats me like an adult.

Dan loves his country and wants to serve. (I don't even know the meaning of the word *serve*—other than meals—when he first says it.) He loves his family. He tells me he wants a "mature relationship," which means we can have fun even when we're not together. He doesn't want to see other people; he just wants us to have our independence.

At Thanksgiving, I'm invited to his family home in upstate New York. While there, I learn that Dan and his family are Jewish, which later amuses my incredulous friends. "*Of course*, he's Jewish. How could you *not know*?"

Dan's parents are warm and welcoming. They make me feel at home, cared for, embraced. I have to sneak out of my room at night to be with him in his room across the hall, and I find this somehow adorable. I'm finally not alone.

In early December, I receive an email from someone I don't know, sent to my newly acquired email address (my first one—it's 1995!).

Hi Katia,

You don't know me, so let me introduce myself. I'm a single dad in search of a babysitter for my daughter Julia, who is two years old. (You might have seen us in the library tonight.) As I was leafing through the Kennedy School photo book, I noticed on your profile that you speak German. We are Austrian and Julia doesn't speak much English yet. Would you be available to help with babysitting, so that I can work on a large research paper for Graham Allison? I would pay you of course. Does $7/hour plus cab rides sound good?

It would be a big help! Let me know if you're interested.

Viktor

A friend who's visiting from Greece is with me in the computer lab when the message comes through. She's convinced the Austrian guy has concocted an elaborate ruse to pick me up.

According to Viktor, his little girl—who lives with him full time—simply pointed to my photograph when he asked her to choose among the three German speakers listed in the book. I agree to the babysitting job—more out of curiosity than anything else—but make it clear I *don't* change diapers.

I arrive at 9:30 a.m. on a Saturday. Viktor answers the door in loose jeans and a long-sleeved T-shirt. He's blond (my type) with sparkling blue eyes, though his face seems drawn. *He must not be sleeping much.* I make a mental note never to become a single parent. A little girl peeks at me from behind his legs. She looks so tiny in her cotton leggings and T-shirt. Julia takes me by the hand and leads me to her room. She's initially shy, but we quickly warm to each other. We play Uno (her favorite) and Hungry Hungry Hippos.

I'm self-conscious about my German, but my two-year-old charge doesn't seem to notice. We have fun together and she understands me well enough. When the unmistakable smell alerts me, I call her father, who's working with his partner in the next room. He smiles and doesn't complain—after all, I warned him upfront.

I only get to babysit Julia once—at least only once for pay.

CHAPTER 6

Swept

"I seem to be torn between 'I wish we'd met
earlier' and 'I wish we'd never met.'"
— Ahmed Mostafa, *Heartbreak & Other States*

"I love you as certain dark things are to be loved,
in secret, between the shadow and the soul."
— Pablo Neruda, *100 Love Sonnets*

VIKTOR TRAVELS BACK TO HIS NATIVE AUSTRIA for
the holidays. Before leaving, he sends a note to thank me for helping him
out with his little girl and says he looks forward to seeing me in 1996. What
he doesn't mention is he's going back to be with his daughter's mother,
Sabine. At the time, of course, this was none of my business. We'd only
just met—as babysitter and employer.

I travel home to Greece for Christmas. My friends and family have all
missed me and it's wonderful to see them. Thankfully, no one comments on
the weight I've put on (I call it the "American food shock"—just one form of
the culture shock variety). Jetlag is a welcome opportunity to (try to) make up
for the past four sleep-deprived months. When I'm not sleeping, I'm either
catching up with girlfriends over coffee after a solid Christmas shopping
spree or sitting down for yet another extended family meal. It feels so good

to be home and let myself be taken care of. Everyone wants to hear about Harvard, but all I want to hear is the latest gossip and eat *kourabiethes*.*

By Boxing Day, the high of homecoming has been replaced with the heaviness of anticipatory grief: I'm homesick before I've even left home.

Coming back to the US is hard. We're in the depths of winter in Boston and drowning in snow—there's a blizzard every other day—and the temperatures stay below zero most of the time. There are no classes while everyone studies for finals, and unless I brave the cold for the twenty-minute walk to the Harvard Kennedy School Library (biking is out of the question and the effort to take the bus is essentially the same as walking), I don't see a soul for days in a row. My little flat is nice and warm in the mornings but freezing cold after 10:00 p.m., when Brianna the Landlady turns off the heat for the night. So, I dress in multiple layers—including a coat, scarf, and hat—and often study bundled up under the bedcovers, so I don't shiver. Soon, my depression peaks.

I become clingy with Dan, who feels my clinginess as a threat to his independence. He tells me I'm "bringing [him] down" with all my "negativity," and I'm far "too needy."

When I most need his support, he backs away, asking for more space or time with his friends, neither of which he seemed to need before. Slowly it dawns on me that my American boyfriend's approach isn't just personal; it's cultural. Who I am—the full version—is not acceptable here. I need to adjust to fit in. But how can I do that and still feel like myself?

When Viktor returns from Austria with his daughter, I receive an email inviting me to something he calls a "Babysitter Gang Brunch" at his place in early February. He's hosting the gathering as a show of gratitude for all the friends who volunteered their time to help him out as a single dad. (I'm the only one in the "gang" who was paid.) I attend the brunch with a mutual friend.

Later that evening, Viktor sends an email asking me out for a drink at Top of the Hub, the bar at the top of the Prudential center in downtown

---

* A traditional Greek Christmas cookie.

Boston. Europeans that we are, we agree this isn't a "date," not in the American sense. We're just two people, having drinks.

Our non-date goes on for several hours. We sit next to each other in front of the small round table, our knees almost touching, the city of Boston at our feet. Viktor tells me about growing up in a big farmhouse in Southern Austria, the youngest of six children. I tell him about growing up in Cameroon and Greece and how I learned to speak German from a half-German boyfriend. He makes a confession: When he asked his daughter to pick a babysitter, he'd gently nudged her to my picture. I feel butterflies in my stomach.

Dan and I haven't formally broken up, but he's been actively avoiding me (and my negativity). After my experience with Alexis, I assume this means we're broken up. Then, just before Valentine's Day, I discover a card from Dan in my mailbox at school. There's a second one there too, from Viktor.

In it, my one-time employer invites me to watch a movie—*Il Postino* (*The Postman*)—on Valentine's Day. Michael Radford's 1995 film is a fictional story centered around the real-life poetry of Chilean poet Pablo Neruda, and it's the ultimate romantic movie. Again, we don't call it a date.

A few days later, I arrive home from class to discover a portable heater has been left for me at the door to my apartment along with a note: "To keep you warm."

I never officially break up with Dan, but now I'm the one avoiding him. *He can't still think we're together*, I think. *If I were a guy, this would be standard breakup procedure.*

Viktor is charming, well-traveled, cosmopolitan. As the son of a diplomat, he grew up in the south of Austria, then lived in Budapest, and finished high school in Helsinki (he speaks almost as many languages as I do). He's interested in politics and highly knowledgeable about American politics, impressive for a non-American.* Viktor wants to be a politician. But first he needs to pay back his student debt.

---

* Today, we are all experts on American politics, but this was much harder to pull off in 1996—pre-internet, pre-social media, and before the 24-hour news cycles so ubiquitous now.

We start writing to each other every night. He sends me poetry. Read: it's all utterly romantic and we fall in love. I'm attracted to his nomadic soul, which fits so well with my own migrant bug. Here, on the other side of the ocean, we're two Europeans and therefore culturally connected. (In truth, our respective cultures couldn't be further apart.) We understand and laugh at each other's jokes. *He will take care of me,* I think.

Viktor is gentle, thoughtful, considerate—qualities that admittedly made me leave past boyfriends because I eventually got bored. But not this time. In Viktor, I find these qualities attractive, even sexy. We can't keep our hands off each other all day and make passionate love almost nightly, after Julia is asleep. He asks me to meet him at his favorite café and I find him waiting for me with a thick poetry book open in front of him.

"Would you like me to read to you?" he asks. *Who does that?!*

We cook together, the three of us, at his place. Julia seems to like me, though I feel incredibly awkward around her—around kids in general. We go to the playground together, and to the mall and the Children's Museum. I feel strange doing all these kid-related things with her (and honestly, I'm a little bored), but I'm so enthralled with Viktor that I go right along.

Julia misses her mom. Every night I sleep over, at 3:00 a.m. to the minute, Viktor gets out of bed to go comfort her. I find this equal parts charming (he's such a good father) and frustrating (I don't like having to share him). I'm moved in by spring break, barely two months after our first non-date date, and just after Julia returns to Austria to be with her mother.

Viktor is my intellectual equal and seems genuinely interested in my work—supportive, which is a new experience. He encourages me to apply for a grant from the German government to do research in Europe over the summer and helps edit my proposal. He draws on his contacts and helps me cultivate my own network and schedule interviews as part of my research.

That summer, Viktor graduates. His parents, sister, and daughter travel to the US for his graduation, where I get to meet them. Afterward, we go away to Mexico on vacation (which my father's credit card largely pays for). Then, we travel to Europe together for research and visit all the places

I'd never have visited on my own. My horizons suddenly feel wide open, as if new opportunities are all around me.

I start to feel excited about the future, our future. I've never felt happier, safer, or more fulfilled. Connecting with someone on every level—especially intellectually—is thrilling.

Later in the summer, we take Julia to Greece for the first time. My family loves them both. It isn't easy, though; she's still a toddler and I find her difficult to deal with at times. She's also the first toddler I've ever spent time with, and I'm in shock by the whole "parenting" thing.

When Julia goes back to her mother in Austria, Viktor and I take a few days just for the two of us. At a little port-side café in Piraeus, we wait for the boat to Santorini. The only available table is in the sun and I'm already in a bad mood (growing up in Greece hasn't made me immune to its intense heat). I sip my iced coffee, but it tastes watery with a hint of dish soap.

"I really miss her," Viktor says softly. "It's always so short—my time with her."

I nod and take his hand. I can't tell him I'm relieved for the break.

"I wish we had more time," he continues. "I've been thinking about this. What would you say if she came to live with us?"

"Sabine would never go for it." My stomach is in a knot.

"I could fight for her. I may have a chance." Viktor, the eternal optimist. He's serious about this.

"Viktor, do you realize that you're asking me to become a parent—for real? I'm not ready to have children. I haven't even started my life, our life!"

"Yes, but you knew that I had a child when you chose to be with me. It's not like I hid her from you."

"But there was never a prospect of Julia living with us. It's unfair for you to throw this at me now." My mouth goes dry, and I feel the blood rushing to my head.

He mutters under his breath. "It's good to know where you stand."

We spend the six-hour boat trip in silence.

I don't know it yet, but this scene will play out again and again in our relationship, usually in the form of arguments over Julia and her mother.

Sitting by the water in Piraeus, I put it out of my mind. What we have is way more important. My parents love and trust him. He's the one. I'm sure of it.

CHAPTER 7

Forever Is a Long Time

"The greatest lie ever told about
love is that it sets you free."
— Zadie Smith, *On Beauty*

VIKTOR STAYS ON AT HARVARD until the end of the year, working as a research assistant for one of his professors. He even pretends to be interested in starting a PhD—all so we can be together a little longer. We try to figure out what comes next for us and it feels terribly exciting.

We start our lives together on neutral territory: Paris. What could possibly be more romantic?

Viktor moves to Paris in January '97 while I start my last semester. We send long emails and pay for exorbitant long-distance calls. But soon, I'm lonely.

While taking an elective at Tufts, I meet a German student, Ralf. We start spending time together and become friends. He writes poetry and we have long conversations about life. Ralf says he wants to be a priest, though the energy between us begins to tip toward the heterodox. *Does Viktor sense something?*

For Spring Break, I fly to France to be with Viktor, who's now working for a big management consulting firm. His first client is based in Normandy, near Rouen, and when he suggests we spend the weekend at his hotel there, I'm not expecting a Small Luxury Hotel—but I'm new to the world of management consulting.

My second day there, we're out for a walk on the grounds when, behind a tree, I see a table set for two. There's chilled champagne and strawberries and a large vase with long-stemmed red roses.

"How strange. What do you think that is?" I turn to Viktor, but he's already on one knee, asking me to marry him.

"I think we should get married next summer in Greece," Viktor says over dinner. I'm impressed at how he's thought this through.

I graduate in the summer and my parents fly in for the ceremony. When my name is called, I march across the stage in my cap and gown, just like in the movies. The proud smile on my father's face feels like everything good.

Before I leave Cambridge for good, I meet with one of my professors. Michael teaches negotiation at the Kennedy School, but he isn't your typical Harvard professor—he's young, down to earth, with a great sense of humor. He's also got kind, sky-blue eyes. Michael mentions an upcoming trip to Greece and I offer to give him "insider" tips. He asks if he can buy me lunch.

We order Caesar salads and lemonades and talk about my final paper on the Dayton Peace Agreement* (he gave me an A). He asks about my plans after graduation. Then things get more personal. Michael tells me he's engaged to be married; I tell him about Viktor. A subtle feeling of disappointment comes over me, but I don't know where it's coming from.

Soon, I pack up everything in my little apartment and join Viktor in Paris. That first summer, his daughter joins us for three weeks. Her father works long hours, so I stay at home with Julia. My newest research question: How do I entertain a four-year-old prone to incredible temper tantrums? For three traumatic weeks.

It can't be easy not to have her *Vati* to herself anymore, or to get so little time with either of her parents. *Who is this strange woman,* she must

---

*   Signed in December 1995, these accords ended the three-and-a-half-year-long Bosnian War.

be thinking, *and why is her German so basic?* The highlight of our day is meeting Viktor for a half-hour lunch at McDonald's. On our way, Julia decides the time is right for a show of protest. She squats in the middle of the sidewalk and refuses to budge.

I don't remember much about the rest of the summer.

In the fall, I find myself sitting alone in a Paris café, looking through the paper at the job ads. It all feels anticlimactic after Boston. Viktor is away Monday through Thursday nights on assignment while I collect rejection letters. My prestigious Harvard degree doesn't seem so impressive in France. I try hard to get a job in defense but in the end, I'm demoralized. So, I go back to finance and take a job at a multinational corporation. It looks good on paper.

History repeats: I'm a model employee. Everyone loves me. I hate the job.

Since I'm new, I feel I have to put in lots of "face time" and end up working crazy hours. When I return home at the end of the day, it's to an empty apartment. Having no energy to prepare or eat dinner, I lose too much weight.

Viktor encourages me and I apply to a PhD program at RAND, a prominent American think tank. I see it as a long shot. Besides, it's in Los Angeles and I can't imagine moving so far away from my family. Then, I get accepted.

"We should move to LA," Viktor insists. So, we move—right after our summer wedding.

My dad has a talk with Viktor. "I'll pay for the wedding," he says, "if you promise to buy my daughter nice jewelry." In my father's book, that's proof of lifelong commitment and devotion.

In June, we have a dream wedding. It's a perfect summer night. I'm wearing my dream wedding dress, which I brought over from Paris. My dad drives me to the church in a stunning, cream-colored classic Jaguar he borrows from a neighbor.

Julia's dress matches mine in color. She holds her father's hand as they wait for me to arrive—late, as any Greek bride. Friends and family from all over the world gather around us in the chapel courtyard. The priest makes Viktor promise that our children will be Greek Orthodox (we've already agreed they'll be Catholic). At dinner, my best friend gives a speech about "all the men" in my life, offending some of my parents' guests. We party till morning and, unlike most newlywed couples, we don't take off, but instead see our guests off before heading to bed. Weeks later, my father admits to me that he'd hired undercover security to make sure nothing spoiled my special night. And nothing did.

In August, Viktor and I make the move to LA. I'm excited to start work as a researcher at one of the biggest, most renowned think tanks in the world. The job comes with the PhD program, which is the only reason I considered applying. It's the perfect next step for my career. It helps that Viktor works for a global firm and is able to transfer easily to its LA office. Although we make this move for me, it's good for him, too. His little girl is in Boston, and being in the same country, albeit on different coasts, he'll be able to visit her more frequently.

For three weeks, Viktor's employer puts us up in a hotel in Santa Monica overlooking the ocean while we search for a place. Viktor has a friend here, a Hollywood screenwriter (whom we hardly ever see), but we don't know anyone else in California. We find an apartment in a high-rise with a pool and gym. I feel like I'm in *Melrose Place*. My dad buys me a used, red Mazda Miata MX-5. I name it Petros, after him. I roam the streets with the top down, wearing a red baseball cap. I feel independent.

RAND is in a vast building that overlooks Ocean Avenue. I meet lots of incredibly smart people there, both at school and at work. And I love my work and I love my colleagues; I feel intellectually stimulated. Great new opportunities open: I conduct studies for the Pentagon and the US Air Force; I present at Sandia National Laboratories; I travel to Europe for research interviews and conferences. I'm a woman in a male-dominated field and loving it.

I'm attracted to defense for the international aspect: it allows me to connect and work with people from many different cultures. RAND is a North American giant and an institution in the field of public policy—but it's also very US-centric. I fit well with the corporate culture, but the foreigner in me craves a more international element. Finding a niche as a European defense expert is a way of keeping that element alive.

I'm thriving, both professionally and personally, but more than that, I feel *at home* here. After every trip away, even when that trip is back home to Greece, I feel really happy coming back to LA. My homesickness fades along with my annual post-holiday blues.

In the mornings, I work out or take a dip in the pool. Then, I throw on my red baseball cap, hop into the Mazda, and head off to class. When we take a trip out to see Disneyland, I carry my books and my yellow highlighter with me.

And all of this feels wonderful. But my first year of marriage isn't holding up its end of the bargain. I work *a lot*—on my PhD coursework and research projects at the same time. I work even more than my management consultant husband—past midnight and on weekends. And he isn't happy about it. He feels neglected, like I don't have time for him. So according to him, *I'm* the one who isn't fulfilling my part of the marriage contract.

Viktor travels a lot, and the distance between us grows. I develop my own circle of friends and my own social life. Mostly, I'm alone a lot—and I hate being alone. I read somewhere that the first year of marriage is "tough." Mine is hell. We fight all the time, whether he's traveling or at home. When he's gone, I mostly sit in our new apartment and stew over how much he travels or how he interacts with his ex, who constantly creates problems for us. In my mind, Viktor doesn't stand up to her when she attempts to blackmail him into getting what she wants—whether it's scheduling or financial arrangements. She uses access to Julia as a weapon (his excuse: he won't see his daughter). It also drives me up the wall that he doesn't defend me; she insults me on a regular basis (his excuse: he doesn't dignify her with a response). Viktor feels cornered by both of us, while Julia pays the price. Almost all our fights have something to do with Sabine's constant interference.

When our first wedding anniversary rolls around, I'm depressed. Viktor is in Florida for a McKinsey training event he claims he couldn't get out of. James—a colleague from my doctoral program who feels bad for me—takes me out for sushi. He tries very hard to cheer me up (James is secretly in love with me, it turns out), but the fact that I'm out with him instead of my husband only makes me more depressed.

When Viktor returns home, he comes bearing a beautiful sapphire ring. (After all, my father made him promise.) But it doesn't change anything; I'm disappointed and angry he wasn't here for our anniversary. I find it difficult to let my anger go.

The summer after my second year, I spend three weeks alone in LA, studying for my qualifying exams. My husband is in Austria with Julia—on vacation in the countryside. Apparently, those exact three weeks are the only time her mother will allow him to take her on holiday. I have a hard time getting over this as well and make sure to tell him so, but he calls me selfish for not understanding his constraints.

I spend the rest of the summer on my own.

I convince my RAND project leader to sponsor me for a conference on international security, which, interestingly, takes place on the remote Greek island called Halki. The event is full of brilliant, ambitious, extremely *fun* people (we work hard and party harder, as the saying goes). I feel alive, which is wonderful. But it doesn't change the fact that I also feel alone.

CHAPTER 8

Paradise Lost

"You know, when there's a noise breaking into your sleep
and you don't want to wake up, you can dream a long
complicated dream that explains the whole noise away."
— Amy Witting, *I for Isobel*

IT'S EARLY 2001 AND WE'VE JUST RETURNED to the States
after spending the holidays with our families. We're out for a walk along
Santa Monica beach when Viktor turns to me as though he's suddenly
remembered something I might find interesting.

"There may be a chance for me to transfer to McKinsey's Vienna office,"
he says. "What do you think about us moving to Vienna?"

He frames it as a possibility, an option, an opportunity even, but offers
no background: Was a relocation offered to him, perhaps because he's
Austrian, or did he ask for such a transfer?

"I don't want to move anywhere right now. I'm really happy here." I stop
walking so he knows I'm serious. "Do you realize that it's the first time in
my life that I'm excited to wake up and go to work? I love our friends. I
love the ocean. I love our life here."

And it's true. I'm blossoming at work. I give briefings at the Pentagon.
And my European projects allow me to travel, to see my family and spend
time in places like Paris and Brussels for conferences and meetings.

Over the ensuing weeks, Viktor brings up Vienna a couple more times. Each time, I dismiss it. I'm not going anywhere.

Then he's given a study in Brussels, a long way from LA. His previous studies were all domestic. But I don't question it. I'm completely absorbed in my work and maybe I no longer mind as much that he's always away. I don't stop to consider why a global company wouldn't choose to recruit someone local (or even someone within wider Europe) for this particular client and must instead import someone—all the way from California.

Then, he comes home to LA one Friday with an announcement. "I'm being transferred to the Vienna office," Viktor says.

I'm stunned.

"What? What do you mean you're being transferred? I told you I don't want to move."

"What do you mean you don't want to move? We discussed it. You agreed. Don't you remember?"

"Besides, Sabine will be moving to Vienna this summer, too. For the first time since Julia was a baby, we will finally be together in the same place. Isn't that great?"

Oh, what a coincidence, I think. I'm incredulous. My heart rate shoots up; heat rushes to my face and I start to sweat. "How did that happen?"

"After three years in Boston, Sabine's tired of being a single mom so far away from her family," he explains. "She needs support to be able to have a life and career, so she's moving to Vienna." He says it as if it's the most obvious thing in the world.

My stomach clenches. There's no way this wasn't coordinated—and without my input.

My next walk on the beach I take alone, torn about what to do. I empathize with Viktor's motives—his desire to be near his child, to finally live in the same city where he can see her easily and often. That's the kind of father I want him to be. But I deeply resent the way this decision has been executed. I'm not made a part of his decision making; my happiness and fulfillment are not factors in the equation for him.

I stare out at the waves. Beautiful California. Since I left Greece, this is the first place I've felt at home. My career is finally taking off. And he wants me *to leave*? How will quitting now impact my professional development?

Seagulls cry out their own woes as the sun prepares to sink into the ocean on the far side. I think of my father, how he left Cameroon for Greece, for my mother. And how he's never been happy for a single day since.

Shortly before we leave Los Angeles, Viktor throws me a thirtieth birthday party. He organizes a surprise dinner with many of my closest friends, after which we head to a famous jazz club. He organizes all of this from Brussels, since he can't actually be there in person.

A week later, Viktor flies back to California to help pack for our move and we attend a goodbye party we throw at the Derby, the landmark LA swing club. Ensconced at the Derby, he tells me it's also a birthday celebration for me. *This rationalization is intended to make him feel better about having missed the actual one*, I think.

Leaving everything behind—my work, my friends, my routines, all my newfound happiness—is indescribably hard. But what choice do I have? Either I follow Viktor to Austria, or I'll find myself divorced. *I love him and I'm committed to our marriage*, I think. *Besides, I want to have children with him.*

I push aside my feelings of betrayal and resentment and set my mind to packing. I pack away my grief, along with the linens and silverware and books, though I won't open that particular box for many years.

If I could predict the future, I'd know Viktor and I will argue incessantly for years about the events leading up to this move. I feel I was explicitly clear about *not* wanting to leave LA but he'll insist we both agreed to the move and he hadn't just hijacked me. I'll grow to doubt my own version of events and my memory will feel increasingly murky. Where I can rarely remember even the basic plot of the movies we see, Viktor is able to recall specific details, even reciting lines of dialogue from films he saw as a child. I'll question myself and privilege Viktor's recollection of things. Did I consent to move or only appear to consent without realizing it? If so, why did it feel like a *fait accompli*?

PART TWO

CHAPTER 9

Neither Here nor There

"Women are supposed to be very calm generally: but women
feel just as men feel; they need exercise for their faculties,
and a field for their efforts, as much as their brothers do; they
suffer from too rigid a restraint, too absolute a stagnation,
precisely as men would suffer; and it is narrow-minded in
their more privileged fellow-creatures to say that they ought
to confine themselves to making puddings and knitting
stockings, to playing on the piano and embroidering bags."
— Charlotte Brontë, *Jane Eyre*

CALL IT A LAST-DITCH ACT OF PASSIVE REBELLION,
but just before our move, I request a transfer to RAND's European headquarters in the Netherlands. I've crossed paths with RAND Europe's president at the LA office, and he kindly accepts my joining the team. He also
extends to me the use of a small RAND-owned apartment in the center of
Leiden and says I can have it for as long as I need to get settled elsewhere.

Leiden is a lovely little town with a famous university, so it's full of
students and has a youthful vibe despite its long history. My two-story
apartment is part of an old building, so it's full of character. There are two
bedrooms and a bathroom upstairs, and a comfortable living room on
the ground floor with large windows that let out onto a shared courtyard.

And it's just a fifteen-minute walk from my office. After living in the US, I'm taken in by the miniature size of everything here—the cute little streets, lined with the tiniest two-story town houses that look almost like dollhouses. Everything is new and exciting. For a while, I walk around in a pink cloud.

I'm over the moon that I won't have to give up my RAND career completely and attempt to put my marital resentments behind me. Things between us are good for a while. Or we do a good job convincing ourselves they are. In the back of my mind, or perhaps my heart, something is always tickling, scratching quietly away at my sense that everything is okay.

I ignore it.

RAND's offices are housed in a modern glass building, very different from the traditional architecture of Leiden. I walk to work from the city's center, crossing the railroad tracks and a sea of parked bicycles. In the Netherlands, many people commute to work from a different city, riding bikes to and from the train station. They come in every color—there are blues, yellows, reds, and bright greens. Some have baskets, in which their riders carry groceries, flowers, and other provisions of daily life. After the endless traffic of Los Angeles roadways, they make a cheerful scene.

For the first time, I have an office to myself. My new colleagues are welcoming and kind, offering to show me around and take me to lunch. I immediately feel I'm a respected member of the team. That said, working with North Americans came more effortlessly for me. I have an intuitive grasp of the culture, more so even than my own European one. Funny that when I was working in the US, I was seen as "the European." Now in Europe, I'm often mistaken for an American. I live and work in this strangely liminal zone, where I'm always the foreigner or outsider—but I love it.

Soon, however, I become acquainted with Holland's infamous horizontal rains, which can drag on for days or even weeks at a time. One night, as I get ready for bed, I hear a soft tapping sound coming from the ceiling above. There's a roof leak; water is dripping into the upstairs attic. Another night, I hear a faint but unquestionable squeaking sound and manage to trace it to the foot of my bed, where two frightened mice stand frozen and staring back at me. Having no previous experience with mice, I panic and call my husband, who's in London at the time. He's equally clueless about what to do in the case of mice. The next day, I go to a store my colleagues recommended and buy a mouse trap.

I have little time to worry about an infestation, however. It is September of 2001 when I transfer to the Netherlands, right before the events of September 11th in New York, Virginia, and Pennsylvania.

In the aftermath of the terrorist attacks, RAND takes a leading role in analyzing the events and what led to them, including US and international responses and counterterrorism strategies. I soon find myself pulled into RAND Europe's counterterrorism task force, working with California headquarters, and reporting directly to the President of RAND Europe. It's a rush.

Yet, despite the excitement and newness of everything I'm learning, my days end the same way: I pick up Indonesian takeout on my walk home after work. Then, I eat it on the couch while watching some American series and reading the Dutch subtitles to familiarize myself with the language. Then I go to bed. Alone.

Viktor and I try to see each other every weekend; either I fly to the Austrian capital, or he flies to see me in Leiden from wherever he happens to be working at the time. My trips to Vienna become the highlight of any week. I leave the office early on Friday and catch the train to Schiphol Airport in Amsterdam for the 4:30 p.m. flight. In contrast to the grim, damp Dutch autumns, Vienna's skies are bluer and sunnier than I remember from past visits. We spend the weekends setting up our new home (a three-bedroom rental flat in Vienna's 7th district that belongs to his brother), spending time with Julia, and catching up with Viktor's old friends from his university days. The distance has mellowed me and made me less resentful toward Viktor. Our time together is enjoyable, and we fight less. Do I long to be with him, or do I long to *not* be alone? I'm not sure I can (or want to) tell the difference.

Monday mornings are always tough. I leave my husband and dash off early to make the 7:30 a.m. flight, then head straight into the office to start my week. The routine quickly begins to wear on me. Perhaps it's the depressing weather, or the fact I'm now thirty, or that I'm alone again most of the time, but I start thinking for the first time about having children.

When I tell him this, Viktor couldn't be more supportive. He's wanted to have kids since the day we got married, maybe earlier. As I think about stepping away from work to focus on having a family, it's with the understanding that this will be a temporary break. I'll work through my pregnancy and take only a few weeks off after the baby is born. My identity is too intimately linked to my work. Besides, I certainly don't see myself as a stay-at-home mom.

I'm a professional woman, ambitious and capable with a bright future ahead of me, I think. *And I'm not giving that up for anything or anyone. All I have to do is figure out what that bright future is.*

I hear my mother's voice in the back of my mind, admonishing me not to let anything or anyone (especially not a man!) get in the way of me fulfilling my potential. Growing up, I saw my mother as financially dependent on my father. Although it never seemed to be an issue between them (he was endlessly generous and made it clear to my mother that whatever was his, was equally hers), it was extremely important to me that I earn my own money. I wanted to be independent, never having to answer to a man. Never having to ask permission to do or buy what I wanted—no restrictions. I wanted an even playing field.

In fact, when we married, I kept my maiden name as a symbolic representation of the fairness and independence I expected to have. Having children won't change that, I decide.

CHAPTER 10

Keep It Down

"'Finding yourself' is not really how it works. You aren't a ten-dollar bill in last winter's coat pocket. You are also not lost. Your true self is right there, buried under cultural conditioning, other peoples' opinions, and inaccurate conclusions you drew as a kid that became your beliefs about who you are. 'Finding yourself' is actually returning to yourself. An unlearning, an excavation, a remembering who you were before the world got its hands on you."
— Kelsey Crowe, Emily McDowell, *There Is No Good Card for This: What to Say and Do When Life Is Scary, Awful, and Unfair to People You Love*

WE DECIDE TO START RIGHT AWAY. And I take initiative this time. I intend to be pregnant by the end of January, at the latest. But, after two months pass without success, I become impatient. What did I expect with all the traveling, stress, and time apart? If I was ever going to get pregnant, I needed to remove those factors.

I ask RAND for permission to move to Vienna, where I can continue to work remotely on my projects. Their answer is "yes"; I'm in heaven. Finally, Viktor and I can start a family. Finally, I won't be alone.

Christmas in Vienna is sublime. My parents come up from Athens and spend the holidays with us. Viktor's parents come, too. The bitter cold is a shock to my parents, but they love roaming the festive Vienna streets, bundled up in the winter coats and hats they never get to wear at home in Greece.

The fact I've never had a regular menstrual cycle has never bothered me before. Now, it's interfering with my plans. I make an appointment with a fertility doctor who begins treating me right away. As we wait to discover whether the first dose has worked, we go away to Thailand for two weeks, just the two of us. It's a pleasant distraction.

We arrive back in Vienna on a crisp, sunny February morning. While my husband unpacks, I take a pregnancy test—*positive!* We're over the moon.

Heading to my first gynecologist visit, I'm excited, happy. But my doctor—an austere, elderly Austrian gentleman—sits me down. "Until you've passed the twelve-week mark," he says, "it's wise not to consider yourself pregnant." His silver eyebrows sprout in every direction. He looks up from his tiny reading glasses: "These first weeks are a vulnerable time and a lot can go wrong."

He's telling me I could lose my baby, I think. I'm infuriated! Barely out of the office door, I call my husband, demanding he leave a meeting to speak with me.

"How could the doctor say that to me? Is it because my German isn't perfect?" I'm incensed. "I'm never going back there! I'm going to find an English-speaking doctor."

My husband tries to reason with me. "Katia, he's one of the best gynecologists in Vienna, the head of the birth clinic at one of the biggest hospitals here . . ." I'm getting nowhere with him.

I call my mom. "Bloody Austrians!" I shout into the phone as I walk. "How arrogant they are!"

People on the street turn to stare in my direction, as they would anyone who's being loud against the shushed backdrop of their soft-spoken culture. Hell, not even Austrian *babies* are loud! I don't care. I'm Greek and we're high-volume—*get over it*. (Viktor often has to remind me to "keep it down.")

I resent having to be quiet.

The culture has challenged me since the day I arrived. Austrians are largely reserved, unlikely to express strong emotions, which feels foreign to me. I wear my heart on my sleeve. I'm spontaneous and "temperamental," as my husband likes to remind me. My volume was never an issue in the US; I fit right in there! In Austria, I collect stares.

We were only a few months into our relationship when we had our first big fight. And more fighting continued from there. It always revolved around the same thing: Viktor's ex-girlfriend (Julia's mom) and her frequent attempts to interfere in our lives. She regularly tried to impose conditions on how we spent our time, always undermining my freedom and autonomy. More than that, I grew to resent Viktor for how he handled her. He didn't (and still doesn't) prioritize *our* needs, much less mine. He's always so accommodating, capitulating to his ex out of fear of losing access to his daughter.

Viktor was already battling his ex when we met, so he's angry to have to fight with me on the other end. Ultimately, an innocent child loses.

In the beginning of our marriage, he would tell me our fighting wasn't "normal." His parents never fought. I saw fighting as a normal part of every relationship since my parents fought often and with great passion. Afterward, they'd make up again and all was forgotten. I didn't see that as a negative thing.

Somehow, I put my anger aside and allow myself to enjoy my pregnancy. It's a wonderful experience of discovery—I learn so much about my body and the human life growing inside me. I read all the books and dog-ear all the pages. Being a parent is a science and an art, and I want to become an expert at both.

Viktor is constantly on the road, however, and soon enough, I become hyperaware of my aloneness once again. At least I have my work. Besides, I also aim to finish the doctoral dissertation I started back in LA.

In my fourth month of pregnancy, I'm awarded a two-month fellowship at the European Union Institute for Security Studies in Paris. It's exciting to have my own little office there, with access to all the facilities and resources of the Institute. It's thrilling to be in a professional environment again, doing interesting work, and feeling appreciated by my colleagues.

I've always had a special connection to Paris. My father feels at home here, too, more so even than in Athens. In fact, the studio where I'm staying belongs to him; he bought it during the Greek stock market boom a few years earlier.

The little apartment is just a few steps off the majestic Avenue des Champs Élysées in a bustling area of town full of cafés, restaurants, theaters, and luxury shops. Despite its busy location, the studio is quiet with its large, floor-to-ceiling windows that overlook a courtyard and let in a lot of light. The living area is no bigger than a small bedroom, but the place is perfectly, creatively equipped. A double bed folds down from the wall at night and can be tucked away again in the morning. The TV and stereo are likewise ensconced in a wall, along with rows of bookshelves, so as not to take up too much space. There's a blue velvet pull-out couch and a round table. The kitchen is small but fully equipped; my parents host dinners for local friends when they stay in Paris.

My father especially loves the studio. It's his *bijou* (his jewel) and his own paintings hang on the walls, so I feel at home here.

During the week, I love walking to work. I could take public transport, but I prefer the twenty-minute stroll across the Champs Élysées and up toward the Palais de Trocadéro. At lunchtime, if I don't have plans with one of my colleagues, I like to pick up a sandwich and a coke and sit on the steps of the Palais de Chaillot, enjoying the magnificent view of the Eiffel Tower below.

As much as I'm learning to enjoy my solitude (perhaps because I know that soon, I'll never be alone again), I also love Viktor's weekend visits.

When my stint is over, I feel almost reluctant to leave Paris and head back to Vienna, which at the time, feels small and provincial by comparison. I will miss the big city vibe. And I'll miss feeling like a professional.

Though, soon, I will have plenty to keep me occupied.

A few days before my due date, I begin having contractions. My parents have come to Vienna for the birth, but still no sign of our baby. Then, five nights after the due date, I officially go into labor.

I wake Viktor and tell him it's time to go to the hospital. When we get downstairs to leave, my father exits the guest room, fully dressed and expecting to come with us. It takes some doing to convince him to stay. "This could take hours," Viktor tells him. "And there isn't much for you to do there but wait, which you can do more comfortably here."

Petros makes us wait nearly eighteen hours, in fact. Nearly eighteen *very* painful hours. Not that it matters in the end. The moment they lay him on my chest is magical. Suddenly everything is quiet. The midwife and my doctor are there, but no one speaks; Petros doesn't even cry. All I want is to protect him and keep him warm and soothe him after the shock that is birth.

Soon, they whisk him away to clean him up and deliver him back to me, swaddled in a white blanket. I'll never forget my first glimpse of his face. His dark blue eyes are wide open and darting from left to right. He is perfectly still but already so curious about the world, quietly taking everything in. We're relieved to learn his vital signs are all normal; everything will be okay. Then the nurse puts the baby to my breast and he immediately latches—it all seems like a miracle.

My parents arrive with Julia at the hospital within half an hour. How could anyone keep them away?! They're all dying to see him.

My colleagues are researchers employed by RAND, but as a PhD fellow, I don't have the right to a formal maternity leave. It's up to me to take (unpaid) time off. I still have tuition to pay, however. As long as I continue to perform project work, though with "looser engagement" now that Petros has arrived, my pay will cover my tuition fees with a bit left over. The choice is between dropping out of the program until I'm ready to work again, or to ask Viktor to pay on my behalf, which I'm not prepared to do.

Viktor soon goes back to Germany to support his client there and my father leaves for Greece after a couple of weeks. My mother stays on a little longer to help me get settled. It's comforting to have her there; she takes care of me while I take care of my baby. Though, an interesting dynamic develops: Mamá knows how best to do things from having raised my brother and me; I claim I know better because I've read all the books. (Later, I will admire how patient she is with me, letting me do things my way.)

I love being a new mother. My favorite part of the day is when Petros wakes in the mornings. Instead of crying out for me right away, he lies contentedly by himself for at least half an hour, observing everything around him, discovering his new world and expressing his delight. As soon as he becomes a little impatient, I go to him and lean over his little cot. "Good morning," I say, and he always looks so happy to see me. His face lights up with smiles and giggles and coos. I can't get enough of him.

Juggling an infant with work is *interesting*. There I am, tapping away on the computer with one hand—finishing a report or creating PowerPoint slides for an upcoming presentation—the other hand holding Petros, attached to my breast with peaceful determination.

Shortly after my mother leaves, my close friend Maria comes to visit and to help me with Petros. Maria and I grew up together in Athens. We were inseparable in elementary school all through eighth grade, when her parents emigrated to Germany. We maintained our friendship in the pre-email, pre-video call, pre-social media times by writing letters and exchanging care packages. Now, Maria lives in the US with her husband and children. I was maid of honor at her wedding.

Her offer to visit is perfect timing. One of my projects is due for a final briefing and I've been asked by a senior colleague to do it. The briefing involves an analysis of trends in the European defense industry. Everything is set up for an afternoon video conference (it's morning in Washington, DC, where the client and my senior colleague will call in to participate). I'm wearing a business suit, even though they'll only see the top portion, and I have just fed Petros, earlier than his usual feeding time. Not much more I can do but hope he'll last for the next couple of hours. My office is in an open space on the upper level of our apartment, so Maria takes Petros downstairs to ensure there is no noise to disturb my call.

All goes smoothly and they are appreciative of my presentation; I feel a huge sense of relief and satisfaction. Despite my unconventional location (I'm no longer based in the US like the client, or even in Leiden with my organization) and the fact I have just had a baby, I can still deliver a high-quality product. Fearing that my leaving Leiden might have led people to question my commitment to the work, I feel a strong need to prove myself.

Satisfied, I turn off my computer and walk downstairs, amazed at how quiet the apartment has been during my call. Maria and Petros aren't in the living room. As I open the kitchen door, the sound waves from Petros's wailing hit me like a brick wall.

Both my friend and my baby are visibly distressed. Maria breathes an exaggerated sigh of relief as she thrusts the baby over to me. "Feed him! *Now!*"

Apparently, Petros had been crying this way since just after my two-hour call started, and there was nothing Maria could do to appease him. I take the still-screaming baby in my arms and barely have time to unbutton my shirt before he grabs with both hands and latches onto my breast.

When he's two months old, we fly to Athens for the holidays—Petros's first flight. It's difficult to describe the level of adoration thrown at a new baby by one's Greek family and friends. Everyone parades through my parents' place to meet the little prince.

As a first-time mom, I'm of course totally freaked out about the idea of my tiny baby handling all these new faces and loud voices—and, more crucially, all the germs! I watch everyone who comes near Petros like a hawk. If they haven't just washed their hands, I promptly send them away to do so. When my godmother comes to visit, she casually lights a cigarette *right next to my boy*. I'm horrified! Granted, she never had children of her own and is a compulsive smoker. Still, I cannot conceive how an educated woman, an academic even, has never considered the facts: passive smoking is harmful, especially for babies.

Here I am, experiencing culture shock in my own country.

Coming back to Vienna after the holidays is anticlimactic. I was only just surrounded by people, love, attention, and support, and now I'm alone again, taking care of a tiny human who depends entirely on me for everything (but isn't yet much of a conversationalist). I miss my family and friends and I know they miss us, too.

The fact that it is the middle of winter doesn't help. I hate the cold; my Greek body—and soul—will never get used to it. So, on yet another bitter, cold afternoon, I decide the time has come: we have to get out of this house! We step out for fresh air and lunch, anywhere I can see real live adult humans and maybe even exchange a few words with them. I pack my book in the diaper bag that follows us everywhere. *Petros will nap in his stroller,* I think, *and I'll enjoy some quiet time.* Easier said than done.

Going out with an infant is a major expedition. First, I feed him so he won't get hungry halfway (I haven't yet mastered the art of public breastfeeding and feel awkward attempting it). Next, I lay out a series of layers to dress him in, culminating in a heavy, dark blue snowsuit. Petros *hates* this snowsuit—it's far too hot—so I have a strategy: I'll wait until the very last moment, then dress him quickly in the snowsuit, and dash out of the apartment. That way, he'll cool down quickly and stop crying.

But just as I get him packed in the suit, then into the lamb-fur lined sleeping bag, and finally into the stroller, I realize *to my horror* that he has just pooped. So, I unpack everything to change him. By the time I'm done, he starts crying; he's hungry again. So, I sit down to nurse him. As soon as he's finished, I start over with the layers. By the time we're ready to leave, an hour (or possibly a year) has passed.

I, the ultimate control freak, am learning from a baby how to be flexible.

There are days when the only people I talk to are long distance—my mother in Greece and the occasional friend. And Petros, of course. I talk to him all the time and have been since before he was born. I read that for a child to learn a language, it's best to start speaking to them in that language from age zero; it encourages passive learning and absorption. So there I am, always babbling to my baby in Greek about anything I can think of.

Τι ωραία μέρα σήμερα. Πάμε βόλτα! (It's a beautiful day today. I think we should go for a walk!)

Κοίτα την κυρία—φοράει ένα όμορφο κόκκινο παλτό. (Look at this lady—she's wearing such a nice red coat.)

Κρυώνεις όσο κι εγώ; Πάμε πίσω στο σπίτι; (Are you as cold as I am? Shall we go back home?)

Πλένω τα χέρια μου τώρα. Όταν μεγαλώσεις, θα σου μάθω να πλένεις και τα δικά σου! (I'm washing my hands now. When you're older, I'll teach you to wash your hands.)

If he's going to learn my mother tongue, I have to keep talking.

As much as I love this time with my baby, I feel desperately alone. When my husband later comes down with a bad cold and decides to take a few days off from traveling, I'm perversely ecstatic. It means I get to spend time with him and Petros together.

The next several years are filled with little more than play dates and pediatrician appointments, punctuated by occasional dinners out with friends. Viktor is rarely around and even when he is, he's still working long hours. I feel like I don't have a partner. I'm effectively a single parent, only I'm not allowed to call myself that. My career is going nowhere. I've given up all paid work but still struggle to finish my PhD dissertation. I become increasingly unhappy.

Still, none of that makes me reconsider my original plan, which is to have at least two children. In 2004, I discover I am pregnant again—with a girl. It has always been my dream to have a boy and a girl, in that sequence. (Growing up, I'd always wished I had a big brother. When I was a teenager, my girlfriends with older brothers had much more liberal family policies about going out and staying up late, because they had the protection of their brothers.) Now, everything feels complete. I'm excited to have a girl for all the usual reasons: I'll have fun dressing her in the cutest little girl dresses, and when she's a bit older, we'll wear matching outfits and do girly things, like go shopping and get mani-pedis together.

My second delivery is likely stress induced. It's November and I'm having coffee with my mom at a little Italian place not far from our apartment. She's come to Vienna for the birth, alone this time. Since my father wasn't allowed to be present for Petros's delivery, he makes a dramatic show of not coming with her. Instead, he spends time in Paris, waiting for word the baby is here before he'll fly to Vienna.

As Mamá and I sip our lattes, the nanny calls my cell, her voice barely audible. Petros has taken a fall from his tricycle and hurt himself.

I pay for our coffees and rush out of the café. Margarita is simultaneously weighing down on me and pushing up against my diaphragm (which is very uncomfortable), but I break into a run. When I make it home, my son and the nanny are still in front of our building and Petros's forehead is covered in blood. Erica is doing her best to blot the wound with tissues. There's a bad cut just beneath his eyebrow—thankfully, his eye is unhurt—which explains the amount of blood pouring down his little face. It looks much worse than it is, though I don't know this at that moment.

That evening, I begin having contractions. I have an uncomfortable night—up and down, up and down—and just before sunrise, we head to the hospital. In the car on the way over, Viktor and I choose from our shortlist of baby girl names. Shortly before noon, our dark-haired Princess Margarita makes her entrance. Her birth is easy compared to Petros's—I'm not even tired!

My mom arrives with Julia and Petros to welcome Margarita to the family and we take our first family photos together, Petros nearly stealing the show with his swollen eyelid. Margarita looks remarkably like her big brother, but she's a very different baby. Petros was relatively low maintenance from day one, but our daughter needs a lot of attention and will *not* sleep unless she's being held. As soon as we put her down, she screams, the pitch of her voice much higher than her brother's.

The first few weeks are as challenging as they are magical: Margarita is captivating and incredibly demanding. She is a vocal child, much more than Petros at her age. She adores her brother—her face lights up every time she sees him—and Petros adores her. His favorite thing to do is to take her tiny little feet and kiss one and then the other, over and over.

The next couple of years pass in a blur. I am completely smitten with my babies and astonished at how quickly they learn and grow and change. Viktor is still gone most of the time, however, so my days are long and full and often exhausting. To balance things, we spend a lot of time in Greece, where my family lavishes the children with love and attention. They speak to the children in Greek and teach them wonderful children's songs and the names of objects. My father quickly teaches Petros to count—in five languages!

In Vienna, I miss the support, which many of my girlfriends in Greece take for granted. With family nearby, they can go back to work whenever they want, resting in the security that their children are well taken care of by someone who loves them. If one of their children catches a cold, they don't have to miss work. I'm incredibly grateful to be able to hire a nanny when I need to, but I'm still forced to scramble when something goes wrong. And every time my parents return home to Athens, or the kids and I return to Vienna, I feel a pang of regret and "expat guilt."

CHAPTER 11

Making Lists

"Grief has no distance. Grief comes in waves, paroxysms,
sudden apprehensions that weaken the knees and
blind the eyes and obliterate the dailiness of life."
— Joan Didion, *The Year of Magical Thinking*

MY FATHER HAS A CAR ACCIDENT.

He isn't injured, and the car isn't badly damaged, but he finds himself parked on the sidewalk and can't remember how it happened.

The doctor schedules a series of tests. When results come in, he asks for more tests—a CT scan, MRI, a lung biopsy. *Biopsy.* The final picture is devastating: my father has a tumor in his pancreas and a scattering of smaller tumors in his lungs. It looks like the cancer started in his pancreas and metastasized.

The pancreas regulates blood sugar levels and the secretion of insulin, so the car accident was most likely caused by a sudden drop in blood sugar, which caused him to faint.

When I hear the news, I already know pancreatic cancer is nearly always a death sentence. It's stealthy; by the time symptoms present, you're already in the final stages. My dad is "lucky" enough to have discovered his cancer by accident—literally. Still, it's among the worst types of cancer you can get.

And Babás knows this. But it doesn't matter; he's in action mode. Just after Boxing Day, and only a couple of weeks after his diagnosis, he starts his cancer battle with the first round of chemotherapy. He's determined to win. He studies every detail of his test results and learns everything there is to know about pancreatic cancer. He calls almost every day to tell me about the latest study or the newest experimental drug that might be helpful to his case. He learns to use email and sends long messages detailing his latest MRI or CT scan results and asking my opinion on the research. Together, we become a two-man pancreatic cancer think tank.

Babás reaches out to his network and identifies the key European experts on his cancer. He visits renowned specialists in Austria and France. Over the next two years, he goes through several rounds of chemo with various drug combinations. He doesn't have much confidence in the Greek system and makes sure to get second and third opinions about every treatment course. Every time a physician or expert offers my father even the haziest glimmer of hope, he lights up like the Paris sky at New Year's, gathering just enough steam to keep fighting.

He refuses to slow down or accept the odds. Even when the chemo side effects kick in, my father stubbornly makes his weekly, sometimes twice weekly, tennis match. And he never skips bridge. Despite his packed treatment schedule, he still travels. He refuses to do otherwise. He comes to visit us in Vienna and spends time in Paris, searching out second opinions wherever he goes.

Every few days, he sends Petros an email, writing in uppercase Greek letters so that Petros, who hasn't yet learned to read in lowercase, can practice his Greek. He tells my son about his "friend" Felix, the "big white bird." Felix flies from Vienna to Athens, he says, bringing Pappoús news of the children and whether they've been good or bad. He praises the kids for their large and small achievements: Petros winning the ski race, Margarita going off to kindergarten. And when he learns of tantrums or poor behavior, Pappoús threatens to "pull on their ears until they resemble donkey ears." He ends every message by expressing his unconditional love.

For my father's seventy-seventh birthday, Viktor and I surprise him. A couple of years ago, my dad wrote a book—a memoir. He was incredibly proud of his book and had always wished his foreign friends could read it, but it was published in Greek. The surprise is Viktor's idea. We hire a translator and find a publisher in Austria to take on the project. In March, my dad opens the mail to find a copy of *If I'd Known* in English—his birthday surprise. I cherish the email he sends to thank us:

My Dear Ones,

Surprise, joy, and a mountain of profound emotions made me cry like a little child when I saw in front of my eyes my book translated into English. A big "thank you" is not enough to express the value of your gesture, so noble and full of warmth.

A thousand thanks,

Dad

In an outbreak of bad timing, Viktor is diagnosed with Hepatitis C and must endure a painful year of treatments. I know very little about the illness, except that my dad had been diagnosed with it a few years earlier and successfully underwent the same treatment; his Hep C disappeared. I assume it will be the same for Viktor, so I don't talk about it much with him. I'm too absorbed in my father's situation to have much bandwidth left for anything else, even my husband.

A few weeks after Viktor starts taking the medication, our fights increase dramatically—in both frequency and intensity. I attribute this to the gradual deterioration of our already dysfunctional relationship. Viktor is often in a bad mood and seems depressed, but I don't connect his moods to the Hep C treatment. Years later, Viktor will tell me I'd been oblivious to what he was going through, uninterested and unsupportive.

"Did you know that some of the side effects of the drugs I was taking are depression and suicide? Do you have any idea what that treatment was like for me?"

I didn't. I hadn't been paying attention.

When the treatments end, Viktor is cleared of Hep C and his mood improves. Our arguments become fewer and less intense. But my husband's resentment lingers.

And now my body decides to chime in. I start experiencing intense lower back and neck pain, which I assume is from lifting the children, who are growing heavier every day. I make an appointment with an orthopedic specialist, who orders an X-ray—but it doesn't show anything wrong with me. The pain persists, so I begin a long-term relationship with physiotherapy. It helps release the tension, but only temporarily; the pain always comes back. I try many different therapists, all of them wonderful. But every time someone manages to "unblock" me and relieve my pain (for which I feel awe and gratitude), the pain eventually returns and I'm blocked again.

It will take another fifteen years before I realize the origin of my pain isn't rooted in my body; it's in my soul. The physical misalignment I try so hard to fix is really about a lack of alignment in my heart. I don't yet know that when you fail to honor your own core values, everything feels off. Without a sense of purpose that comes from within—and not from anything outside of you—it's impossible to find meaning and fulfillment.

But it will be years before those realizations come. For now, I just feel . . . off. Unhappy, resentful, trapped. Like a victim.

Margarita starts kindergarten, Petros begins first grade, and I start exploring career options.

Viktor's father is a former Ambassador, so he tries to set me up with some of his dad's old security and defense contacts in Vienna. The market in Austria is minuscule and saturated, however, and there are no realistic prospects for me here. So, I look outside the country, assuming if I get a great offer elsewhere, Viktor will agree to relocate.

After all, I moved to Vienna for him.

My big target is the European Union—specifically, the European Defence Agency, or EDA. If you work in the field, the EDA is the place to be. And it has been my dream since I gave up my work at RAND and we moved to Europe. The EDA is a new and ambitious organization; it's technocratic, so the solid analytical skills I built at RAND would be appreciated. And the EDA seems poised to make a difference in European defense matters (in contrast to the usual EU bureaucratic inertia).

But the prospect of landing a job at an EU institution without political backing is another matter. To stand any chance as a candidate, you have to be supported by your national delegation, or at least the bilateral ambassador to the country. I've never worked for the Greek government and have no contacts in the Greek political establishment. I'm a complete outsider.

I'm also pretty apolitical. Politics wasn't discussed at the dinner table when I was growing up. My parents never revealed what party or candidate they voted for in elections. They never expressed strong political opinions or argued about politics with their friends—perhaps the most popular national sport in Greece, if one excludes arguing about soccer. But it's more than just lack of interest. There is an underlying disgust among Greeks, a belief that politics is "dirty"—no surprise, given the widespread corruption in Greek politics—and a belief that engaging in politics can only lead to disappointment. Or, worse, to trouble.

When my friends started joining party-affiliated youth organizations in our late teenage years and all through university, I stayed out of their discussions. I simply didn't know enough—or care. It's ironic that I attended the John F. Kennedy School of Government, the ultimate sanctum for political junkies. It's an even greater irony that I married one of those junkies, a man whose dream has always been to become a politician.

When Viktor first told me about this dream, I didn't take him seriously. When I later realized he *was* serious, I told him he'd be wasting his time, brains, and talent on a lost cause that would get him nowhere. He's an idealist but all politicians are self-centered, self-interested egomaniacs with no integrity, I insisted. They'd have him for lunch.

It's been a source of tension between us ever since.

But right now, I'm not thinking of that. I'm wondering how to navigate the political gauntlet required to land a defense job. I send a letter to the Greek Ambassador to Belgium, asking him to support my candidacy, but he politely turns me down. He has no clue who the hell I am and neither do any of his people; I'm mortified. But I'm my father's daughter; I refuse to give up. Defense is my future.

For the last couple of years, I've been scanning job vacancies and networking with colleagues who keep me up to date on what's happening. I apply whenever I see a relevant position open up. My credentials get me shortlisted twice. When I receive my first formal offer, I'm over the moon.

Viktor says he's happy for me, but he doesn't think it's a good time to move. So, I turn down the job.

When a second offer comes, it's much harder to say "no," but Viktor still isn't budging. He's just started a big new job himself, and he doesn't want to be separated from his daughter again. Our kids are still only four and two years old, too young for me to be gone full time. If I take the job, I know I'll probably never complete my dissertation. Regardless, I still want Viktor to take me in his arms and tell me we'll make it work somehow, just like he did when I got accepted at RAND and he declared we would move to LA.

I call Michael, my former Harvard professor who's become a friend and mentor over the years. He's been helping me with part of my PhD dissertation, so he's familiar with my work. Michael is unequivocal: I can't take a full-time job with two young children and an unfinished dissertation. I'm only months away from completing my PhD, so I need to finish it. If I don't, he says, I will regret it for the rest of my life. And he's right.

I decline the second offer and hope there will be a next time. But despite knowing it's the right thing, I feel misled—betrayed even. Why did Viktor let me go through the whole process—*twice*—if he couldn't support my taking the work? I feel blindsided. I worry that declining two offers has made me seem unserious and unprofessional. How is it that with my education, connections, and hard work, I have to ask a man's permission? Worse, why do I always have to compromise my professional dreams?

When we got together, Viktor and I never explicitly discussed our career paths or what we wanted from life. If we had, we might have realized how different our goals were.

My dad continues his cancer treatments into spring of 2008, and Viktor introduces the idea of us potentially moving to Greece. He knows how much it means to me to be close to my family. He can see how much I look forward to every trip and how down I get when I come back to Vienna. The only thing that cheers me up is planning the next trip. Maybe he thinks Greece can salvage our relationship, or the move will make up for the wasted job offers. It's almost impossible for Viktor to get a job in Greece, but he's willing to commute, he says. I can't believe my ears.

My husband likes to make lists. To assess pros and cons, to weigh options according to a set of criteria. He even makes lists to evaluate our relationship—what we have and what we need from each other. So, we sit down together and make lists: one for the pros and cons of moving to Greece and another to assess our relationship.

We make tentative plans and projections: where we would live (close to my parents); who would help us take care of the kids (the dear family friend who helped raise me and my brother); what schools the children could go to (the German school). I start spending more time in Greece and making contacts with potential employers there. And I'm grateful for the precious time—at least one week per month—I get to spend with my dad.

Somewhere in the midst of all this, a former colleague who now works for the EDA calls. A new position just opened up and he encourages me to apply. The job is perfect for my profile, but I hesitate. I've already turned them down twice; I doubt they'll invite me for an interview. My friend insists I apply anyway. It's a different department and no one will remember I applied—that was so long ago. So, I do. And I get invited for a round of interviews in June and shortlisted for another round in early July, right before we leave for Greece and summer vacation.

We arrive at a seaside resort near Athens, an area called Anavyssos, one of the many small towns along the coast of Attica. We book a nice five-star hotel for its proximity to Athens. There's a beautiful, clean sandy beach and the water is clear and shallow, perfect for families. We spend our days by the pool, then go for a dip in the sea. Afterward, we head back for lunch at the pool restaurant, and then back to the pool after naps. Late in the afternoons, Viktor likes to take the kids to the tennis court to throw some balls. I skip that, since like most Greeks, I avoid any form of physical exercise that isn't swimming while the sun is in the sky. But with the big white parasols, comfy beach chairs, warm sand, and cocktails at sunset—it's heaven.

It's mid-afternoon on a scorching Greek summer day. My two little ones have gone up to the room for a nap. Viktor and I have an understanding: a couple of hours out of every day are my time. No feeding chicken nuggets and french fries, no entertaining with books and games, no chasing little feet around the swimming pool. While the kids nap with their dad, I usually read a book. Or if the heat hasn't made me lethargic, I go waterskiing, zero kids in tow—a luxury.

Our little oasis is only forty minutes by car for my parents, so they join us for a few days. Babás needs to stay close to the hospital where he gets chemotherapy so he can be treated in the event of complications, which occur often. This morning, for example, he suddenly came down with a fever and chills and couldn't join us at the beach.

By last summer, he'd already lost all his hair, but he still looked fit posing for photos with his grandchildren. This year, he has his hair back, but looks tired, gaunt. He doesn't have much energy for photos. Successive rounds of cancer treatment over the past year and a half haven't brought any improvements. His spirit was upbeat and hopeful when he started, but now he seems almost resigned to his fate.

I think back to a picture of my parents taken in Bratislava, a few weeks before his diagnosis. They look relaxed, happy, healthy. My father was still his strong, temperamental, larger-than-life self. The strongest man I know. Now, my dad—my rock—is weak and scared. Cancer is winning.

I'm grateful to Viktor for wanting to spend our summer vacation here, despite there being many more beautiful and exciting places we could be. He loves my dad and spending time with him now is almost as important to him as it is to me. My dad loves Viktor, too; he's always treated him like his own son. He relates to my husband's ambition and his willingness to put in hard work. And he knows he can rely on Viktor to take good care of me, to take over for him.

In Greece, we joke that only tourists and fools are out at 3:00 p.m. on a summer afternoon, but here I am. I order an iced latte at the bar and the waiter offers to bring it out to me, so I go back to my lounge chair in the shade and open my book. *Istanbul* by Orhan Pamuk. I'm hoping to get a sense of what my mother's life there would have been like.

As the waiter sets down my coffee and hands me the bill to sign, my cellphone rings.

"Hi, is this Katia?" The caller has an English accent.

"Yes, that's me."

"This is Boris calling from the European Defence Agency in Brussels."

I sit up. Boris tells me I was one of two finalists for the senior analyst position. He's the head of the department.

"Do you have a minute?" he asks.

"Of course, Boris."

"I'd like to make you an offer to come work for us." He says he'll send the contract by email today and I have a week to respond.

Boris's offer couldn't have come at a worse time.

Our presence in Greece is one of the few things that can cheer up my father and pull him out of his despair. We can already see the difference in him. At home, he spends his days in bed, staring absently into space. But here, he's much more present and cheerful, more like his humorous self. He flirts with the waitresses and the ladies at the front desk. A couple of days ago, he even sprinted across the grass in the hotel garden to show us he could still jog!

If I take the position, I won't have this time in Greece with him. Besides, an international move with two small kids and without the support of my parents? It's impossible. I'm crushed.

After their nap, Viktor comes down with the kids and I tell him about Boris's call.

"That's awesome news, Katia!" He's upbeat and optimistic. I'm stunned.

When I explain why the timing is all wrong, he makes every effort to point out how we can make it work.

"You don't have to start until October first, so we can move sometime in September. I'll take time off to get us settled and make sure the kids are comfortable in their new school while you start your job. We can bring over our babysitter from Vienna for the first few weeks to help out."

This offer is a dream come true—it's what I've aimed for all these years—but taking it feels wrong. My dad is my priority right now and this time with him may well be our last. It isn't negotiable.

I feel clear about my decision but it's no less devastating.

A week later, I call Boris and explain I won't be able to accept their offer due to my family's situation. There's a brief pause—he wasn't expecting I'd turn down the job, and rightfully so. Still, he's kind and understanding and invites me to stay in touch. As I hang up the phone, I can hear the thud as the door to my dream closes.

Very soon, our plans to move to Greece vanish, too. It's early autumn, 2008, and the global financial markets are in meltdown, with the Greek economy soon to follow. I fully recognize why we can't make the move, why Viktor shouldn't take any professional risks amidst so much uncertainty. But I'm angry, frustrated, and resentful toward him anyway.

I'm also incredibly sad. My father is dying, and I can't be with him. I'm a thousand miles away in a different country, only able to see him for limited periods of time. He's deteriorating and I can't be there for him on short notice. It feels wrong.

Viktor and I are in stalemate. The atmosphere gets so bad between us that we decide to see a couples' therapist. Session after session, we tear into each other, digging our heels in on our respective positions.

"But you were the one who suggested we move to Greece more than a year ago!" I say. "Now you're going back on your promise."

"Things have changed since last year, Katia. I can't find work in Greece and, if I want to be able to support us, I'd need to be in an airplane all the time. The commute would kill me!"

"My *father* is the one who's dying, remember?" Sarcasm has always been my weapon of choice.

I have no sympathy for my husband's plight. I feel like a child who's been promised something only to have it ripped away. And I dislike our therapist—she gave me a bad vibe from day one. I find her to be distant, judgmental, and lacking in compassion. After every session, I leave her office fuming or drained or both, and I spend the rest of the day in a passive-aggressive fog.

After five sessions, we haven't moved an inch from where we started, so I refuse to go back. We're perfectly capable of eviscerating each other without spending 150 euros per hour for an audience.

In parallel with my Greek job search, I've been pursuing an opportunity in Austria. One of Viktor's contacts is an Austrian Army General who heads the National Defense Academy, the *Landesverteidigungsakademie* or LVAk, part of the Austrian Ministry of Defense. I meet with the general and it goes well. He finds a way to put me through the recruitment process, despite my being a foreign national.

In true public sector bureaucratic fashion, the interview process takes several months, but by September, I'm offered a position as a "researcher and officer instructor." The prospect of teaching terrifies me. I negotiate that I be allowed a week off every month—unpaid of course—to be with my dad. To her credit, my new boss, an accomplished and compassionate woman, is both understanding and accommodating. I take the job.

At LVAk, communications are in German—not just for meetings, but my research and *writing* will be in German. It's a steep learning curve but I'm grateful for the challenge and see it as an opportunity to build on my language skills. I'm even more grateful for Google translate.

Two weeks after I start, I fly to Greece for a week to see my dad. Viktor follows with the kids a couple of days later. Babás is weaker than he was a month ago. He's lost even more weight; he can hardly eat now. His skin is grey, almost translucent, and he's taking morphine for the pain. It comes in a lollipop, and he asks for them several times a day. His eyes are manic until he shoves one in his mouth. Then, he closes his eyes and waits for it to take effect, to bring him some temporary relief.

If he's not in bed, he's sitting in front of the TV, staring at the dark screen; he doesn't even switch it on. He now uses a cane—the same one his mother used. Often, when he walks from his bedroom to the living room, he asks my mother—or my brother, if he's there—to walk behind him, their arms wedged under his armpits, for support.

I place a folding chair next to his bed and sit with him, working while he dozes. I type with one hand and hold my dad's hand in the other. We sit this way for hours. It calms him.

I'm amazed with my children. My dad looks so frail and ill, but they're not afraid to be near him. Several times a day, Margarita climbs in bed next to her grandfather for cuddles. And Petros draws pictures for him that we tape to the closet door across from where he lies, so they're the first thing he sees every morning.

We go back to Vienna at the end of that week, but I've already planned my next visit for November. It's important to give my dad something to look forward to, but I need it just as much as he does.

It's a Monday morning, four days before our next trip to Athens. I'm stressing about getting everyone out the door and to school on time. Suddenly, the landline rings and I freeze. I can't think of anyone who'd call us this early in the morning. Except . . .

It's my brother. "It's over," he whispers, his voice breaking.

I fall to my knees.

"What do you mean?" I ask, even though I know exactly what he means. "When?" My head is spinning. My consciousness has no space for this reality.

"Just half an hour ago."

I search my memory for the last time I talked to my dad. I think that's what we do when someone passes. We try to keep a record of our memories, to hold on to something now that the person is gone. No memories, no person. Well, it wasn't yesterday. Even though I call home every day, lately twice a day, yesterday I only talked to my mother. My dad didn't come to the phone. I didn't make much of it at the time. I'd talk to him the next time, when hopefully he'd be feeling better. I wish I'd known.

Viktor kneels down beside me and takes me in his arms as I sob. The kids join us on the floor, hugging me, looking puzzled. "Why are you crying, Mamá? What happened?"

Ginny, our cleaning lady, is here. She doesn't speak Greek but seems to understand what's happened. She gets down on the floor, too, and cries with me. She lost her sister only a few months ago—she understands grief.

We don't have a lot of time; the funeral is tomorrow. It's probably a remnant from the old days, prior to refrigeration, but Greek funerals take place right away. Viktor books the four of us on the 1:30 p.m. flight to Athens, which leaves us only a couple of hours to notify schools and our employers and pack. The kids don't own anything black.

When we arrive at my parents' house in Athens, my dad is no longer there. The family is gathered around my mom—my brother and his wife, who's expecting their first child; my aunt and uncle; and my cousins.

The funeral is a blur. My dad didn't have a lot of family (he was an only child), but he had many dear friends, especially from his time in Cameroon. They all come to pay their respects. Some of my closest friends are also there, not just to support me, but because they loved my dad. Seeing how much he was loved warms my heart and makes me miss him even more.

Some of the family is shocked to see our kids there. In Greece, children don't attend funerals; they are to be protected from unpleasant experiences, especially death. Growing up, I missed out on the chance to say goodbye to loved ones, and I don't want to inflict that on my children. They will say goodbye to their Pappoús with the rest of us. Viktor and I are on the same page about this, at least.

We stay with my mother for the rest of the week to make sure she's okay. And in less than a month, we return to celebrate Christmas. "Celebrate." It's the worst Christmas of my life. Mamá is depressed and spends most of her time in bed. Viktor and I go through the motions for the kids' sake, but I resent him for insisting we perform all the usual holiday rituals. All I want to do is hide. Of course, he's right—the rituals help us to cope.

CHAPTER 12

Shaking the Bars

"The memory is a living thing—it too is in transit.
But during its moment, all that is remembered
joins, and lives—the old and the young, the past
and the present, the living and the dead."
— Eudora Welty, *On Writing*

I'M STANDING IN FRONT OF MY BATHROOM MIRROR,
finishing my makeup. The babysitter has arrived and is preparing dinner
for the children. My husband and I have been invited to an event hosted
by an elite club of high-ranking executives and entrepreneurs—Viktor is
being vetted for membership. The group prides itself as a family-friendly,
if not family-centered, organization, and my husband is excited for the
opportunity. But before they accept him as a member, the club has to
meet me. I'm not looking forward to being judged by Vienna's business
crème de la crème.

I'm dressed conservatively, in a little black dress and heels. As I reach
for a pair of earrings from my jewelry box, I notice my coiled dragon
ring and smile. It's not a ladies' ring—more like something someone
with a lot of tattoos and piercings would wear. It's simple: made of silver,
no stones, no sparkle. I saw it in a shop window a couple of years ago
and couldn't resist. I love how it encircles my ring finger, the opposite

87

of a traditional engagement ring. Part of the appeal of buying it was anticipating Viktor's reaction. I knew he'd disapprove, the same way he disapproves of the tattoo I got on my hip last year. Neither fits with the image he likes me to project—elegant, worldly, sophisticated. But I love the contrast—wearing something like this ring and knowing I *am* sophisticated, stylish, educated. And I have an inner wild child who likes to surface occasionally.

It might be fun to show up to this dinner wearing that ring. Would my high-society interviewers be shocked to see it? I hope so. I slip the ring on my finger and call out to my husband: "I'm ready, let's go." It's a minor act of rebellion, but it's something.

Thankfully, he doesn't ask me to go to many of these dinners. He knows how angry it makes me to be seen and addressed as "the wife." I've earned the right to my own name, my own identity. Not that long ago, I was giving briefings at the US Department of Defense. Now, I go to dinners where no one bothers to ask me what I do.

I hate feeling invisible. Unseen.

The evening isn't as painful as I dreaded; everyone's pleasant enough. I end up chatting with the only other foreigner in the room, of course. Funny, she's also the only nonmember. She's the event organizer. Before dinner, as we're standing around with our drinks, I observe her as she flies around the room, making sure everything is in place and everyone is happy. She doesn't speak German, but English—with a slight Spanish accent. Her warm smile is comforting in that frosty room.

I'm placed at the same table as Viktor, but we're not seated next to or even across from each other. We've been skillfully planted among our examiners. The elegant man to my left is in his sixties. I turn on my charm, which lubricates the conversation. The woman to my right, his wife, is quite a bit older than me. I put on my good-wife-and-mother face. Viktor, of course, is his usual charismatic self, so I'm not at all worried about how he'll fare through the evening.

After dinner, the organizer introduces herself to me. Her name is Ana; she's from Barcelona but moved to Salzburg when she fell in love and married an Austrian. Ana tells me she loves my dragon ring—the only genuine thing about me this evening. I smile and feel an instant connection.

I'm done being good. It hasn't brought me anything but resentment—and a burdensome sense of victimhood. My life doesn't feel right to me, but my small act of rebellion feels good. Rattling the bars of my cage feels good.

By winter, our marriage is in crisis.

Viktor allowed me time to grieve my father, but my break is over. Now, all the grievances, the frustrations, the unsatisfied desires—they're erupting like Vesuvius. On the surface, we share the same values: family, loyalty, companionship. But in practice, we interpret those values in vastly different ways, at least according to my husband. I do things out of a deep desire to protect and care for my family. But Viktor sees me as overprotective and controlling. He says I'm robbing our children of their independence.

Viktor's definition of betrayal is restricted to physical infidelity. But to me, betrayal is about more than sex or even romance outside the marriage. It's about not keeping your promises, not prioritizing your partner's happiness. For me, companionship goes beyond physical intimacy and affection. It's about valuing the other person's autonomy and considering them an equal partner in decision making. Viktor honestly believes he's prioritizing my happiness, of course. But I'm not happy, so it's not working.

We talk past each other, each stubbornly holding to our point of view. Most of the time, we're too triggered to consider the other's perspective, or even make a good case for our own. Nearly all of our arguments turn into a censure on character—and I'm always found lacking. Viktor's list of my character flaws is extensive: I'm selfish, unreliable, distant, withdrawn, ungrateful for all the privileges life has afforded me. His attacks on my character go deep; the hurt feels irreparable. He's not merely critiquing my behavior; he disapproves of who I am.

In rare moments, I can see why he thinks as he does. I'm not ungrateful, but I *am* unhappy. All the time. And he's right; I'm easily upset. Even with the little things: the late taxi, the mannerless waiter, the kids fussing over their dinner.

Sometimes, he leaves long handwritten letters on my nightstand, attempting to make sense of his emotions, our relationship. Other times, he sends long emails. When he loses his patience, I get short, caustic notes. Anti-love letters. In them, Viktor picks apart whatever I've recently done or said, or *not* done or said. Sometimes, his notes are a referendum on my past behavior, something that left him hurt, angry, or both. I feel like I'm constantly failing him on multiple fronts and the pressure to respond feels too heavy. Sometimes, I don't even reply. Even if I did, he'd complain, so what's the point?

Maybe I don't want to salvage us anymore.

But he won't let me off the hook. He says he wants to trust me, but I know he doesn't. Maybe he has good reason; maybe I *am* unreliable. I start to worry my upbringing has given me bad habits—bad habits that are now part of my identity. I apologize for not being a better partner or a better mother to our children, for forcing him and the kids to suffer through my moods and feelings of inadequacy.

I have nightmares nearly every night now. In one of them, I'm being squeezed between my car and a large truck. I wake up panicked; I can't breathe. Maybe I'm having a midlife crisis.

I try to offer Viktor my contrition. But it isn't genuine, and he's a smart, intuitive man. I find another letter on the nightstand. In it, he suggests a separation.

But somehow, we keep going.

Against all reason, I find myself wanting—no, deeply longing for—a baby. My biological clock doesn't give a damn about the state of our marriage. I yearn for intimacy, connection, unconditional love. At thirty-eight years old, it's now or never. Surprisingly, Viktor is open to the idea; he's always wanted a big family. Against my better judgment, I wonder whether a new baby could help bring us closer.

At work, I'm lost, directionless, and unsatisfied. Bored out of my mind and with no other prospects. And I hold Viktor responsible for it. After nine years in Vienna, I'm no less bitter than the day we arrived. Having a baby will allow me to take a break. And maybe I could use the time away to work on my book. At my age, I don't expect to get pregnant quickly, so I have time to get used to the idea, to imagine and plan.

After putting the kids to bed one evening, I sit down at my desk. Viktor is away on a business trip, and I take the opportunity to catch up on some research. When he's home, he disapproves of my working after dinner, but tonight, I'm free to do as I please.

As I'm skimming through an academic paper, a Skype notification flashes at the top right corner of my screen: "Your contact, Michael, is online." I must have left the application running in the background. A few minutes later, I receive a message from Michael, asking if I have time to talk. I'm surprised; we haven't been in touch since my father passed away over a year ago, and even then, we communicated only by email.

Tonight, we catch up. I tell him about the kids, my work at the Ministry, Viktor's daily commute to Bratislava. Michael tells me he and his family are now settled back in the US after a year in Switzerland, where he was teaching at a renowned business school. I tease him about not having visited while he was in Europe and relatively close.

As we talk, the energy shifts. It's suddenly heavier, more serious.

"I'm going through a tough time at home," Michael says. "I feel like my marriage is falling apart. I thought that you might have some insight to share, as a woman."

I listen as my friend tells me the story of his broken relationship. He sounds broken himself. He talks about his pain, his anger, his sense of powerlessness, his fear for the future of his family. Slowly, a weight seems to lift. Michael exhales.

"Thank you for listening."

"I'm really sorry, Michael. This is so challenging, and I wish there was more I could do to help."

"You *are* helping. I needed someone to hear me, to validate what I'm experiencing. To tell me that I'm not crazy."

"You're not crazy, Michael."

This is our first deep, personal conversation, and it's the first time Michael is asking for support from *me*. He's been my mentor, so the shoe is usually on the other foot. It feels like a new level in our friendship, one I hadn't expected.

Together, we brainstorm ideas for how he might salvage his relationship, his family. I try hard to offer possible solutions. We agree to talk again in a few weeks.

We're a few days into a family vacation for Easter in Thailand when I decide it's time. I brought the pregnancy test with me, "just in case," so I head to the en suite bathroom and take it.

We're here with friends—another couple and their two children. The house where we're staying sits right on the beach. It has a large swimming pool, surrounded by towering palm trees and a luscious tropical garden. There's a massage room and a woman who comes daily to give everyone massages. A lovely local couple shops and cooks for us and the food is to die for. The house is designed for outdoor living, so we spend most of our time by the pool and take our meals together on the patio.

After a few minutes, I look down at the plastic stick in my hand—*positive*. I gasp. It's only been a month since we stopped using birth control. I expected the process to take months. Am I ready? Are *we* ready?

There's a knock at the door.

"Mamá, where are you?" Margarita is looking for me. "We're all having breakfast."

I follow my daughter outside but spend the rest of the day in a state of shock, grateful to my husband for keeping the kids occupied. They spend most of the morning splashing around in the pool with the other children.

In the afternoon, my friend and I make good on our promise to take the kids to a nearby mall. A driver drops us off and we arrange to be picked up in a couple of hours. I order a coffee, and Helen and I sit down to watch the kids jumping in a bouncy castle.

"I'm pregnant." It just comes out.

Helen's face lights up. "*What?* Oh my god, congratulations! Have you guys been trying for a third?"

"Well . . ." I let out an awkward smile. And then a sigh. "I'm thrilled . . . but I'm also freaked out. We didn't exactly have time to try, if you know what I mean." I ask her to keep my secret until I've had time to tell Viktor.

I'll tell him in the morning, I decide. I want one last night.

We've just come back from breakfast to put on our swimsuits when I tell Viktor the news. His eyes go wide. Then, he laughs.

"Well, that didn't take long!"

"What can I say, Viktor? We still got it."

"Did you just find out? Can I see the test?"

"No, I took it yesterday. I threw it away."

"Who else knows?"

I find the question odd yet intuitive. I'm annoyed at the inquisition. When I tell Viktor I've already shared the news with Helen, he gets upset.

"I don't get it, Katia. How could you tell someone else before you tell me? The *father*? And why did you wait a whole day before telling me?"

If I were him, I'd be angry, too. Instead, I'm sad about what my behavior says about the state of our relationship. I explain I was shocked and needed time to process, but I'm aware of how lame and unconvincing my words are. I was stunned by the positive test but didn't go to him—my partner, my husband—with the news. I just needed some space to come to terms with it. Once Viktor knew, it would be announcements and plans and celebrations. I wanted to be ready.

When the time comes for our daily gin and tonics on the deck, I request only a splash of gin. Helen's husband, not one to miss a clue, gives me an impish smile.

"Why, Katia, are you pregnant?" He's not expecting my positive reply.

There are exclamations and a toast—to our new baby. We celebrate with a special dinner that evening, but the air between Viktor and me remains cool over the next few days. He's not yet ready to forgive me.

After breakfast one morning, I go to the little office to check my email on the house desktop. It's hooked to a spotty dial-up connection—sadly, no Wi-Fi. I sit down and wait for Gmail to open. Once it does, an instant message pops up. From Michael. He's at home in Massachusetts, about to take off on a world tour—Hong Kong, Singapore, London, Frankfurt—sponsored by a big investment bank. Two straight weeks of lectures, masterclasses, and meetings with high-level bankers. It's already late in the evening for him and he's working out some last-minute details on his trip.

> *"Man, I'm not looking forward to all the travel. But I do have a free weekend between my European destinations. I was thinking, I've never been to Vienna . . ."*

Michael pauses for a beat.

> *"Will you be back from Asia by then?"*

We haven't seen each other in years, though in just the past few weeks, our paths keep crossing.

"*Yes, we'll just be getting back to Vienna by then,*" I reply. "*I'd be delighted to help you plan a fun weekend.*"

Michael flies to Southeast Asia the next day but sends an email as soon as he's in Singapore. We connect again the morning after that. And the next. What started as a spontaneous Skype call becomes a daily ritual. Every morning, I sit down in front of the villa computer and pull up Gmail, and he's there. After working out the logistics of Michael's upcoming trip to Vienna, we keep chatting—about literature, poetry, life. We don't talk about his marriage.

I start really looking forward to these chats, but I don't tell Viktor about them; Michael is my mentor and friend, and it's not like we're doing anything wrong. Still, part of me feels a little guilty for the omission.

This time, we don't wait for the customary three-month mark. As soon as we're back home in Vienna, we announce our news to family and close friends. There's a lot of joy—mostly from Viktor's side—and disbelief from my side. I had previously declared there would be no more children, so no one was expecting it. Besides, with Viktor on the road so much, my mother has seen firsthand how overwhelmed I've been attempting to manage two kids, the household, and work. Adding a baby to the mix sounds almost masochistic. But it doesn't feel that way to me. I want this baby with my whole being, so I'm ready. I'm also scared to death. How *will* I manage?

CHAPTER 13

I, the Non-Adaptive

"Though fairy tales end after ten pages, our lives do not.
We are multi-volume sets. In our lives, even though one
episode amounts to a crash and burn, there is always another
episode awaiting us and then another. There are always
more opportunities to get it right, to fashion our lives in
the ways we deserve to have them. Don't waste your time
hating a failure. Failure is a greater teacher than success."
— Clarissa Pinkola Estés, *Women Who Run with the
Wolves: Myths and Stories of the Wild Woman Archetype*

AFTER SUCH A MAGICAL VACATION, the idea of going
back to work, where I feel miserable—completely bored and wholly
unchallenged—just feels wrong. This pregnancy comes as a relief; it gives
me so much to look forward to, including maternity leave. I shouldn't complain. At the end of the day, I have a job. In *my* field. And no one except for
me is forcing me to go. I'd love to leave, but I'm terrible at ending things,
at walking away. That would be like unchecking boxes—unthinkable! I've
spent my adult life focused externally—on what the "right" path for me
is, on what others expect of me—rather than internally on what I really
want to do, on what *I* feel is right for me based on what's fulfilling. What
energizes me? What brings me joy? I don't even know.

At least I also have Michael's visit to look forward to. I'm thrilled to be able to see him in person again, to catch up. Viktor agrees to take care of the kids on Saturday so I can see Michael. I offer to show him around the city, but from the moment we meet, we can't stop talking. Instead of the sightseeing I promised, we spend the day in a couple of my favorite Viennese cafés.

One is the legendary Gerstner on *Kärntnerstrasse*, where we sit over steaming cups of hot chocolate and *Apfelstrudel*. Michael asks how I like living here, and I tell him the truth. After nine years, Vienna still doesn't feel like home. It's been hard for me to come to terms with living in Austria. I have difficulty understanding why I've struggled so much and for so long, while other foreigners I know don't seem to share the same difficulties.

Talking about this with Michael helps me structure my thoughts. He asks me to take two of my friends and compare their experiences living in Vienna. I choose Aliki and Jasmine, whose experiences of Vienna couldn't be more different. Aliki feels settled, but for Jasmine, Vienna still feels foreign. At Michael's suggestion, I label them: Aliki, "the integrated," and Jasmine, "the non-adaptive." Slowly, we build a list of characteristics that set them apart and help explain the differences in their experiences. We talk about contrasting cultures, stages of adjustment, family dynamics, the meaning of "home," and how the definition we use affects the adjustment experience.

I don't have a notebook with me, so I scribble notes on paper napkins; I don't want to miss anything. I've never thought about these concepts and neither has Michael, but we're having too much fun exploring the ideas to stop. I feel *alive*, like my brain is on fire for the first time in years. I feel competent, confident, and hopeful, like I know what I'm talking about. I feel like the old Katia, the me before Vienna. Before marriage, even. I feel seen and appreciated.

By the time Michael and I are done with our hot chocolate, we've come up with a framework for understanding adjustment.

He leans forward. "This would make a great book, Katia."

The next morning, I pick up Michael at the Hotel Sacher where he's staying. I'm used to seeing him in business casual, but he's wearing jeans and a brown leather jacket that looks like it's been his favorite for a while. His hair is still damp from the shower.

We walk over to Café Mozart, next to the State Opera, for breakfast. It's still too early for the tourist crowd; I've never seen the café so quiet. In contrast to yesterday's "working coffee," today is more personal. It feels more like a meeting between friends than between a mentor and his mentee. We talk about our lives and aspirations, our plans for the future. I confide in Michael. I tell him about my marriage struggles, that things aren't good and haven't been for a while.

"I'm pregnant," I say. I search his eyes and see a touch of sadness.

"Oh, Katia. I'm so sorry. This must be so hard."

I laugh nervously. "I know I want to have this baby. Of that, I have no doubt. It's just . . . all the rest of it. Things at home aren't easy right now. I'm not happy and neither is Viktor. I'm scared about the future. If my marriage breaks down, I'm not sure I'll be able to move on with my life. Who's going to want to be with someone like me? I'll be forty soon, with three kids."

Michael smiles warmly. "Someone will want to be with you, Katia. Many will. That's not something you'll ever have to worry about." I smile back, relieved and touched by his kindness. He believes in me and that feels good.

Maybe things aren't as dark as I've been seeing them.

It's Michael's turn. He tells me his marriage has rapidly unraveled. My friend is in distress and I can't fix it, but I can be present with him as he talks.

"You've done so much for your family, Michael. You're a wonderful father, a loyal husband. You deserve to be happy."

Finally, he smiles again. The heaviness lifts.

We leave the café and head toward Vienna's famous outdoor market, the *Naschmarkt*. We'll meet my husband and the kids for lunch at Café Sperl. It has a children's corner with books and toys and uncharacteristically friendly staff (Viennese cafés are infamous for their rude waiters). Once there, we start many conversations and finish none of them; we are constantly interrupted.

After lunch, Viktor offers to drop off Michael at his hotel, so we all climb in our minivan, Michael in the front with Viktor. When we arrive, Michael gets out and I wave goodbye to him from the back seat. Suddenly, my stomach clenches and a feeling of sadness washes over me. I don't know what to do with this feeling.

That evening, I write in my diary, trying to make sense of what I felt. It's clear to me our relationship has shifted from friendship to . . . something else—a sort of complicity, a deeper connection that seems to have come out of nowhere. None of it makes sense. I feel more exposed, more vulnerable, than ever, when what I want so badly is to feel taken care of, cherished, and appreciated. And Michael is in the same place, but the timing is unthinkable. Yet, it feels like the most natural thing in the world.

On Monday morning, Michael leaves to get back to his world tour and I spend the next few days in a fog. Everything around me is moving in slow motion. I go through my morning routine with the kids, sit down to do my daily writing, pick them up from school, and take them to music lessons, the playground, or play dates with friends. But I'm not really there for any of it. I'm somehow surprised, confused, devastated, and delighted, all at the same time.

My normal everyday life has suddenly divided in two, as if each is running in a parallel universe to the other.

CHAPTER 14

A Story of Two Universes

"If we listened to our intellect, we'd never have a
love affair. We'd never have a friendship. We'd never
go into business, because we'd be cynical. Well,
that's nonsense. You've got to jump off cliffs all the
time and build your wings on the way down."
— Ray Bradbury

MICHAEL SENDS EMAILS FROM THE ROAD that arrive
in the evenings, once he's alone and back in his hotel room. He says he's
relishing the time to himself—time for self-care and rest—which has given
him new mental space and energy. He tells me how good it felt to talk in
Vienna, how grateful he is for my friendship.

"I have faith that things will be okay," he writes.

"They will be, for both of us," I reply. *"One way or another."*

*"Would you be interested in reading something together and talking
about it afterwards?"*

Michael's grandfather loved Shakespeare, so we agree to read *Henry
V*. He sends me act one. I've never read Shakespeare and feel awkward
admitting my ignorance, but I learn so much from our discussions.

One evening, Michael sends a poem, "Meeting Catherine." In it, the
speaker is hopelessly mesmerized by Catherine's "incandescent" beauty. I

was baptized as Catherine, or Aikaterini, the archaic form for Catherine, so as I read the poem, I'm amused. I search for the author's name, but it wasn't included.

"Who wrote this?" I ask.

Michael tells me he used to write poetry when he was young. Now that he has some time to himself on this trip, he's been feeling inspired again. I'm too shy to ask for more details. It's one thing to have these secret feelings, and quite another to engage in the potential reality that they are reciprocated. That would be flirting with betrayal. I'm *pregnant*, for God's sake.

Michael must sense my confusion; I'm taking longer than usual to reply. He sends an instant message instead of another email, apologizing for making me uncomfortable. Like the speaker in his poem, he has feelings for me, but no hope or expectation that I reciprocate.

My stomach knots as I type my reply. "And what if I do?"

Oh God, what the hell am I thinking?

Michael is even more surprised than I am. "I never expected this to be anything but one-sided."

Michael confesses he's in love with me. Suddenly, butterflies crowd my stomach—until my brain takes over. "You were a friend in distress," I explain. "And I offered you my friendship, a sympathetic ear, a female perspective . . ."

But my butterflies won't be quelled.

"It happened in Vienna," Michael says. "As we talked over hot chocolate, I started to feel differently about you." The way he looked at me in the café should have given me a hint—if I'd been looking for hints.

"For me, it was waving goodbye to you at the hotel."

Our feelings for each other are beautiful and uplifting and pure, but nothing can come of them.

Michael senses my overwhelm. "We need to catch our breath," he says.

Later that night, I have trouble falling to sleep—my mind won't stop racing. Viktor notices my discomfort and sits up on his elbows.

"What's going on?" His voice is gravelly from sleep.

"Just pregnancy hormones."

A convenient excuse, though not entirely untrue. I've been on the verge of tears all the time lately, and he knows this, so he accepts my answer and goes back to sleep.

I quietly reach for my diary—writing always helps me grapple with difficult emotions—and head into the other room. I bought a new one ahead of our trip to Thailand—a crimson, cloth-covered notebook. I turn to a fresh page.

> *I wasn't even aware I had these feelings for Michael. Then Vienna happened and it was already there, a done deal. It's so confusing; we're two people in troubled situations who are finding comfort in each other. How is it possible to have these feelings while carrying a child? I don't understand it. But I can feel that Michael wants to cherish me, spoil me, love me; and I want so badly to be loved, spoiled, and cherished.*

> *I also know this can never happen. But what happens to me now? What happens to my marriage, my family? How can I make these feelings go away?*

We leave for a weekend to visit Viktor's family in the South of Austria. I'd rather stay home and not have to pretend everything's fine, but that's not an option. I pack my diary in a small, zippered pocket of my travel bag. I'm still hopeful for some epiphany on how to deal with all of this.

Then, Saturday happens.

Late in the afternoon, Viktor asks me to come upstairs, *now*. When I enter his childhood bedroom, I see his face is flushed and agitated.

"Is something wrong? Did something happen?"

"Yes, something *happened*. I read your diary." I stop, frozen in my tracks. "You've been acting weird all week, and I knew there was something wrong. *How could you*, Katia?"

In a jolt of lightning, I see an image of our broken family. I imagine myself raising our children—and this new baby—alone. *I never wanted to hurt our children*, I think, as guilt washes over me. When I surface again, there's just a feeling of low-simmering rage. *He has never read my diary before. I've never once had to hide it from him.*

Blood rushes to my forehead and my limbs feel suddenly cold. I try to control the shaking; I know better than to let my anger control me. I know what I have to do, so I swallow my pride.

"I'm . . . sorry." The words feel stuck. "Can you forgive me?" I feel exposed and raw. He thinks he's been right about me all along—Katia, the unreliable, the dishonest, the disloyal. And I *hate* it.

"Nothing physical happened between Michael and me—just the exchange of a few messages." According to Viktor's own interpretation of betrayal, this doesn't even count.

"I'm so . . . sorry. I don't know what got into me. I'd never want to do anything to hurt you . . . to hurt our family." I feel sick to my stomach.

But I'm not sorry. *You did this to us when you betrayed me, when you hijacked me to Vienna,* I think. But I'm stuck and I know it—I'm pregnant and have two young kids.

My rebellious streak gets the better of me. "Maybe we need to think about what brought me to this, why I felt the need to confide in someone else."

"You're not sorry, Katia!" Viktor's face is redder now. "If you were, you would own this. You wouldn't stand here and try to make excuses for yourself."

He lists my faults once again. I'm too defiant, too proud, too unwilling to accept responsibility, even as I ask for his forgiveness. I counter that we've been going through tough times and maybe he's had some role, however small, to play in this.

"No," he spits. "This is entirely your fault and no one else's."

I know this isn't going away. Though I'm reluctant to spend the next however many months, or even years, apologizing. I just want some peace. I want my children to be okay. I want some semblance of normalcy.

I type out a long email to Michael. I explain that Viktor is enraged we've been communicating, and I'm not sure what he plans to do about it. I refresh the page until I see his reply come in.

"I've already heard from him. He wrote to tell me that I should be ashamed of myself and that I should stay away from your family."

Things between us have to change and we know it.

In a final email exchange, I reflect on what's happened between Michael and me, and how I feel about him. But I don't see a future between us. We're both married. We have families we're not prepared to sacrifice.

"We should be putting our emotions aside," I write. "We should be focusing on what's ahead of us. You have to figure out how to save your marriage, and I have to focus on bringing this new life into the world."

It feels like I'm being forced to sever one of my own limbs. Michael suggests it's better to make a clean break, not to torture ourselves further or risk destroying everything we've built. I don't try to change his mind. We stop communicating.

The weeks that follow are rough. Viktor ceaselessly tosses snide remarks in my direction, even in front of our friends. I repay him with the cold shoulder. The tension between us is palpable and it's exhausting. I don't have anyone to confide in and I miss Michael. I don't regret my decision to end whatever there was between us, but it hurts.

Life is busy with work and the kids, which helps. Time helps.

In early summer of 2010, three months into my pregnancy, I give notice to my boss. I'll start maternity leave in October, I explain, but I don't specify how long I'll be gone. In Austria, my position is secured for two years. But if I can help it, I'm not going back. This pregnancy is my golden ticket out.

CHAPTER 15

Reinvention

"I have yet to hear a man ask for advice on
how to combine marriage and a career."
— Gloria Steinem

WHEN MICHAEL AND I STOP COMMUNICATING, I
become desperate for a diversion. So, I take out the notes I kept from our
café meeting and begin outlining a plan for a book on the expat experience. Then, I set about conducting dozens of interviews. One of them is
with Paula, a thirty-five-year-old Brazilian mother of three; Vienna is her
third expat assignment. Paula is at once kind and utterly vibrant, and she's
become one of my closest friends in Austria. As we sit across from one
another in my living room, I ask where she feels most at home.

"There's not one place. I make sure I feel at home wherever I am." Paula's
eyes shine as she speaks. "I moved so much as a child that creating home
has become a necessity for me, almost a form of survival. Home has to
be a safe space, otherwise it's corrosive."

Paula's words stay with me. And so do the words of many others I
interview.

For the first time since leaving RAND, I feel alive and connected to my
chosen work. The insights I glean from the book interviews begin changing
the way I see my life. I even start to see my time in Vienna through a different

lens. Up to now, my frustration and sense of homelessness felt self-indulgent, even ungrateful. When I talk to other foreigners who've had a hard time adjusting, just like I did, I see I'm not alone. I feel understood. I also talk to expats who feel settled and at home, and their stories stop me in my tracks. I start to feel more empathy, more connection with others like me.

Not a single day goes by that I don't miss my home or my family in Greece. I miss the light and the warmth, the food, the music; but most of all, I miss the people—the belonging I feel when I'm there that comes from understanding the cultural references, getting the jokes.

While writing the book, I feel a sense of responsibility. I become aware of all the ways I can use my own experiences and lessons learned to help others navigate their challenges and feel more at home—in Vienna and in the world. The project becomes more than a means for me to understand my own experience or satisfy my curiosity as a researcher. It becomes my contribution to the expat community. For the first time, my work has a purpose that's precious to me. I feel inspired and motivated; I feel more myself—and that's like coming home.

Despite this newfound shift, my relationship with Viktor continues its freefall. He struggles with my lack of communication and the distance it creates between us, something he details in the emails he writes to me. He says I'm communicating with everybody *but* him. I'm likewise miserable and the fact I'm pregnant only intensifies the suffering. Hormones are partly to blame, along with the issue of mismanaged expectations. I want to feel taken care of by the father of my children; I want him to bring me my favorite treats, or take over with the kids on Sunday mornings so I can sleep in. But Viktor is no longer trying to be nice to me, much less anticipate my cravings and desires. Once again, I feel alone.

The urge to reach out to Michael ebbs and flows, but it's always there. I know in my heart he would understand and find the right words to comfort me. But I resist the urge with everything in my being.

Still, even though I'm struggling, I'm grateful. Six months into my pregnancy, I have the biggest belly that has ever existed in the history of pregnant women! I got my wish, my own little (or not so little) miracle.

After a tense and exhausting first trimester, my energy levels return. I start to "glow," to feel more balanced, more patient, more appreciative. I devote this new energy to self-care—body, mind, and spirit. I eat healthy (no more morning sickness); sleep as much as I can manage, given the kids' schedules; and exercise regularly, returning to a yoga practice I once enjoyed and taking long walks to clear my mind. I feel my heart bursting with love for this little being growing inside me—a boy!—and I know, if nothing else, he will be loved. Unconditionally.

Our son arrives on a Saturday morning in December. By far the biggest of my babies, his birth feels like a celebration. I've done this twice before, so I'm comfortable with my body and unintimidated by the process; I nearly breeze through the labor and delivery (if twelve hours can be considered a breeze). Despite the pain and discomfort, it's a thoroughly happy process. Viktor and I are both excited and relaxed, a pleasant change. All our children have Greek names, so we name our little giant Nicolas, which means "victory of the people" in ancient Greek.

Now that Nicolas has arrived, I'm hopeful things with Viktor will smooth over. For a few weeks, we go through a honeymoon period in which we're nice to each other. But our relationship soon returns to its prior state, one filled with tension, resentment, and even contempt. It doesn't matter; I'm completely absorbed by Nicolas—feeding him, taking care of him, watching him become a little person. I know he is my last baby and my last chance to breastfeed, so I relish every minute. And I'm reluctant to share him. Though, with a new baby and two children to care for, I hardly have time for anything or anyone else.

Sometime early in 2011, Viktor goes back to his normal travel schedule and I'm alone with the kids. *Three* kids, which is intimidating at first. (It's true that with a third, the chaos and complexity rise exponentially.) But I grow to love our little routines and rituals: our walks around Vienna, our playground time, or just eating dinner together. The kids and I exist in our own little bubble; we are a team.

Evenings are lonelier, but I try to fill them. When Viktor is home, we run on parallel tracks, never meeting. While he relaxes with a book, I spend my evenings in the office on my laptop. I feel a bit guilty for this, though not guilty enough to change my behavior or my part in the uneasy dynamic between us.

By early spring, I feel ready to get back to work, so I schedule the next round of interviews for my book. I'm excited to get back on track. And back into shape, which seems to come more easily this time. I stay committed to my yoga practice, and soon, a friend asks if I want to try the new pole dancing class at our gym. I'm surprised to learn pole dancing is a form of fitness, and I'm intrigued, so I join her. Much like the dragon ring, pole dancing is a subtle act of rebellion. I love the exercise in contrast: the shy, respectable wife and mother; the respected military analyst; the utterly unrespectable hobby of pole dancing.

When I mention my new hobby to Viktor, he seems amused. But I wonder what he really thinks.

For my fortieth birthday, my dear friend Nick (who's also turning forty) and I throw a big party in Athens in July. It's challenging to organize from a distance, but after some research, we find the perfect venue—a minimalist outdoor space built above a small cove, with a gorgeous view of the Athens riviera. At once trendy and romantic.

The evening of our party is magical. When we arrive at dusk, there are flickering candles everywhere and the soft beat of ambient music plays in the background. Waiters stand ready with trays of cocktails and finger foods. Best of all, we're surrounded by friends and family who've shown up from all over the world to celebrate with us. I feel beautiful in my open-back, beaded gold dress and heels. I even bought a new bright coral red lipstick for tonight. (Hey, you only turn forty once.)

As the evening progresses, the music and the guests get louder. At midnight, our joint birthday cake arrives, and it looks like it's been set on fire (I insisted on forty candles—no reason to be modest). Nick and I give a short speech together to thank our guests and blow out the candles (no small feat) and it's back to dancing till the early morning hours.

I decide this will be my best decade yet.

CHAPTER 16

Imperfect Ingredients

"Home wasn't built in a day."
— Jane Sherwood Ace

ONCE BACK FROM OUR SUMMER VACATION in Greece, Viktor proposes we make another list—the very one I've been waiting ten years to make. A list of cities we'd each consider moving to.

I'm the one who's dying to get out of Vienna, but Viktor produces a list of *twenty-nine* options, all the places he could imagine living, arranged in order of priority. My own list names only three: Los Angeles, United States; Athens, Greece; and Zurich, Switzerland. LA and Athens already feel like home, but Zurich is a place I could quickly warm to, not least because of its proximity to water. The first time I visited Zurich, I felt an almost visceral connection to the lake, as if I were back on the Mediterranean where I grew up.

After the difficulty I experienced feeling settled in Vienna, I'm no longer willing to take relocation risks. Viktor isn't happy with my limited list of possibilities, but he isn't surprised—and he knows my mind can't be changed. Thankfully, Zurich appears on his list, too. Soon, he starts reaching out to the professional headhunters in his network, looking for an opportunity that could take us to Switzerland.

As the self-development gurus teach: for the universe to hear you, you have to be specific about what you want. We name our city, and it doesn't take long before Viktor receives an attractive offer for a senior vice president role with a generous compensation package, including a provision that covers relocation expenses and private schooling for the kids. But there's a catch: the new job involves extensive travel—three to four days a week on average, even more than he traveled for previous employers. Ordinarily, that stipulation would force me to veto the offer, but I have Nick in Zurich and his family are like family to us; I won't be alone. So, we schedule a trip to Switzerland, just the two of us.

In the world of expats, this sort of visit is called a "look-see"—the kind you make before accepting an offer. We want to get a personal feel for a place and see if we can imagine ourselves living there. Visiting Switzerland in the middle of winter isn't ideal; temperatures across the canton of Zurich are well below freezing and, for a moment, I feel desperate. But my displeasure with the cold is soon overpowered by a far greater feeling: the desire to escape Vienna. By the time we board our return flight, I've made up my mind.

"I'm in. Let's do this."

Viktor smiles, relieved. We agree to move at the end of June, once the kids are done with the school year.

Zurich feels different. This time, I'm part of the decision; I'm *choosing* this move. The more conscious choices I make in different areas of my life—to relocate, to write a book, to leave my job—the more empowered I feel. I'm excited to turn a new page, personally and professionally, and get away from the negativity I associated with Vienna. My perspective on my career has started to change, too. I now see possibilities and opportunities I hadn't seen before. For the first time, I desire to create a home for myself and my family. I am intentional about it; I will no longer depend on someone else to push or organize things for me. I will take charge.

I want the kids to feel supported as they adjust to the new environment, especially my oldest, my sensitive nine-year-old, Petros. I'm sad that my children will miss their friends in Vienna—the only place they've known. As much as I want to leave, I'll miss some things about Austria, too, especially the friends I've made. Of course, I worry about the effort it will take to set up a new support system in a new country and how I'll cope with three children, with their father away all the time.

The effort of making another international move will interfere with the work I've been carving out for myself. I've finally found a rhythm, a daily routine I enjoy. Every morning after dropping the kids at school, I walk to a little Japanese tea place around the corner and pick up a large matcha latte. By 9:00 a.m., I'm seated at my desk. This time to myself in the mornings has become precious. It allows me to explore my own thoughts, visualize the future, and stay motivated and connected with my work. The move will change things and push back my plans for the book, at least temporarily.

It doesn't matter, I decide. I'm now a *Zürcherin*.

But first, Viktor and I have to share the news. As soon as we're home from our look-see, we sit down with the children. I want to sound enthusiastic, convincing.

"We have news! Daddy just got a new job!" I keep my eyes fixed on Petros as I speak, watching for subtle facial expressions, minute shifts in body language. "And his new job is in Zurich, Switzerland, so we're all going to move there. What do you think?"

Petros looks down and away, squeezing his lips the way he does to stop himself from crying. I've been nervous about how he'd react to the news, more so than how his sister would. My son has just started Gymnasium, the Germanic equivalent of middle school. (In any language, middle school is the pits.) Having skipped second grade, he's the youngest in his class by a long shot and adapting to the social changes has been challenging. And now, we're asking him to start over.

Our girl has a different reaction, as I knew she would. "Can we find a house with a garden? Can we find a house next to Nick and the kids? Can we . . . ?"

Her ebullience may not last indefinitely, but Margarita is younger and more easygoing than her brother. She's a natural extrovert who easily makes new friends, so we know she'll have no trouble fitting in wherever she goes.

We decide together to make another reconnaissance day trip to Zurich with the kids. We want them to get a feel for the city and to visit prospective schools with us. We take off early on a Monday morning. The kids barely slept—too much excitement!—but we have no difficulty getting them up and out the door to the airport for the short flight.

Once landed, we take a taxi from Zurich Airport to the center of town to meet Alexandra, the relocation consultant Viktor's new employer has hired to help with the move. Years ago, we decided on a bilingual—English and German—education for the kids, and we want that to continue. So, we've selected three bilingual schools that came highly recommended. Alexandra has made the appointments and will drive us to each.

The Swiss school structure is different from the Austrian in that primary school lasts six years instead of Austria's four. This means Petros will have to do another year of primary school (the sixth) before reentering middle school. He seems positive about this prospect, since it buys him a year before yet another complicated transition. Margarita will start third grade, so no important reset there. And we like all three schools we visit.

Afterward, Alexandra drives us around a bit so we can explore potential neighborhoods. I notice how polished and well maintained everything looks—from the buildings to the gardens to the people on the street. But by far its best feature is that Zurich lies on the shores of a magnificent lake. I love being near the water.

As our return flight lifts off, my daughter's hand in mine, I close my eyes, relieved. I've moved so many times, but this move feels different—it's the first time I feel excited about creating a new home. I've never been good at visualizing, but I know our future home will have high ceilings and spacious rooms, yet it will still be cozy and warm. I will have an office and we will be close enough to the city. In all my years with Viktor, I've resisted having a house with a garden, despite how much he's always wanted the natural space. In Vienna, any property with a lawn would require living out in the suburbs, which would have felt all the more isolating to me. I prefer living in the heart of the city, close to the action. But since Zurich is small, having a proper house with a garden will still feel close to civilization (i.e., my daily Starbucks). So this time, I concede; my husband can have his garden.

A few weeks later, Viktor and I fly back to see potential properties. I'm hoping to walk into the perfect house for us and know in my gut we've arrived. The reality on the ground is a bit more disappointing. All the homes we view are either spacious and isolated or central and cramped. The last place we visit is a good compromise, but it's only available for two years—not ideal. (We laugh when we learn this is because the owners are away on an expat assignment.) We could hold out and wait for a better home to become available, but that might not happen in time.

In the cab on our way to the airport, Viktor notices I'm near tears.

"Let's go for that last one!" He wants to make it better. "It's spacious, in great shape, has a decent sized garden, and even a cute little home office with a view of the lake. Two years is a long time."

He's right. Maybe it's a good thing it's only a two-year commitment. It gives us time to get to know the city and search for our perfect fit. True, it didn't give me that instant "welcome home" feeling, but I liked the big windows and the way the rooms were bathed in light. Light is important, especially in a country where the winters are long. It's not exactly walking distance from the center of things, but it's only a ten-minute drive.

Time to grow up, Katia, I think to myself. The perfect home is what you create with imperfect ingredients.

Viktor smiles, relieved. "I'll let Alexandra know."

Turns out the Swiss think *very* highly of their gardens. Our rental contract stipulates we agree to hire the landlords' current gardener to do complete lawn maintenance at least twice per year. This, they say, is to ensure the grounds are kept "up to standard." When Viktor solicits said gardener for a quote for the work, we learn his two little annual visits will cost us about 10,000 Swiss Francs! Viktor tries to assure the owners that a gardener won't be necessary—he's very much looking forward to caring for the lawn himself. We are informed, however, that the owners "would like their standards to be kept," and their minds won't be changed. Welcome to Switzerland.

Our move is scheduled for early July. I approach it with intention and a mindset of possibility. With the big tasks—finding a school and a home—taken care of, now there's all the paperwork: residence permits, insurances, banking. Viktor's new employer also provides us with an immigration lawyer, someone to help us navigate the bureaucracy of becoming Swiss residents. In my book research, I've come across horror stories stemming from immigration issues, such as highly qualified expat partners who found themselves unemployable because of their visa status in a particular country; or others, who were forced to leave their host country after an unexpected divorce because their visa was tied to that of their partner. It's important to me there be no ambiguity around this matter for myself. Thankfully, the attorney reassures me that my permit allows me to do whatever I want, as long as it's legal.

Viktor's new position begins in mid-April, after which he's away from home again—a lot. Even so, he handles the logistics of our move: he selects the movers and schedules the date; takes care of all our immigration paperwork; and deals with taxes, health insurance, and bank accounts. Periodically, he hands me a set of papers that need my signature. I'm grateful he's got it all taken care of.

For my part, I set out to learn what will help make Zurich feel like home for the children. I want to maintain as many of their current activities and routines as possible, so I research what's available in our new neighborhood. Apparently, Taekwondo, which Margarita has been practicing in Vienna, isn't a thing in Zurich, but no matter; I sign them up for football (soccer), piano lessons, and Greek. I also focus on what we'll need to make their rooms feel comfortable and cozy. Nicolas is still young enough that he doesn't require much beyond the presence of his parents and a cozy corner to play.

I go through the same process for myself, consciously looking for the pieces that will make this a home, like a desk for my office, where I can enjoy quiet mornings to myself to reflect and write. I search for a yoga studio and even waterskiing lessons on the lake, which I'm most excited about. Despite the hectic nature of preparing an international move, I feel calm and grounded.

There are lots of goodbye dinners and activities with friends before we go. It feels both joyful and bittersweet. I organize guest books for our friends to write in; souvenirs for each child (a map of Vienna for Petros, a Taekwondo belt for Margarita) signed by their friends; and a picture book for each child, in which I collage photos that show their whole lives in Vienna.

CHAPTER 17

Stumbling Pas de Deux

"Every dance is a kind of fever chart, a graph of the heart."
— Martha Graham

WE MOVE INTO OUR NEW HOUSE in Zollikon on the first weekend of July. I make a promise to myself that, this time, I will empty every box. Luckily, the two older kids are eager to help and our nanny is with us to keep our youngest occupied. It takes about a week, but things finally start to feel normal again. The kids love our little garden and spend most of their time outside, playing football, enjoying the swing set or the new ping pong table. I take a seat on the steps overlooking the garden, a wine glass in hand, and watch the children kicking the ball back and forth. I suppose this house-with-a-garden life isn't so bad.

A week or so later, Viktor and I attend the parents' orientation evening for the kids' new football club. We sit down among the group of total strangers and the coach asks if there's anyone in the audience who doesn't speak Swiss German. (I speak High German—the kind you learn at language school and what's spoken in most of Germany. Swiss German is a dialect—spoken, not written—and only loosely based on High German. They are really very different animals: different pronunciations, words, language structure, and grammar rules. My fluency in High German only allows me to recognize a few words here and there, assuming I can decipher the Swiss pronunciation.) I look around and not a single person raises a hand. *Shit.*

I'm too embarrassed to raise mine, so I'll have to rely on Viktor. Being a native German speaker should count for something, right? Nope. We spend the rest of the hour not understanding a word, sneaking funny looks at each other and trying not to burst out laughing.

We've barely arrived in Switzerland but soon pack up and head to Greece for summer vacation. We'll have to be back in Zurich by the time school starts on August 20, a date that feels uncivilized to my Greek soul. (In Greece and Austria, school doesn't start before early September.)

When we return home, the children start school and Viktor leaves soon after. It's up to me to make sure our train keeps to the rails. After a few hiccups with Swiss daycare options, Viktor suggests we hire a live-in nanny from Greece—someone I'll feel a natural connection with, who'll be great for the kids' language skills. I love the idea, especially if she's willing to spoil us with Greek cooking. We luck out on all fronts with Marina. She's a warm, immediately likable woman in her mid-fifties, and she knows how to run a household. I'm happy to let her boss us all around if it means I can work in peace.

Eventually, the kids and I will figure out the train system, but for now, I handle the morning and afternoon school commute. The drive takes us along Lake Zurich, which gives my soul the chance to take in its calming waters—not quite a Mediterranean blue, but a beautiful blue nonetheless. The lake is framed by the snowy peaks of the Glarus Alps, a gorgeous scene that brings a new, grounding energy to our lives.

In Vienna, I walked, biked, or scootered everywhere; and when it was unavoidable, I took public transportation. In Zurich, I drive everywhere: through forests, along narrow winding roads, past meadows populated by sheep and cows. Early mornings, I navigate through the sometimes dense fog that rises off the lake. I struggle initially to get us to all the kids' "away" games, but Google Maps becomes my best friend.

For a while, I'm barely treading water with all the driving, practices, and games; the parent-teacher evenings; and other activities—but we manage.

I keep an eye out for potential challenges; I want to ensure the kids are adjusting smoothly to all the changes. I don't have time to feel the initial loneliness that comes from being in a new place, and soon, we're hosting a line of friends from far away—my friend, Aliki, and her daughter, Stella; my childhood friend, Iris, and her family (now expats in Belgrade, Serbia); and some of Petros's school friends from Vienna. We have fun showing everyone around the city and, in the process, get to explore it ourselves.

After acquainting myself with the nearest Starbucks and browsing Google for a yoga studio, I stumble upon an ad for adult ballet classes. I still miss ballet, a keen longing that shows up as the lump I feel in my throat every time I attend a ballet performance. *My skills are too rusty,* I think. Besides, I could never put myself through the embarrassment of being the only adult in the room. But the studio in the ad is called "Ballet for Everyone," which sounds promising. It's taught by a former professional dancer, Virginie, and it's only a ten-minute drive from home.

I email Virginie to request more information and she replies to invite me for a trial lesson. I'm forty-one! The last time I was in a ballet class, I was twelve. Thankfully, my longing is stronger than my fear.

I buy a pair of cream-colored ballet slippers and show up at the old villa where the studio is located. In the changing room, I sneak peeks at the other women around me. There are about ten of us in all; some appear to be in their early twenties, while others must be in their mid-sixties. And a few look to be around my age. As we change into leotards, tights, and ballet slippers, I notice everyone's movements—graceful and precise, ballerina-like.

I don't expect the class to feel effortless, but it does. We start at the barre and move through the basic positions and movements, exactly as I remember them. I place my hand on the barre and perform my *pliés,* as if my last ballet class took place only last week, not thirty years ago. We move to the center of the room to learn some choreography, and the familiar French names all come back to me: *chassé, glissade, pas de bourrée, arabesque.* I pull my shoulders back, draw my stomach in, and lengthen my neck. As I stretch my right leg into a *tendu,* I feel every muscle tensing, from my thigh to my calf to my ankle and toes. I let myself move to the music.

Ballet requires you to be present with your body, to feel every minute muscle. To be tight and controlled, leaving nothing to chance. At the same time, it requires you to be light as a feather; to be ready to fly. As I reconnect to the physicality of my body, I'm a ballerina again. I'm *alive*. And I'm hooked. Monday morning ballet becomes a new part of my routine—a source of comfort and joy, and a way to stay sane through the ups and downs ahead.

Only a few months into his new job, and barely a couple of weeks since our move, Viktor asks me to sit down with him after the kids are in bed, to talk. He's experiencing the vagaries of office politics.

"I'm being de-layered," he says.

"What do you mean, delayed?"

"No. De-*layered*. Basically, the CEO has decided to hire someone else to be my boss. It came out of the blue."

Viktor's current position reports directly to the CEO, so this will mean an additional level of hierarchy between the two of them.

"That's surprising. Why would he do that?"

Viktor rolls his eyes.

"The official excuse is that my job is too big. I'm not sure what the real reason is. But this isn't what I signed up for. If I'd known this would be happening, I wouldn't have taken the job!"

This is effectively a demotion and Viktor feels understandably blind-sided. He opens his laptop and hands it to me. The screen displays a draft email he's writing to the CEO.

"What do you think?" His expression is pensive, serious. "I believe his decision is a bad move—not just for me, but for the business." It's unusual for my husband to ask my opinion on something work-related.

He presents his arguments, which are solid, but the CEO goes ahead with his plan.

Viktor and the new boss don't hit it off. From what he tells me, they're very different personalities. He feels actively undermined on nearly a weekly basis. At first, I assume it's a classic case of two alpha males jockeying for respect and marking their territory. Then, one evening in early fall, Viktor asks me to sit down after dinner again. He seems more down than usual.

"My boss has decided to move me from my current role." He almost spits the words. "He's offered me two options: head of North America or head of Asia."

Both positions are narrower in scope than the job he was hired to do—effectively, another demotion. And either position would require us to move again.

"*What?* Move again? We've only been here for, like, a month!" I've barely finished unpacking our last boxes.

"We're not going anywhere."

He shows me the draft of another email he plans to send the CEO. "I've already cleared this with my lawyer.

"I think it's time to pull the plug." There's no emotion in his voice. "I know when I'm being pushed out. I've tried to fight this, but it's no use. I need to get out before it's too late. If I stay any longer, the way it's going, I risk getting fired by the end of the year. That won't look good to my next employer." He seems exhausted.

I get it. The smartest thing to do is leave now, while he still has a great track record, and not give anyone the opportunity to tarnish his name. That said, we've only *just* moved to one of the most expensive countries in Europe and my husband is telling me he's quitting his job. I've heard about this happening to other expats—they move somewhere for a job and then the job falls apart. That's why we chose to move three months *after* Viktor started with the company, to make sure this wouldn't happen to us.

My gut tells me he's in dangerous territory.

"You should absolutely pull the plug."

Viktor's CEO makes a brief effort and encourages him to reconsider, or at least to stay on for a few more months. But Viktor and I agree he can no longer trust the company. He stands by his decision. With his attorney's guidance, a settlement is negotiated and his departure is publicly announced. There are a series of articles placed in the media, some of which are critical of the company's inability to retain valuable talent.

Even before his departure is official, Viktor reaches out to his network and signals his availability to headhunters. In the interim, he has a lot more time on his hands, so—much to my chagrin—he decides to help found a political party in his home country, Austria.

Since we first met, Viktor's interest in politics has been a constant source of disagreement between us. It's not that I don't want him to fulfill his dream; it's about what the contours of his dream will mean for *my* dream. And becoming a politician's wife is decidedly *not* my dream. It would upend our lifestyle; it would mean having an absent husband. I'd virtually become a single parent! It would also mean being under constant scrutiny, exposed. I don't want to be alone, left to "hold down the fort" while he goes off to build a political career. That's not *my* dream. And I let him know it.

"You really believe you can 'change the world' by becoming a politician? You can't. You're too much of an idealist to survive in politics, Viktor. Politics is corrupt. All politicians are ruthless. They'll eat you alive."

"I'm not stupid, Katia."

"No, you're not, but you have principles. That won't work in your favor."

"You grew up with Greek politics! *Of course* you're cynical."

"Austrian politics is unbearably provincial," I shoot back. "It's not worth your time or talent."

It goes on like this for a while, until one of us gets tired of rehashing the same outworn arguments. We agree to disagree. Regardless, Viktor proceeds with his plan. He and a friend from his university days conceive a new liberal political party in Austria. Together with other like-minded Austrians, they organize a conference set to take place in late October. I don't pay much attention to their plans, so I'm taken by surprise when their efforts make the news. Now, even when he's home, Viktor is constantly on the phone, answering media requests and giving interviews.

I'm too busy shuttling our children to school and activities to ask questions, even if I were remotely interested. Still, one has to put her feelings somewhere. As the month wears on, I feel perpetually exhausted and emotional. By the time I'm done clearing the dinner table, I hardly have the energy left to make it through the kids' evening routines. I become edgy and short-fused with them—no patience for their last-minute requests (an ancient ploy in which children attempt to delay bedtime for as long as possible). At first, I don't lend it much weight. Feeling annoyed has become my natural state; I'm triggered by anything having to do with Viktor and politics.

Even when my period fails to come on time, I'm not alarmed. I've never been regular, and Viktor and I are careful. Besides, I'm forty-one! *How easy can it be to get pregnant now?* I buy a test from the pharmacy anyway.

Come Monday morning, I'm seated, legs crossed, on the edge of the bathtub, waiting. Five minutes is an eternity. Finally, I reach for the test, which I've temporarily hidden behind a shampoo bottle, and take a look. I stare, unmoving, for a long time—two, possibly four, eternities. *You have got to be kidding me.*

I feel the knot forming in my stomach, but I don't have time to panic; I have a full day. Writing, then grocery shopping, then school pickups, then activities—violin for Margarita, football practice for both. Thankfully, Marina will take over with Nicolas. On Wednesday, my good friend Johanna will come to stay for a few days with her two young boys. I need to prepare the guest room and think through a meal plan, perhaps some fun activities. I sit down at my desk, but I can't write, so I call my aunt. I need some practice before I tell my mother.

"You guys have been naughty again, huh?" Her voice brings me back into my body. "Listen, these things happen. Now, what are you going to do?"

"I still have to tell Viktor, of course. But we can't possibly go ahead with another pregnancy. *I* can't go ahead with it."

I've only just started getting my life on track. The kids are at school for a reasonable amount of time. I have support for Nicolas. I'm back to writing. I've even started working with a coach to figure out what direction I want to go professionally. I can't—*won't*—go back to being a full-time mom. Besides, how can I bring a new child into this world the way things are with Viktor?

"Do you have a doctor there?"

I don't. Before we got here in July, I had already lined up a pediatrician, but I hadn't anticipated needing a doctor so soon myself.

"Maybe you could find an excuse to come to Greece and just have the procedure here with our doctor?"

The kids have school and Viktor is traveling for the next few weeks. "I can't just leave the kids with the nanny. I'll have to figure it out."

I don't feel guilty; why should I? Viktor is the Catholic between us, not me. I see my options clearly. And I hope he'll be on board with my decision.

"Okay, but if there's anything you need . . . you know, right?" I know. But the knot in my stomach doesn't.

We hang up and I dial my mom. I'm late for our morning call and she senses there's something wrong. When I tell her my news, she's immediately supportive; she understands. Abortion isn't a taboo in our family, though I don't know of anyone who's had one.

That evening after the kids are in bed, I close the bedroom door and turn to look at Viktor. When I tell him I'm pregnant, he hugs me, laughing.

"We did it again, didn't we?" I'm surprised by the lightness in his voice.

"Viktor, we can't keep this pregnancy. I hope you see that."

He sighs and looks at me, the twinkle gone from his eyes. "I know," he says. "But we need to be more careful."

The next day, I find the number for a clinic in the ninth district. They ask when my last period was and give me an appointment for a consultation at the end of the week. The ninth district is on the other end of town. I'm too scared to drive in case I lose my way or can't find parking, so I take public transport. (Taxis, like everything else in Zurich, are insanely expensive.)

The clinic is located on the ground floor of a glass building. There's a sign above the door that reads, "Doctor's Practice." The receptionist gives me forms to fill out and, when I'm done, takes me in to see the doctor, whose hands remind me of my grandmother's. He's in his sixties, wearing round glasses and a kind smile. As the doctor describes the procedure, I feel reassured; he's surely done this thousands of times before.

My appointment is set for the following Friday.

The day of, Viktor drives me to the clinic and we go in together. The receptionist takes my name and points us to the waiting room. A few minutes later, a nurse walks toward us and asks me to follow her. Viktor stands up with me, but heads for the door.

"You're leaving?" I try not to sound accusing.

"I have a meeting in town," he says. "This will take a while. They'll need you to stay until you've recovered from the anesthesia. Give me a call when you're ready and I'll come get you."

I say nothing in response. I just turn and follow the nurse into another room, where a second nurse is waiting. They're both dressed in green surgical gowns, their hair tucked under blue caps. They wear blue rubber gloves. In the middle of the room is a chair. It looks like a dentist's chair, except for the stirrups.

The second nurse asks me to undress. At least they both speak in High German for me.

I'm asked to sit in the chair and lie back. Suddenly, I'm shivering. The room is chilly, or my nerves make it feel that way.

"Don't worry. It won't take long and it won't hurt." The second nurse's eyes are kind, almost motherly. "You will sleep right through it."

The IV is administered and the nurses take their places on either side of my chair just as the doctor enters the room. Perfectly synchronized, like a Swiss watch.

"*Grüezi, Frau* Vlachos." The doctor greets me, already dressed in green.

Seconds later, a cold sensation flows through my left arm and my eyes close.

When I wake, it feels as though I've dozed off for only a couple of minutes. The nurse with kind eyes is there, smiling. I start to cry. I don't feel particularly sad, but I can't control the tears.

"I'm so sorry, I don't know why this is happening." I'm weeping now.

"It's okay," she reassures me. "Sometimes the anesthesia does this."

She helps me stand and walks with me to the recovery room. "I'll let you rest now. I'll be back to check on you in a bit."

When she leaves, I'm completely alone. Again.

The next day, I jump right back into the usual busyness of drop offs and pickups, music class and football practice. As planned, my friend comes to visit. I'm exhausted during her stay but force myself to rally. From the outside, everything looks great. Normal.

CHAPTER 18

Finding My Tribe

"True belonging doesn't require you to change who you are; it requires you to be who you are."
— Brené Brown, *Braving the Wilderness*

WITHIN THE FIRST COUPLE OF MONTHS, the two younger children seem to have adjusted well to their new home base. For Petros, it takes longer, though that doesn't come as a surprise. For the first few weeks, he seems easygoing and lighthearted. School seems to be going okay and he enjoys playing football with his new club. An independent spirit by nature, he's thrilled to explore our new surroundings. So, when he becomes irritable and short-tempered, I attribute it to hormones. Petros is ten now and closing in on puberty, after all. Then, he becomes defiant and aggressive over seemingly minor concerns—mostly directed at me. I'm the parent he spends most of his time with, so I understand why his rebellion is focused on me.

One day in the early fall, we have an argument over something forgettable. I watch as my son opens the front door and walks out, slamming the door closed behind him. By the time I realize what's happening, he's gone. I panic; he can't possibly know where he's going and he's ten years old.

I call Viktor at the office. He tries to reassure me, but I can tell from his voice he's worried too.

"I'm coming home," he says. "Call me if Petros comes back in the meantime."

But nearly an hour passes and our son doesn't come back. When Viktor arrives, he calls the police. A short time later, a Swiss policeman appears on our doorstep—right about the time our son decides to return.

When Petros realizes why the policeman was called, he freezes. I'm crying and shouting through my tears; I can hardly breathe. Petros doesn't say a word. Hard to tell who he's more afraid of—the police or his mother (I suspect the latter), but suddenly, he bursts into tears.

"I'm so sorry. I really didn't mean to worry you. I'm sorry, Mamá!"

I take him in my arms and let him sob against my chest.

That evening after things have calmed down, I go to his room to say goodnight, just as I do every evening. This time, I sit down.

Petros doesn't usually make eye contact with me when we talk, but tonight he lifts his head from the book he's reading, and I can see his big hazel—green with brown—eyes are watery (the color of his eyes has always been a mystery to me).

"What happened today, Petros? Why are you so angry?" My voice is soft, gentle. I just want to understand.

"I want to go back to Vienna. We never should have moved here."

"I understand. But why didn't you say something before? I didn't realize things were that bad."

"I want to change schools." He's near tears again. "I'm miserable here. They all speak Swiss German. And they've all known each other since kindergarten."

"I'm so sorry, Petros." He's lonely and unhappy and it breaks my heart.

He glares at me. "It's *your* fault we're here."

"My love, we moved here for your dad's work."

"Yeah, but you agreed to come! You could have said 'no,' so that we didn't have to move."

I open my arms. "Come here. Do you want to hear a bit about what I'm working on these days?"

Petros looks at me, puzzled. "Sure?"

"You know I've been writing about people who move from one country to another, right? Just like we did."

He nods.

"Most people who move countries have a hard time at first, too. They go through something called the 'U-curve of adjustment.' Look." I trace an imaginary line on the wall beside his bed. "A U-curve looks like this. You start on a high note when you arrive to a new place. Everything is new and exciting, right? Then, you start to feel sad, homesick. You miss your old home, just like you miss Vienna now. That's how you know you're at the bottom of the curve. But the good news is that, from here, you eventually start to feel better and better. You start to feel at home. I've been through these stages myself several times, every time I've ever moved."

Petros's eyes widen. "So, that's where I am right now?" He touches the bottom of my imaginary U-curve.

I nod.

"And this is where I'll be later?" He points to the top.

I nod again.

"Okay," he says, and snuggles beneath the covers.

The next morning, Petros comes down to breakfast wearing a smile. He seems lighter, less angry. He even offers me the top of his head to kiss, which I usually have to ask for.

Once all three kids seem to be doing well, I reclaim my mornings for research and writing. I pick up my matcha at the local Starbucks and sit at the new desk in my tiny (but all mine!) office. I stare out the big windows toward the lake. It's my time.

I get back to work with my life coach, Gaby, who cheers me on and holds me accountable. I start writing blog posts a couple of times a month and begin tackling broader themes like belonging, home, adjustment, relationships. I search out other expat bloggers and follow them, becoming familiar with their writing. Soon, I discover news of a conference hosted in the US by an organization catering to the needs of the global community—expats, global nomads. The organization is called Families in Global Transition, or FIGT. A fellow blogger I read regularly is one of the speakers this year.

"It's a life-changing experience," she writes. "Not to be missed."

I click on the link. The FIGT conference takes place in Silver Spring, Maryland, just outside DC. Viktor assures me he can take care of the kids for four days, so I book a flight. It's time to invest in myself and my new future.

After New Year's, 2013, Viktor tells me he's thinking of taking on the role of business manager for the political party he's been working to get off the ground. I'm not sure what a business manager does but I know the party is based in Austria, and therefore, so is the position.

"Can I do this?" he asks.

I stare at him, but all I can see are my old fears and resentments. Fear of being alone again, of being left behind, solely responsible for our children. Even with help at home, I never really get a break—from the schoolwork, the activities, the doctors' appointments. Why can't I have a partner who is physically present to share the load? Or just to share the simple things, like walks by the lake. Someone to have a drink with on the patio in the evenings, where we can discuss our day.

"How much travel are we talking about?" My voice is cold. "Will you be able to look for jobs while you're working on this full-time?"

"I'm just volunteering to take over the role until we find someone to hire full-time. I'll have to be in Vienna a couple of days every week."

"For how long?" I demand.

"Not sure. Probably until the summer." It's January. "There could be elections in June. We need to mobilize the party and be organized in time. Just so you understand what's at stake here, Katia."

"Thanks, Viktor. So, you're taking on an unpaid position, plan to finance the travel out of our budget, and are unlikely to have the time to focus on looking for work here in Zurich. Is that right?" He can feel my contempt.

"Katia, you're making this bigger than it is. I'll optimize the cost of travel between trains and flights and stay with friends or my brothers in Vienna. And of course I'll have time for interviews. I've already been talking to headhunters. What do you want me to do, sit around waiting for jobs to come along? At least this way I'll be doing something productive."

He has a point, but I'm too pissed off to see it. I'm worried about the money. How far is his severance package going to take us before we start drawing on our savings? This is Switzerland, after all. And I don't want to be left alone with the kids—again—and this time not even for a real job.

"I wonder how you'd feel if I had the same reaction to your book project."

"Book *project*? Seriously?" He makes it sound like a hobby, not real work. He's never said it, but I often get the sense he sees my work as less important than his because I don't yet earn an income from it. Now this.

I storm off.

The next morning, Viktor sends me an email, outlining his plan with the dates he'll need to be away in the first quarter.

"Can I do this?" he asks again.

I don't reply.

It doesn't matter; Viktor takes on the party management role. For several weeks I give him the cold shoulder.

In February when the kids are on break from school, we travel to Austria as a family to visit Viktor's parents. The days are still short and the afternoons get dark by only 4:00 p.m. On the drive, Viktor and I get into an argument. We speak to each other only in French, so the children won't understand, but it's futile; our tone is unmistakable. In the backseat, Petros stares silently out the window. Nicolas is asleep and Margarita pretends to be.

I go silent, refusing to engage further.

"You only see me as a source of income." Viktor's words stun me.

After we had Petros, Viktor encouraged me to quit work and focus on finishing my PhD. Attempting to work, write a dissertation, and care for a newborn, with my husband always traveling—it was an impossible task. So, I followed his suggestion and gave up my salary. At the time, I was certain money would never become an issue between us. Besides, Viktor had always assured me his income was "our money." Had I known this was coming, I would never have given up my independence. Now, I feel trapped by my decision, dependent on someone who resents me.

But in place of outrage, I feel clarity. After years of wavering between insecurity and guilt, I finally know exactly where I stand—and I know what I have to do. The burning sensation in my stomach, the discomfort I always feel when Viktor and I argue, is gone. I straighten my spine and take a deep breath, exhale, and feel my whole body relax. I suppress the smile that comes to my lips, and for the rest of the drive, I don't say another word.

In the meantime, I cope with the reality of our marriage by escaping it as often as I can. I take short trips alone to visit my family in Greece. These weekends away are a complicated endeavor. In addition to planning the logistics, I have to first clear the dates with Viktor, organize extra childcare, and prepare detailed instructions for the kids' schedules and activities. All Viktor has to do to travel is announce the dates to me. But I'm determined to make my trips happen—and they're worth it. Even a few days of not feeling annoyed or resentful are good for my soul.

At home in Greece, I find joy in all the things I miss: chatting with the owner of the kiosk where I buy the Athens newspaper (she always remembers me); sipping cappuccino and sharing gossip on the terrace with a dear friend; the sun soaked days of January; writing at the neighborhood café, where everyone around me speaks Greek; sitting down for a 4:00 p.m. Sunday "lunch" with my family.

I come home calmer, recharged.

Viktor enjoys his time with the kids, but my trips are tough for him. He sends an email to say he wishes I showed the same enthusiasm and determination for planning time away with him as I do for planning time away *from* him. He reminds me it's hard on the baby for either of us to be away, but I deflect: Why can't he just let me enjoy my time off, for once? Still, I know he's right; I'm not making much of an effort in our marriage. He notices on my weekend escapes, I come alive. These days, I am far more myself when I'm away than I ever am when we're together.

"You make everyone feel like you're in prison," he writes.

I do feel trapped. I hadn't realized it was obvious.

He feels like he's in a prison of his own, forced to account for all the time he spends elsewhere.

"It's called having a family," I reply.

We send short, snide messages back and forth throughout the day, accusing each other of double standards, unable to agree as to who's the bigger victim in our marriage.

"I never take time for myself." It's his usual refrain. "I'm expected to work full-time and take care of your and the children's needs. The rare times I do take off, you're resentful about it. I don't know how long I'll last, physically, living like this."

"I'm the default parent, Viktor. I can never devote myself to my work for more than a couple of hours at a time. I might as well give up any hope of a career." My usual refrain.

What we're *really* arguing about is how unappreciated and disconnected we feel. Even though Viktor knows how unhappy I am—we both are—he says he believes in the depth of our love for each other and its power to conquer all. Many of his emails end with an expression of his faith in us and our commitment to each other.

He can't see how far apart we've drifted.

For the next nine months, Viktor will be traveling weekly to Austria, visiting different parts of the country and staying a couple of days at a time. I manage, of course. The two older kids are easier, and I have help. What makes me resentful is the fact that he chooses to be away. He chooses to leave us for work he doesn't even get compensated for. I recognize he's following his passion, something that fulfills him and makes him happy. And I know I should be supportive of that and happy for him. But I can't be. In my book, volunteer work is not an acceptable reason for leaving us, for leaving me.

The live-in nanny becomes my household companion. When Viktor's three-day trips turn into weeklong absences, my mother comes to Zurich to help out—and to keep me quiet. To fulfill his promise, Viktor occasionally meets with headhunters, but nothing concrete comes up. I suspect he's in no hurry.

In March, I leave for the US to attend the FIGT conference. I'm excited for the opportunity to meet fellow global nomads, to share my work, and to get inspired. I feel like a child, about to go on a long-promised vacation.

As excited as I am, I'm also nervous and self-conscious, unsure what to expect. It's been years since I was last in a professional setting—how good will I be at presenting myself? To prepare, I order new business cards, describing myself as a researcher and writer. And I remove my husband's surname (up to now I'd used a hyphenated last name, even if on all official documents I could only have my maiden name). When Viktor sees the new cards, he's hurt.

"You're cutting yet another thread that ties us together." He's right; it's a deliberate act of rebellion. But I refuse to admit it.

Instead, I minimize. "A shorter name is easier for people to remember. I'm just simplifying things."

Viktor sees through it. But I keep the business cards as they are.

Before I leave, I make a detailed schedule for each child, complete with the addresses of their various activities (many), phone numbers of local contacts (not many, we're still new here), emergency numbers (ambulance, police, fire department), and a detailed feeding schedule for Nicolas. I even create an excel sheet with an overview of every single appointment for the next five days (I'm a visual type; I assume that will help).

The second I'm seated in the taxi and heading for the airport, I take a deep breath. *They'll survive.* Once on the plane, "Greek mom" switches off and my professional self switches on. *I did it.*

I haven't been back to DC since I defended my doctoral dissertation six years ago, which feels like another lifetime. Yet, everything is familiar—from the stern look on the immigration officer's face to the Dulles International Dunkin' Donuts shop where I grab a vanilla coffee. An hour later, I check into my hotel and get changed into a dark blue blazer and jeans, a safe choice when you don't quite know the dress code. As I head off to a networking event at the conference venue across the street from my hotel, my heart is full.

As soon as I enter the conference room—notebook in hand, name tag around my neck—I notice the vibe and it feels good. Jenny, a blogger whose posts I follow, greets me at the door, smiling.

"Welcome! Come on in!"

I introduce myself and she pauses for a minute. "You have a blog too, right? 'Diary of a Move'?"

"Yes! How did you know?" I'm stunned.

"I read a post you wrote about home a little while ago. Loved it!" She motions me in, smiling.

I scan the room. It's a small, intimate space, not one of those oversized hotel ballrooms. There are about a dozen people, most of them standing near their seats and chatting. I notice a blond woman who also appears to be here by herself, so I sit down beside her.

"Hi, I'm Katia." I offer my hand and smile.

"Hi Katia. I'm Brenda and," she pauses, "you look familiar."

"Hmm. It's my first time here."

"Mine, too!"

Turns out, Brenda is also familiar with my blog. She tells me she's read my post on the challenges of long-distance relationships, where one partner works outside the country of residence.

"I really enjoyed that post. Great insights!"

I thought my only readers were my family and a few Facebook friends. It never occurred to me I was reaching other expats. It feels really good.

Brenda points to a woman near the entrance, chatting with the author. "That's Ruth Van Reken, the founder. She's a legend."

When I finally meet Ruth myself, I experience firsthand all the qualities that make her a legend—her infinite kindness, wisdom, and humility combined with a strong desire to serve her community. Ruth inspires my work and changes the way I see myself and my own journey.

The next few days are full—from early morning to late evening—with various sessions and workshops, fascinating conversations over coffee, and spontaneous dinner dates—all with people I've only just met.

I attend sessions on blogging, cultural intelligence, intercultural competence, global relocation trends, and building a portable career. I write down words and concepts that keep coming up in those sessions: dislocation, transience, mobility, identity, loss, grief, resilience, reinvention. I fill my notebook with insights and learnings, like the idea that concepts of home evolve. You don't need land to feel rooted; you can find belonging in many other ways. I learn intercultural competence is not just about gathering knowledge on another culture, but about cultivating the empathy and curiosity that allows us to shift perspectives and frames of reference. Everything I learn refines the language I use to talk about my experience and those of other expats. I swap emails and business cards. I don't even feel the jet lag until my head hits the pillow at night.

The writers' event is intimate; there are about fifteen of us in a small room, chairs positioned in a semi-circle around the host, author Pico Iyer, who immediately puts us at ease with his humor. His tone is unassuming and low key; he even strikes me as shy. For a while, he ceases to be the "famous author" and simply becomes Pico, a writer, wearing jeans and a sweater, talking about his craft.

The next day, when Pico takes the stage to deliver his keynote to a room of over 150, he seems as comfortable and at ease as he was in yesterday's intimate circle. His words about the contrasts and paradoxes of leading a global life are poetic. Every word has its place and every sentence is crafted with skill and care, memorable. I fill six pages of my notebook with his words.

"Home is a moving target, a work in progress, a stained-glass window."

"Home is the place where you become yourself. It has less to do with a piece of *soil* than a piece of *soul*."

"Surviving as a foreigner requires accepting our own foreignness."

For Pico, being a foreigner is what comes naturally; it's his sense of home. Listening to him speak, I feel validated, seen. The poetry of his language speaks to my soul, and I leave his talk deeply inspired.

I'm also impacted by everything that happens outside of the sessions. For a shy introvert, I feel welcome and at ease almost instantly. The usual awkwardness and feeling like an outsider vanishes. Everyone I meet is friendly, unpretentious, warm. They seem engaged and genuinely interested in my story. They are researchers, coaches and counselors, international businesspeople, missionary kids, military brats, bloggers, writers, and other creatives or performers, all of whom lead globally mobile lives themselves or are there to support those who do. They've come from Kenya, Korea, Australia, America, the Netherlands, and elsewhere and are the most welcoming crowd I've ever met. Most have lived in several countries, have multiple passports and citizenships, and more than one place they call home. I feel humbled and embraced; I have found my tribe.

The more I share my story with others, the more natural and uncompli-cated it gets. I don't need to explain myself; they see me—as an individual and a professional.

On my overnight flight back to Zurich, I pore over my notes, my mind overflowing with new ideas, projects, and connections to follow up on. I don't want to forget anything. In lieu of sleep, I begin writing a new section for my chapter on couple dynamics about the importance of addressing dual-career issues early on.

When my plane lands in Switzerland, Viktor is already on his way to Austria. But I don't let it bother me; I want to hold on a little longer to the good feelings I've brought back from my conference.

CHAPTER 19

Doomed

"You never really know a man until
you have divorced him."
— Zsa Zsa Gabor

FOR SEVERAL MONTHS NOW, we've stopped entertaining guests
in our home. Hosting dinners is a tense, stressful experience. It's exhausting
enough to manage marital tension in front of the children, but adults see
right through the façade. It's always the same thing: I'm annoyed because
I feel I do all the work; Viktor feels attacked and stops helping altogether.
We snap at each other until the first guest arrives, at which point we put on
our Gracious Host masks and pretend everything is perfectly fine. And it
works, at least until the first snide-remark-followed-by-sarcastic-counter
is made, at which point, everyone at the table stops talking.

Last summer, we attended a dinner for members of the board of direc-
tors of a Zurich media company. Viktor had just been offered the job of
CEO—with one irritating proviso: the board wished to meet his wife.

When Viktor told me this, I rolled my eyes. "Doesn't that sound a
little sexist to you? What on earth do *I* have to do with how suited you
are for the role?"

Long ago, Viktor had agreed never to ask me to perform "corporate
wife duties." He knew how much I resented the role and the presumption

that a woman should have to play it. But this was a big job, his first CEO position, so I agreed to put my principles aside for one night and support him. What I *wasn't* going to do was hide who I am or pretend to be the "good Swiss wife." This time, instead of a dragon ring, I wore a black cocktail dress with a plunging neckline. It was classy but provocative. Now I was evaluating *them*: Would they be able to see the woman beyond the dress?

They must have, because Viktor got the job.

At the beginning of 2014, I sit down at my computer and secretly type, "female divorce lawyers in Zurich" into the web browser. Several names come up and I choose the one who looks the kindest in her photo. I don't tell Viktor I'm planning to see a lawyer, but I put the appointment in my calendar; I'm not trying to hide it.

The attorney I meet is as polished as her sleek office in the city center. I share with her the key facts of my situation, and she gives me an overview of the process of separation and divorce in Switzerland. I'm not quite ready to file but she agrees to represent me should the time come. In the meantime, she suggests I create a budget for myself and the children. I pay for the consultation in cash and leave her office with a budget template and renewed conviction. Over the weeks that follow, I keep meticulous notes for every Swiss Franc I spend—from Starbucks and Amazon to grocery shopping and tram tickets.

Shortly after I visit the divorce attorney, I receive a late-night email from my husband. He's on an annual ski trip with the two older children, a vacation we would ordinarily take together. This year, I've decided to bring Nicolas to Greece and let the three of them enjoy the slopes without us. Viktor writes to explain his disappointment with my decision in an email that continues for several pages. Halfway through the first page, he says it's time for him to "come clean" about our move to Vienna. I sit up in bed and reread the sentence. That was the move we vehemently disagreed on, the one in which I felt my choice had been hijacked in a *fait accompli*; the same international move he swore we'd discussed beforehand and that I had agreed to make. The same move about which I felt gaslighted, made to distrust my own memory.

Now, Viktor tells me the truth. Yes, we had discussed moving back to Europe, but I had refused and we'd left it at that. Until my husband announced to me he was being transferred to Vienna. I had never explicitly agreed. Viktor had made a unilateral decision. It was a decision made *for* me, not *with* me.

His email offers no apology; it merely lists all the reasons he'd felt we should leave LA. His primary justification is it had been a "precarious time" for him professionally. So, to spare us any potential financial insecurity, my home and my career were taken from me.

As I read this, it's nearly 2:00 a.m. in Athens. My youngest one is sleeping peacefully beside me. And I want to scream.

For months, we grapple with the damage that's been done to our relationship and the question of where to go from here. As usual, we communicate largely by email. Our exchanges are often bitter, aggressive, filled with blame. Although we make an effort to end every message on a positive note, professing our love for each other and our commitment to our family, it doesn't matter. We both know we are failing.

By April, Viktor and I are sitting in a therapist's office for the fourth of five weekly sessions we've committed to. Jessica, our therapist, is from California. She's warm and friendly but careful to maintain professional distance; she shows compassion for our respective plights and is careful not to take sides. She earns my respect early on, she doesn't just let us rant for fifty minutes, and she asks questions that force us to get to the heart of our grievances. Her questions are direct and often uncomfortable, but there is an underlying kindness and desire to help that we can feel.

Viktor and I pour our hearts out during the sessions, bringing out every instance of disillusionment, betrayal, and resentment for Jessica to view.

"Do you want to make our marriage work?" Viktor is exasperated that we haven't gotten anywhere after three sessions.

"I don't know." It's an honest reply.

A few minutes later, he asks again. "Katia, do you want to make our marriage work?"

Is he hoping for a different answer?

"I don't know." That's all I've got.

"What do you mean, you don't know? Why are we here then?" His face is red.

We're here to find a way to end it, I think. *We're here to find a way to protect our children and our relationship as their parents. We're here because I need a third person to hear me and tell me I'm not crazy, I'm not exaggerating, I'm not the bad guy. We're here so I can tell you things I don't dare when it's just the two of us.*

The following week, in our fifth and final session, I'm sitting on the edge of my chair, looking at my hands. Viktor is looking at me. All week, we've avoided talking about our last session and now he's asking that same question.

"Do you want to make our marriage work?"

I feel two pairs of eyes looking at me, waiting.

"I don't know," I say again.

My brain knows these three words are likely the final blow, but my heart is numb.

"I don't have another answer, I'm sorry."

My gut says our marriage is beyond saving. We've grown too far apart, broken too much glass.

In a recent email to Viktor, I shared a passage from a book I was reading—Ann Patchett's *This Is the Story of a Happy Marriage.* The words had been haunting me ever since.

> *"Does your husband make you a better person?" Edra asked. "Are you smarter, kinder, more generous, more compassionate, a better writer?" she said, running down her list. "Does he make you better?"*
>
> *"That's not the question," I said. "It's so much more complicated than that."*

"It's not more complicated than that," she said. "That's all there is. Does he make you better and do you make him better?"

There was a time when Viktor and I made each other better. We don't anymore.

Jessica's voice is firm when she speaks. "I think you should consider separating."

Viktor and I just stare at her, stunned into silence by six simple words.

Jessica's face softens. "There's too much baggage between you and it doesn't look like either of you is willing to let go. I think you may be better off separating."

I didn't expect this. I assumed, if we decided to separate, it would have to come from one of us. But we'd asked for her expert opinion and now she's given it.

When we leave her office, neither of us speaks. Months go by, and we simply don't talk about what was said. But we both know we're postponing the inevitable.

Meanwhile, our lease is expiring soon and I have to search for a new home for us. The last two years flew by, and now we need to deal with reality. There's a good chance our family structure will undergo a transformation in this new home, and I want our children to feel safely anchored in the midst of uncertainty and change. So, I say a prayer.

The last property we view is just down the road from where we currently live. From the outside, it's old, but simple and tasteful. We make the walk through the garden, up the stairs, and through the front entrance and I stop. *This is the one,* I think. *I can see us living here.*

The Universe hears my prayer.

With everything that's going on, including Viktor's new job and the upcoming transition to a new home, I fall behind on my writing. I feel like I'm losing all the momentum and inspiration I brought back from the FIGT conference. I miss one self-imposed deadline after another; I'm demoralized and frustrated when I need to be energized. My life coach, Gaby, helps me connect to the part of myself I'd lost and now rediscovered through writing—my professional self, my competent self. She helps me connect to my "why," the contribution I want to make, the urgency for getting this book out there for my tribe. But the writing happens in fits and starts; there's no flow or consistency. To keep my deadlines, I know I have to prioritize the work—but I'm stuck.

This time, instead of wallowing in either self-pity or resentment (or both), I choose to hire a specialist to help me. I haven't heard of the term "book coach" before, but why not? Maybe a book coach can help get me out of this rut.

Amy and I connect instantly. Maybe it's her warm and friendly manner; maybe it's her genuine interest in the theme of my book. She knows what it's like to be an expat—she used to be one herself (what are the odds?). She gets the concept and purpose of my book. Now all I have to do is send her what I've written so far.

I'm sitting in front of my laptop in a hotel room somewhere in the countryside, outside the city of Lausanne. Viktor and the older kids are playing a card game on the floor nearby while our youngest naps. For spring break, we decided to take a road trip through the French part of Switzerland. I spent a few summers here in a chalet just above the city of Montreux at a sort of alpine summer camp. I haven't been back since I was a child and thought it would be fun to show the kids.

I wasn't planning to work while we're here, but I don't want to lose the momentum with Amy. She's already seen my outline and has asked me to send her my introduction and the first four chapters. I upload the documents but can't bring myself to press "send." Amy is a published novelist. What if she doesn't like it? Will she tell me?

I'm also terrified of having my book out in the open, of sending my baby to a total stranger who lives on the other side of the world. What if she steals my ideas?

"Am I being paranoid?"

"Yes." Viktor chuckles. "No one wants to steal your book, Katia."

I press "send." It's time to take myself seriously as a writer.

We move to the new house at the end of June and I set about turning it into a home. I hang up my dad's paintings throughout. The larger paintings go in the living room, and the children get to hang the ones he made for them in their bedrooms. Our house is filled with his colors. I unbox the wooden mask and the small ebony statues, artifacts my dad brought with him from Cameroon. I grew up in a house full of these things and I want my children to be surrounded by them, too. They take their place in our library.

I buy a big, solid wood dining table, one that's stable, grounding, and welcoming. The one I choose was repurposed from an old Belgian monastery door. It's massive—three meters long—and gray-brown with streaks of blue; thick, solid legs; and plenty of imperfections that make it even more beautiful. I dream of lively Sunday lunches with family and friends—just like in my childhood—and, for a moment, I imagine what starting over together could look like.

But my dream is quickly vanquished by reality. I've only just managed to settle back into a good writing rhythm when Viktor asks whether his two nineteen-year-old nieces can come and stay with us. For three months. I'm exhausted from the move and have been trying to turn my attention back to my writing. If they come, I'll be the one caring for everyone's needs, not him. I will lose momentum again.

Viktor doesn't see it like that.

"You won't have to work harder. Lizi and Astrid can help with the shopping and cooking, even some babysitting. You'll have *more* time for your book."

I want to believe him, but I know it will never happen like that. As the mother, I'll be expected, however implicitly, to take care of everyone.

"Please give me some time to think about it."

Viktor agrees but doesn't give me time. He tells his nieces to come and alienates me from them in the process. I become the bad guy. Worse still, he invites them to arrive on the same weekend my brother and his family will be visiting. We'll already have a full house.

"Family means that one is always welcome," Viktor says. "Should I tell them they're not?"

I've been overruled. I see I have no agency in my marriage (if I can't control my own home, what control do I have over my own life?). In the past, I would have convinced myself I was merely overreacting, blowing things out of proportion. I would have felt guilty and capitulated. This time, it is abundantly clear to me my needs are not a priority. My husband is no longer trying to keep us together; it's become his way, or no way at all.

As hard as I've worked to make our home a safe space for the children, it hasn't felt like a safe space for me.

So, I'm done.

When the holidays arrive, I'm exhausted. There is the meal planning, the shopping lists, and the schedule juggling in addition to all the holiday prep. It's not so much the physical effort but the mental space that effort occupies. And, of course, there is the weight of knowing Viktor and I have reached the end of the line, for good this time.

Now, we only communicate by email; the days of talking to each other are gone. When I complain about my exhaustion, he criticizes my parenting.

"Your overprotectiveness robs our children of initiative and makes them codependent. That's why you're always overworked and short on patience with everyone."

I read somewhere that when the arguments get personal—when attacks are made on the other person's character, their values—the relationship is doomed.

CHAPTER 20

Breaking Free

"Perhaps home is not a place but simply
an irrevocable condition."
— James Baldwin, *Giovanni's Room*

IT'S BEEN SEVEN YEARS since I was in one-on-one therapy. I last went when my father was terminally ill and I was spending one week out of every month in Athens. When I was home in Vienna, I felt stressed and irritable and had a hard time controlling my emotions. Whenever it felt like Viktor wasn't pulling his weight at home or when the kids were being messy and refusing to do their chores, I would lose it. I heard myself shouting at everyone too often and started to feel like the worst parent who'd ever existed.

Now, I'm sitting at the desk in my office with the door locked. The laptop screen is open to Skype and the face I see belongs to my new therapist. A good friend recommended her. She's based in Tel Aviv, Israel, a total stranger to me, but we connect immediately; she's compassionate and empathetic and seems to understand where I'm coming from. She sees patterns and dynamics without my having to explain the detailed backstory.

I initiated therapy again because I need help coping with the decision to separate. The guilt is overwhelming; I'm consumed by it. There's also the low drone of incessant fear and anxiety.

"We have to work through the guilt first," Sarah says, warmly. "Then we'll deal with the fear."

I nod. "You're the boss." Guilt is a big part of the fear.

"What do you need to forgive yourself for?" she asks, looking me straight in the eyes.

I've already condemned myself for something that hasn't happened yet.

"For being selfish. For harming my children." I feel a knot in my throat.

I have just told her I'm unable to continue the way things are. The events of last November between Viktor and me have shown me I am no longer in control of my own life.

"I have no agency. I can't be myself in this marriage. But I'm terrified that I will damage my children if I leave. I'll be the cause of their unhappiness and could never forgive myself."

"I want to challenge your definition of 'selfish,'" Sarah says. "Is it okay to take care of yourself? How about taking care of your emotional needs? Is it selfish to want to be in a relationship that nurtures you and makes you happy?"

"You're saying there's such a thing as 'good' selfishness?" I ask, a cheeky smile on my lips. That's never occurred to me. I've always been the selfish one in my family and, believe me, it's not a good label to have. Early on, I realized it was futile to protest or try to convince them otherwise. So, I embraced it.

"Yes, Katia, there is." Sarah smiles back.

We talk about what I need from a relationship, what my soul needs to feel nurtured and loved. Those needs don't feel selfish.

"The kids will be okay, Katia," Sarah reassures me. "It won't be easy, but they have you and they have their father. Try to rest in that thought."

It's comforting—but not quite enough to unhook the guilt.

"Do you want your children to think this is what a happy marriage looks like?" Sarah asks.

I consider the ever-present tension in our home, the steady stream of passive aggression, divisiveness, and contempt.

"No, certainly not. I don't want my daughter to think that marriage is an act of self-sacrifice either."

Maybe it's possible to release the guilt.

Next up: fear. I'm overwhelmed by fears—the fear of financial insecurity, the fear of judgment, the fear of being alone. How will I support myself and the children? What kind of job should I even apply for? What will my family and friends think of me when I tell them about the divorce?

Those fears are workable, I realize. It's the fear of being alone that weighs heaviest. It sits on my chest and makes it hard to breathe. How will it feel to be without a partner again? Will our friends choose Viktor over me? How will I manage on my own in Switzerland, with my family thousands of miles away? Worst of all, what will it be like when I have to be without my children? I've never been apart from them for more than a few days. Now, I'll have to share them, to divide my time with them down the middle. I can't possibly imagine our five-year-old being away from me for weeks at a time, or on holidays. I can't imagine having to be apart from any of my children.

Sarah smiles. "Divorce is inherently scary, Katia. The fear goes through you, all the way to your heart. There's nothing wrong with being afraid. You need to go through it. You need to acknowledge and stay with the fear, so you can get to the other side.

"Now is the worst time," she says, "because it's all taking place inside you. Nothing has happened yet. It won't be like this forever."

I look forward to the "other side."

I'm standing at the front end of the conference room where my session is about to start. I'm at a Marriott Hotel in Virginia, attending my third FIGT conference in a row. This year I'm one of the speakers.

I finally got the courage to apply and was over the moon when I received my acceptance letter. I've spoken at conferences before, but this is the first time I'll be presenting my own work, and my new professional identity, to the world. This time, I'll be speaking from my heart about things I have experienced personally. Things I care about deeply. Public speaking has always been an uncomfortable part of my work; I did it only because I had to. Now, I choose to. I have a message I want to share and it's worth confronting my fears.

The room comfortably fits eight large, round tables, each sitting eight people. The layout makes it much easier for people to engage with each other. The lone downside to this setup is there's nowhere for me to place my presentation notes. The tiny table at the front of the room barely fits my MacBook and the projector. Even if I never need to glance at my notes, I prefer the security of having them close. I feel my heart rate rise for a moment, but I take a deep breath and tell myself, *I'm speaking from my heart today. It'll all be fine.*

As people begin entering the room, I smile awkwardly. Some are familiar faces. I breathe deep again and remind myself this is the friendliest, most tolerant crowd a speaker could ask for. I remember the advice I was given while preparing:

"Pick one person in the audience and talk to *them* first."

When Viktor offered me a couple of sessions with a speaking coach, I initially declined. I was reluctant to owe him any favors given the state of our marriage. But this was too important. I wanted everything to be perfect when I shared my work with the world. So, I booked an appointment. Herbert was a warm gentleman in his seventies. Even though we met at his home office, he greeted me wearing a suit and tie. His voice was kind.

He asked me to deliver the first few minutes of my speech while he recorded me with a video camera set up on a tripod near his desk. As I practiced, my palms were sweaty and my hands trembled as I gripped my notecards. Afterward, we watched the recording together.

"You're a natural speaker," he said. Apparently, Herbert hadn't noticed my shaking.

"Now, *that's* something I've never heard before."

"You just need a few tweaks here and there. Really, you've got this."

Ever since that unfortunate incident in high school, I've been telling myself I suck at public speaking. And I've avoided it at all costs. I've kept my voice down and my profile low. But now I've found something I really want to speak up about, what do you know? It turns out I'm not so bad after all.

"Pick just one person and engage them. Convince them. When you've achieved that, move on to the next person and do the same. You can win over even the most difficult audiences this way. It's not so much about what you say, but how you build an emotional connection to your audience."

Herbert drew two figures on a piece of paper. Their heads were connected by a black arrow. "These are your words, your arguments," he pointed to the arrow. "It's important to have a convincing speech, but it's your emotions, your body language, your personal stories that will win them over." He took up a red pen and drew a heart at the center of each figure, then a line connecting the two hearts. "Connection is heart-to-heart, not head-to-head," he smiled. "Got it?"

"But I was so nervous just speaking for you! Couldn't you tell?"

"I didn't see any of that. Neither will your audience."

Herbert taught me a special breathing technique for calming my nerves, one I've used many times since to help reduce stress. He then wrote key tips in capital letters on notecards for me (PAUSE! EYE CONTACT!). He also taught me to be present, to control my thoughts, to radiate positive energy. His version of speaking was a meditative experience.

Standing in the familiar hotel conference room, I think of Herbert and relax. Then, I start my presentation. So far, so good.

Midway through, I ask the audience to share their own stories with each other. The room starts to buzz with energy, voices, laughter, and hand gestures. Two women stand up from their chairs and hug each other, their eyes brimming with tears. Later, when I invite the audience to share what came up for them, the two women are the first to raise their hands.

"We just realized that we were at the same school, in Cairo, at the same time! We have so many memories of that place."

At the end of my talk, several people from the audience come to thank me. I'm even told by one or two that I'm "a great speaker." (*Say what?*)

Others ask when my book is coming out. A fellow researcher gives me her card so she can share some resources.

My heart is full and I can't stop smiling. This event is a bright light for me in an otherwise dark year.

The next couple of months are busy. Viktor is on the road to political conferences and speaking engagements. Even when in Zurich, he has frequent evening events—dinners and speeches—but I never join him. On weekends, we split the kids' football games and rarely do much as a family, except the occasional parents' evening or school picnic.

We discuss exploring potential separation scenarios. I propose a "transition summer," where we stay together as a family, rather than spending time separately with kids. Viktor is bitter about the effort I put into planning the logistics of our separation. Couldn't I be putting that energy toward rebuilding rather than tearing apart? We don't dare discuss specifics, such as whether one of us will move out or when. It's like trying to find our way out of a maze, too scared to touch anything around us.

In early June, we meet at a small Japanese restaurant near his office—for "a date." An attempt to give the marriage one last try. The building is rather nondescript from the street, so I'm surprised by its elevated, if cramped, interior. We take the last two seats at the large running sushi table. As soon as we're settled, Viktor grabs two dishes and sets them before me. It isn't our usual sushi fare.

"Try this one." He points to a plate of green seaweed topped by a (barely) poached, runny egg. "It's really good."

I gather he's been here before, probably with a colleague. The egg looks raw to me.

"Thanks, but I'm not crazy about the combination. You have it." I pass the plate back to him.

When the server comes, Viktor orders a bottle of warm sake.

"So here we are." He smiles awkwardly. "When we got married, I never thought it would come to this. Did you?"

"No one does, Viktor." The cynical remark falls out as if by habit. To his credit, Viktor ignores it.

"The question is, what do we do now? We need to make a decision."

"I don't know," I say. "Are you willing to change anything?" I look down at my plate.

"Depends on what you want me to change." He's no longer smiling. "If you're asking me to change who I am, then no. I can't."

"Does who you are include obstructing my right to make decisions for my own life?"

Our server returns with the sake. She places two cups in front of us and pours.

"Or does who you are include seeking my input? Or protecting me and my aspirations? Is there room for *that* in who you are?"

"You're blaming me for being generous, for prioritizing my family's happiness," he says. What I hear him saying is that I'm *not* generous, that I *don't* prioritize my family's happiness.

"What about prioritizing *my* happiness?" I ask. "Am I not family?"

"Don't be ridiculous, Katia. I've always prioritized your happiness. I'm sorry, but this is who I am," he repeats.

"Well, then *I'm* sorry, but that doesn't work for me."

Our sushi date only reveals how entrenched we both are in our own feelings, and how unhappy we are with each other. We can't expect the other to be someone they're not. That's nothing new, of course. But in the past, we were more willing to make compromises. We were willing to hold on to the good we saw in each other and overlook the rest. Now, neither of us is willing to compromise. Neither of us is willing to change for the other. Jessica was right—we have too much baggage.

"I don't know about you, but I don't recognize myself any more in this marriage. I don't like who I've become." I avoid eye contact. If I look at him, my emotions will overwhelm me.

"So, I guess that's it?" he asks.

"I guess that's it."

True to form, we disagree about when to tell the children. Viktor wants to tell them right away. I want to wait until Petros is done with his exams, to minimize the disruption. Viktor gets impatient but I stand my ground. He accuses me of seeing our marriage as a continuous power struggle, a zero-sum game where there must always be a winner and a loser.

"Why do you always have to get your way, Katia?"

"Why do you always have to paint me as the villain?"

But I do get my way in the end. And in Viktor's eyes, I'm responsible for tearing our family apart. Part of me believes him.

On a Saturday morning in early July, Viktor and I sit down in the living room with our two older children. Margarita sits on my lap; Petros sits next to his father. Nicolas is upstairs in his room, playing Legos. The window of opportunity before he gets bored and comes to find us is only a few minutes wide. A window of opportunity to break their hearts.

Viktor and I cooperated on a script, taken from a book I'm reading called *Putting Children First*. The author offers different scripts for different age groups, so the one we'll use for Nicolas is different.

Viktor clears his throat. "Kids, Mommy and I have decided to separate. We won't be living in the same house anymore."

Margarita's eyes widen. Then, she bursts into tears.

"But why? How?" Her little body is shaking. "Why do you have to do this?"

"We can't explain it to you right now, my love. This is between Daddy and me. I'm so sorry."

"Can't you just stay together? Please!"

I have no answer that will assuage my ten-year-old's tears. All I can do is hold her tightly in my arms. It feels as though someone has reached into my body and torn the heart from my chest.

"I'm so sorry," I say again.

Damn right you're sorry. The voice inside my head won't let up. *See what you've done?*

Viktor continues with the script. "We may not be together anymore, but we both love you very, very much. We will always be your parents. That's never going to change."

Still sobbing, Margarita moves into her father's arms, as if she's already trying not to show favoritism for one of us over the other.

I turn to Petros. His face is turned away, toward the window.

"Petros?"

He refuses to meet my gaze, though I can see his nose is red and his eyes are glassy. Still, he doesn't cry—he just presses his lips tightly together.

"Are you okay?" I ask.

"It's okay, I understand. I understand." His voice trembles as he speaks.

My heart is now being bludgeoned with a hammer. Did Petros see this coming? Or is he trying to keep the peace, trying not to burden us with his feelings? The book says kids often make up entire stories in their minds about why their parents' divorce is all their fault. I don't want that for our children.

I turn to face them both. "Nothing about this is your fault. Daddy and I haven't been happy for a while, but that has nothing to do with you."

"But you never fight!" Margarita protests.

"We never fight in front of you," I correct her. "That doesn't mean we're happy."

"Well, thanks for ruining my last week of school!" Margarita snaps.

"I'm sorry, my love," I say softly. "There's never a good time to do something like this."

I'm barely holding it together.

Now that the children know, we have to tell our friends and family. Viktor wants to make a communications plan for this, including splitting between us who tells whom. He creates a spreadsheet, complete with everyone's email address. It resembles one of our party guest lists. *Hi everyone, come celebrate the ruination of our marriage!*

I probably shouldn't let Viktor control how we tell others the news, but I don't have the mental space to formulate separation announcements, nor the energy to negotiate with him. Besides, I have to call my family.

When I tell her we're really done, Mamá isn't shocked; she's seen it coming for a while. But when I tell my brother, he cries. Both are deeply sad for the children, of course. Neither asks how I'm doing. They don't have to tell me, like Viktor did, that I'm selfish for doing this to my children, for breaking up the family. But I know it's what they're thinking.

The day school is out, the kids and I leave for Greece. We kick off vacation with the usual week of waterskiing, and my mom joins us for the first time. It's nice to have her with us; her presence creates a sense of stability for the children. The second week, their father joins us. We've rented a villa on Naxos, our favorite island, along with friends.

It's a strange vacation, the last one I'll ever spend with Viktor. There's no hostility between us, but we make no effort to be warm toward each other, not even to keep up appearances. No need now that everyone knows. We want the children to feel secure, however, as though everything is "normal"—for just a little while longer. So, we choose to sleep in the same bed.

As I said, it's a strange vacation.

Soon, Petros becomes angry and defiant, spending too much time on his phone. Margarita becomes anxious and clingy. I ask Viktor to join me in reassuring them, but he refuses.

"You got us into this, Katia. Don't ask me to pretend that we're still married."

"I'm not asking you to pretend. I'm asking you to co-parent with me."

"I'm as hurt as the kids by your decision. You're on your own."

You can't have it both ways, Katia, says the voice in my head. I can't have both my freedom and Viktor's support.

Two days before my birthday, Viktor returns to Zurich. The children and I stay in Greece a few more days. They surprise me with a birthday card and small trinkets from town, and my friends organize dinner at a favorite restaurant, where they order me the most delicious orange cheesecake. In my annual birthday photo, I'm wearing a green, strapless cotton dress, with my arms wrapped around my babies—all of us looking tanned and carefree. You'd never guess our family had just fallen apart.

Yet, back at home in Zurich, Viktor is moving out of our home and into an apartment just down the road. I'm grateful for the proximity, which will make it easier for the kids to go back and forth.

On a Friday in mid-August, the kids and I fly home. The new school year starts on Monday. Viktor picks us up at the airport and drives us home, though it isn't his home anymore. We order dinner and their father stays to eat. When it's time for him to leave, neither of us knows what to say. I give him a moment alone with the children to say goodbye. The two older ones are quiet and Nicolas is starting to fuss. He's tired and doesn't really understand what's happening.

"I'll see you tomorrow!" Viktor tries to sound cheerful, but his voice breaks.

No one cries but the air is heavy with emotion.

Before they go to bed, I cuddle each of my children. I don't mention their dad's new apartment or the separation. I just focus on staying present for them. I want them to know they can always count on me to be right here next to them. Every time I feel my throat tightening, I force myself to take a deep breath. I open my eyes wide to prevent the tears from falling. Only later, when I'm finally alone, do I allow myself to cry.

The next few days are an adjustment. It's not like we were used to having Viktor around all the time, especially during the week. Still, knowing he's no longer part of our household feels weird. Now, there are only four of us at the dinner table. Only one car in the garage. When Nicolas is fussy in the evenings, or when the older kids have activities at completely different times or locations, there's no one to tag team with me. When I need a moment to myself, I'm on my own.

Those are the hard parts. But there's also relief—a new feeling of lightness and freedom. A new beginning. The tension in my stomach slowly dissipates and there's a new feeling of expansion in my chest, as if I'm carrying a little less weight. It's liberating to be fully in charge of my decisions; to not have to get permission from anyone; to not feel judged. I no longer have to justify my parenting choices. I just follow my instincts and do what feels right.

I work hard to keep a sense of continuity for the children. Margarita is starting a new school, but her brother is already there. Nicolas's nanny returns after the summer break. I set up play dates with their favorite friends and otherwise keep them to the same routines. Except for one: every other weekend, they are with their dad.

When Viktor's first weekend with the kids arrives, I find myself completely alone, without them for the first time. It's just me and my big, empty house. I haven't made plans, so there are no coffee or dinner dates to occupy my time—or my thoughts. It occurs to me I don't have many friends I can spend time with on my own. Viktor and I always socialized with other couples or families. The only friends I visited without him were my girlfriends, and that only happened during the week. On the weekends, they're with their families, just as I was. On my own, I'm too shy to reach out to anyone. I don't want to make anyone feel awkward. So, I stay home, alone and miserable.

On Saturday, I manage to keep busy with grocery shopping, bill paying, and gathering up the things Viktor left behind—his football shoes, books, music, and other little things I find here and there. I'm trying to create a clean slate (though, I'll be finding and returning things to him for years to come). I'm grateful Margarita has a football match scheduled so I can go watch her play. When it starts getting darker—both outside and inside—I convince myself to reach out to my friend Paula from Vienna, who's also going through a separation.

"I have a lot of free time," I write. *"Don't know what to do with myself. How did you cope with not having the kids all the time?"*

"Oh, sweetie," Paula replies. *"I'm also alone tonight. Kids are at their dad's. Can I call you?"*

I'm grateful for her call.

"This is the worst part," she says softly. "But it will get better every day. Now is your mourning time—think of it like a funeral. Bury it deep. Then, it's time for your rebirth.

"Soon, you'll learn to appreciate your alone time. It's precious! I know you can't see it now, but you'll start looking forward to your weekends alone. Think of all the things you've always wanted to do but never had time to do."

She's right. I'm grateful for her kindness and wisdom, for her friendship. "Careful not to lose too much weight . . . *eat!*" She promises me it will get better. "Look at me!" she says, "I'm off to the gym right now."

I smile.

Over the next couple of weeks, Paula and I check in with each other mornings and evenings. We share our stories, our frustration, our anger, our sadness. She gives me encouragement and I offer her a safe space to vent. We help each other through each day, each milestone on the journey of divorce.

Sunday night, the kids come home. I don't think I've ever felt happier to see them. They've had a busy weekend. Viktor doesn't have the problem I have about reaching out to friends. He's organized a full program for himself and the kids—swimming dates, bike rides, Sunday brunch—for every weekend he has them. As stupid as I feel about sitting home alone, I can't yet bring myself to reach out to our mutual friends in Zurich, especially knowing Viktor already has. I worry he's trying to win them over to his side. *He can have them*, I think. *I won't fight for them. If they want to be my friends, it's their choice, not mine.*

I focus instead on educating myself about our finances. I write down all our bank account details and information about our insurance policies and pension plans. I track our account statements and credit card bills for the past year, poring over them line by line, entering numbers into a spreadsheet based on the template my attorney gave me. And I stick carefully to the budget I made for the children and myself. It's tedious work, but in the end, I'm proud of the insight it gives me into our finances.

I learn to do all sorts of things that used to be Viktor's responsibility. I learn to pay bills online; submit doctors' bills to insurance for refunds; take the car in for service; change lightbulbs around the house, which, strangely enough, gives me a real sense of accomplishment. It's a steep learning curve, but I manage to climb it. Viktor comes by to mow the lawn the first couple of times it's needed—he's always liked to do it—but then stops, so I learn to do that, too. Rather than feeling overwhelmed, I feel empowered.

I leave the photographs of Viktor up, including the ones of us as a family, but I make other small changes. I buy fresh flowers every week (before, flowers had always been brought to me by Viktor). Their presence lifts my spirits. I make a few changes to my bedroom, like buying pristine white bedsheets and throw pillows for the bed. Since the separation, I've had a hard time sleeping, so I joke to friends that I intend to turn my bedroom into an altar of peace and serenity.

Margarita continues to struggle, becoming anxious whenever I go out for the evening. And like me, she has trouble sleeping. Viktor blames me as the cause of her anxiety, pointing to what he considers my overprotectiveness. He believes I got it from my mother, who, according to Viktor, is also "scaring the kids" by seeing danger everywhere. He doesn't recognize it's normal for a child to go through a period of feeling frightened and insecure after her parents separate.

Meanwhile, we continue to navigate as co-parents. We agree to celebrate the kids' birthdays together, as well as the Christmas holiday. We schedule weekly fifteen-minute calls to touch base on how they're doing and any logistics that need to be discussed. His secretary sends me Google calendar invites.

When I meet with my attorney, she urges me to "be open to compromise" on finances and "not to push him against the wall." I get the feeling she's being deferential to Viktor because of his prestigious position in Swiss society that comes with his job. I don't intend to push anyone against the wall, but I *do* intend to get a new lawyer. I need someone who's willing to fight for me, not look for compromise before it's even offered.

This time, I hire someone with expertise in international family law. The moment I walk into her office, I get the sense I'm in the right place. My new lawyer looks sharp and elegant at the same time. Her handshake is firm and her manner warm but no-nonsense. She has a reputation for being tough and exudes the kind of self-confidence that comes with solid training and many years of experience. She tells me she has no tolerance for arrogance or injustice; she's exactly what I need.

After our meeting, we shake hands and I leave with a smile on my face. For the first time in a long time, I feel a protective arm around me.

CHAPTER 21

Reemerging

"I think that any time of great pain is a time of
transformation, a fertile time to plant new seeds."
— Debbie Ford

ONE GREY NOVEMBER MORNING, I'm sitting at my desk in
my attic home office. I'm on the phone with an interview subject, Maria,
a Greek expat who's in the midst of a nasty divorce from an abusive Swiss
husband. She's fighting for child support while working three part-time
jobs to make ends meet.

While preparing for my next conference presentation, I feel pulled
to talk about what I'm going through—divorce. Divorce is challenging
enough, but as expats, it's even more difficult. We're often forced to go
through it in a foreign place, far from our extended families and other
external support systems. By focusing on my community, rather than just
my own experience, I knew I stood to gain new perspective and insight.

Maria's husband kicked her out of their home, without a job or any
financial means. She had been a stay-at-home parent while raising her
children, so she had no income of her own on which to survive. She told
me her husband has been manipulating their children, alienating them
from her. Apparently, he's doing the same with their mutual friends,
lying about Maria to them and gaslighting her into submission. As she

relayed all of this, she spoke in a calm, quiet voice. She was matter of fact, even stoic.

"My family is in Greece," Maria says. "My parents are simple people. They can't support me financially or otherwise. Thankfully, I have friends here who lent me money for the down payment, so I was able to rent a small apartment."

When I ask if she has anyone to turn to for emotional support, she laughs softly. "Between work and the children, I don't even have time to call anyone. I don't really talk to my friends.

"If this had happened while I was living at home in Greece," Maria says, "the children and I would have been able to stay with my parents. I'd have been able to reach out to my network to get a job. I'd have been able to walk away from the marriage earlier, not wait until I could afford it."

Her story leaves me speechless, except to express indignation on her behalf. When our call ends, I can feel the heat flushing through my body. I want to punch someone.

In comparison, my own divorce is a walk in the park. I can afford a lawyer, a therapist, a life coach; Maria has none of those. My husband is willing to sit at the table and negotiate; hers walked out of mediation after the first session and never came back. ("Hell," she said, "the *mediator* even quit after an encounter with him.") Most importantly, my children are protected from any form of conflict, because their father and I agreed early on to keep our disagreements entirely out of earshot. For Maria's children, their parents' divorce is front and center.

As I speak with more expats dealing with divorce in a foreign country, I notice a significant contrast between those who can afford professional help and those who barely manage to make ends meet and must scramble to find any kind of support. I speak to a stay-at-home mother whose husband suddenly left her for another woman. Because of this, her residence permit as a dependent was no longer valid and she was forced to leave the country. Her story, like Maria's, fills me with deep sadness, anger, and a sense of powerlessness. Neither she nor Maria currently have the luxury to create new, more fulfilling, freer lives post-divorce; their entire focus is survival.

Their stories leave me with a complex set of emotions. I feel at once grateful for and ashamed of my own relatively privileged experience. As I work through the interviews to prepare my talk, I feel a sense of urgency to help raise awareness around the many challenges divorcing expats face and the lack of resources and support available to them. I'm stunned when I think about how seldom this topic gets addressed; it's simply not discussed in expat circles. Sure, we talk about what it's like to be a trailing spouse or to raise children abroad, but we don't talk about what happens when a relationship falls apart and you're far away from home. The dark side of expat divorce is *verboten*, seen as too disturbing or even potentially contagious. Whatever the reason, expat divorce is taboo. And I want to change that.

My mother arrives in Zurich in early November to celebrate the kids' birthdays and stays for the holidays. This year, I want to create new rituals and traditions, apart from Viktor.

When we lived in Vienna, Christmas was always his thing. I never bothered to put up decorations. And every year, I complained about how late we waited to decorate the tree (it's the Austrian tradition to do it just before Christmas Eve, and even though I managed to get him to reluctantly do it a couple of days earlier, it still didn't leave us much time to enjoy it before we had to take it down again). Viktor refused to allow electric lights on the tree; it could only be lit with candles on Christmas Eve. Then, there was a lot of singing and some reading from the Bible. The whole process was lovely but far too constrictive for my tastes.

This year, I head out to buy the tree as soon as they become available in mid-December. The salesman helps me load it onto my car, but I take it down and haul it up the stairs to our living room on my own. I nearly die in the process, but I and the tree survive. I turn on Michael Bublé's *Christmas Album* and the kids and I decorate the tree, wearing orange Santa hats. *Our* tree has twinkling electric lights all over. They make my soul brighter.

Christmas itself is awkward and sad. I invite my brother and his family to stay with us so the kids have family around for this difficult first holiday.

Viktor isn't crazy about the idea, but I insist. We celebrate all together, him included.

Our mediation sessions also start in December, on Nicolas's birthday. The mediator has excellent credentials and came recommended by my attorney. Her job is to help us come to an agreement, not to defend the interests of either side. Still, I won't commit to anything without consulting my lawyer. I head to the first meeting with a four-page list of documents, including my budget proposal. I take a deep breath and try not to get overwhelmed. I don't know it yet (probably for the best), but it will take us a whole year to negotiate the terms of our divorce.

By New Year's, I discover I have more time and energy for myself and my work. I get far more writing done than before. The book is progressing nicely. Maybe Paula was right about the silver lining.

I head for the back corner of the room and sit down cross-legged on my mat, next to the big floor-to-ceiling windows that overlook the lake, my usual spot. I've never been a front-row student, and I like the warmth of the sunlight and the view of the horizon. The stillness of the lake calms my mind.

There are about thirty of us in class today. It's a big space, but it still feels cozy and intimate with its warm wooden floors and airy curtains. Everyone around me is settling onto their mats, doing stretches, exchanging greetings and quick gossip. One woman is lying on her back in *Shavasana*, "corpse pose." I breathe in the sweet incense and rest my eyes on the bouquet of pale pink roses beside the massive sculpture of Buddha. Kevin, our yoga teacher, gently taps his mallet against a brass Tibetan singing bowl, a signal that class is about to start. The commotion stops and the room becomes so quiet I can hear the person next to me breathe.

It's only Wednesday, but it's been a long week. Yesterday was our third mediation session and, two and a half hours into it, Viktor walked out, saying it made no sense to continue and we should just go to court. I refused to budge from my position on the amount of child support he should pay. My goal is to ensure the children's needs are fully covered.

During the mediation sessions, I manage to stay calm (mostly), confident, and strong. But the minute I leave the mediator's office, I fall apart. The idea of facing Viktor in court terrifies me; the outcome is too uncertain, and the legal fees would be colossal.

Kevin sits cross-legged on an orange velvet cushion at the front of the room, elevated slightly on a small platform. He's in his late fifties; tall, fit, and clean-shaven. A gentle man who radiates calm.

Kevin's voice is deep and echoes through the room. "Good morning, everyone." He presses his palms together in *namaste* and bows to us.

Kevin always starts the class with a few words—thoughts for the day, a reading from a favorite yoga master, a funny anecdote. Today, he reads us a poem. The words are poignant and powerful, and as he speaks, my throat tightens and my eyes fill with tears. I close them tightly and try to will the tears away, mortified. Mercifully, Kevin picks up his harmonium and invites us to chant the opening "Om." I'm too choked up to chant, but I'm grateful class is starting.

When I'm on the mat, I feel grounded, literally; I feel peaceful. The poses and movements are gentle and flowing, but also challenging. I enjoy feeling myself grow stronger, noticing my progress—holding a pose a little longer, bending deeper, keeping my balance when previously I couldn't.

Kevin's classes are a lifeline for me. Some mornings, I show up exhausted, having spent most of the night before agonizing about the future or the damage I'm inflicting on my children. Other mornings, I'm so sad that my chest becomes blocked, and I have difficulty breathing. Sometimes I just want to get away from it all and spend an hour not thinking about divorce agreements, budgets, or mediators. I sleep too little and eat even less. I don't talk to many friends about what I'm going through. For me, yoga is a rare act of self-care (the other being my weekly ballet class) so I can keep going.

Later, Kevin and I will become friends and I'll tell him how grateful I am to him. Without knowing it, he helps me make it through divorce.

Our separation agreement stipulates we split the children's school breaks, but when their two-week break starts for winter vacation, Viktor agrees to let me have them both weeks. I take them to Singapore, where my friend Nick and his family relocated the year before. It's my first big trip alone with the kids. When I finally book our flights, I feel both exhilarated and apprehensive.

Viktor always organized and handled everything when we traveled— from the flights to accommodations to car rentals. My input was largely around our itinerary while away, scheduling activities and meetings with friends. Making all the arrangements myself for the first time, I feel almost like an adult. This is a family adventure just for the four of us, and it feels good. At the same time, I worry I'm making a mistake—that I might be in store for a stressful two weeks. Nicolas is only five and we'll be making a twelve-hour flight in economy. I've heard the jet lag on arrival is brutal.

Happily, we survive the flight and our time in Singapore is fabulous. The kids love the warm climate. They love spending time with their friends. They love trying out the local delicacies and spending hours in the pool. I enjoy myself too; it's nice to be with dear friends again. I've missed having Nick close, especially while dealing with divorce. Other than Paula, I've been reluctant to confide in anyone. (In retrospect, I probably didn't give my friends the chance to connect with or support me.) Now that I'm here, it feels so good to process my experience with someone I know will never feel burdened by my emotions or uncertain about his loyalty.

It also feels great to just be with the kids, away from everything and everyone else. Away from the grind of school and homework and activities. Away from the divorce, the budget, and the parenting schedule. Away from Viktor. I don't have to share them. I don't have to prove anything or answer to anyone. I just get to enjoy my children.

We stay up late and sleep through the mornings (the jet lag is indeed brutal), rarely getting out of the house until the afternoon. There's a lot to see and do but we also take time to just be—to swim, play video games, or laze around on the patio. We are a new constellation, just the four of us. I feel lighter than I have in a long time.

A couple of weeks after we return home, I fly to Amsterdam, where the 2016 FIGT conference takes place. The venue is a beautiful, historic building from the early twentieth century, the De Bazel. From the outside, it looks massive and imposing, with its strict geometric lines interrupted by delicate stained-glass windows and sculptures of austere colonial generals. Inside, everything feels unexpectedly close. The room where I'm set to give my presentation isn't much larger than my living room, so there's not much space between me and my audience. I don't mind the smaller scale; it makes for a more intimate experience.

As the room fills, I notice some familiar faces. When everyone's settled in, I begin.

"I'd like you to imagine yourself in Lily's shoes," I say. "Imagine that, over breakfast one day, your husband makes an announcement. He's leaving you for another woman."

Lily, a Chinese expat in her mid-forties, was living in Ethiopia with her husband and three kids. Suddenly, she found herself with no visa, no job, no financial or other support for herself and her children, and in a foreign country. I describe the tough choices Lily had to make, how scared she was, how deeply she sank into depression, but also how hard she worked to pull herself out.

"Lily's story isn't unique." I pause and look at my audience, letting my words sink in. I see some people nodding.

Then, I describe the practical challenges of expat divorce—unfamiliar language and legal systems, lack of support, problems with residence and work permits, custody, and other complications when children are in the picture. I move on to the deeper emotional issues expats face. I even share some of my personal story. I want to break the stigma. Maybe by freeing myself—from the taboo, from the shame—others will feel freer, too. There's a moment during my talk when I'm stunned to recognize the passionate, articulate advocate is as much a part of me as the quiet, shy introvert. Perhaps the former is the bigger part and just got crushed early on. I feel empowered, more authentic, more myself.

As I wrap up, a feeling of relief washes over me. I did it. There are lots of hands in the air. Someone—a lawyer—emphasizes the importance of knowing what your rights and obligations are in your new country. Someone else talks about having a backup plan for when things go wrong. Another mentions the importance of having your own bank account with emergency funds set aside.

Afterward, people come to the front to speak to me.

"Thank you for starting the conversation!"

"It was about time someone talked about these issues."

"Thank you for sharing our stories."

Once again, my heart is full. It's nice to have my work acknowledged, but the true reward comes from doing something that matters.

Later, while talking to a sophisticated Turkish divorcée, I ask her what resources might have been helpful to her as she went through her divorce.

"I could have used more guidance through this process," she said. "I could have used a divorce coach!"

A divorce coach: I've never heard those words together. But after some research, I learn it's actually a profession. Unfortunately, most divorce coaches seem to be based in the US. A lightbulb goes off for me. Divorce coaching. Could I use my personal experiences and knowledge of the process to help others cope with the practical and emotional challenges of divorce? Maybe I could help other expats feel more supported and less lost.

The thought of having to go back into defense research depresses me, though I didn't think I had much of a choice. As a newly single person, I need the financial security. Could divorce coaching be a viable alternative? I search online for accredited training, but nothing specific to divorce coaching comes up—at least nothing that appears credible or solid enough for my tastes. I close the screen. *I'm too overwhelmed with the prospect of getting through my own divorce right now,* I think. So, I set the thought aside.

On a Monday morning in April, I wake with a headache. My limbs are heavy and it's hard to open my eyes. When I try to move my neck, a piercing pain runs from the base of my skull to the bottom of my left shoulder blade. It's as if there's a string connecting all of the muscles and nerves on my left side, and any movement I make pulls the string, stretching everything taut at once. This is not the first time I feel this pain, so I know: I'm completely blocked.

During periods of intense stress, my body revolts. I know from experience the only thing I can do is suck it up, take a couple of ibuprofen, and get on with it. It will pass in a few days. There's no point in making an appointment with my physiotherapist; she's always booked at least three weeks in advance. By then, I won't need her.

Last week was hard. On Wednesday, Margarita had an accident. She fell while doing tricks on her scooter. When she called from the local skate park, the pitch of her voice told me something was wrong. Sure enough, she'd fractured her tibia.

She'll be fine, thankfully. But it's been challenging. Her leg will be in a knee-to-toe cast for the next six weeks. She can't step on the foot, so she uses crutches. Stairs are complicated (and our house has a lot of them), so I move her to the guest room on the ground level. She needs to be driven to and from school. So every day, I carry her backpack as we slowly make our way from the car to her class on the sixth floor of the school building. In the evenings, I help her shower, carefully tucking her cast into a garbage bag and securing it closed with rubber bands. By the Monday I wake up blocked, I'm drained.

I manage to drag myself out of bed, wincing with every move. The kids have to get to school and my ballet class is at 9:30 a.m. I consider skipping, but it doesn't feel right. This is my time. If I give it up, even just this once, I'll be betraying myself. I can't take care of everyone else if I never take care of myself.

When I enter the ballet room, my legs are heavy and my energy is zapped. *You just need to make it through the next fifty-five minutes,* I think. I drop to the mat as Virginie starts the music for our warmup. It's jazzy, sensual, in contrast to the classic piano pieces that will follow when we go to the barre. As she takes us through a series of gentle stretches, my limbs, chest, and neck slowly expand and awaken, as if my body is unfolding itself. The pain is still there, but with every deep stretch, I feel myself dissolving, releasing whatever it is that's blocking me inside. The endorphins start to work their magic. By the time I get to the barre for my *pliés*, my energy has shifted.

When class is finished, I'm lighter, more supple. Saner. Reconnected.

Right about the time Margarita's cast comes off, Nicolas breaks his arm in gym class. It happens while I'm in a yoga class with my phone off, so his teachers call an ambulance. Thankfully, they also manage to reach his dad. When I turn my phone back on after class, there are seven missed calls. From now on, I keep my phone next to me, no matter where I am.

At least this time, I'm well-versed in the care of fractured limbs. Poor thing is still wearing his cast when we leave for our annual vacation in Greece.

CHAPTER 22

Hope

"A party without cake is just a meeting."
— Julia Child

ONE AFTERNOON IN THE SPRING OF 2016, I'm upstairs in my office, browsing through my LinkedIn feed when a new message pops up on my screen. It's from Michael. He's just read through a series of articles I posted on the subject of expat divorce.

"I hope it's okay to reach out," he writes. *"I saw on your profile that you live in Zurich now."*

Michael has been teaching part-time at a business school in Lausanne, which is little more than two hours away.

"I pass by Zurich on my way to the airport all the time," he continues. *"Would you like to have coffee sometime?"*

Instant butterflies. All these years, I've been so good at keeping my emotions tucked away in their own little compartment. So good, in fact, I forgot there was anything inside. I say "yes." A wave of anticipation takes me by surprise. For the rest of the day, I wear a giddy grin. Thankfully, the kids don't notice.

Michael and I meet on a crisp April morning, almost exactly six years after the last time we spoke. He's just wrapped up the executive program he teaches and his flight to Boston isn't until late afternoon. We meet for coffee at my favorite café in Zurich's Old Town. It's called Cakefriends—and I'm a friend of cake. We order two coffees and a slice of frosted chocolate cake for me. It all feels so natural, as if no time has passed since we last sat together over steaming cups. As if our last meeting caused no disruption to our lives.

Now, looking at Michael in the flesh, I try and fail to suppress a smile.

"What?" he asks, smiling back. I'll have to get used to not being able to hide anything from him.

"Nothing. I was just thinking about the last time we met at that café in Vienna. Feels like ages ago. And like yesterday."

"Not a day has passed," he says, looking straight into my eyes. My heart skips.

The last time we met, I was pregnant with Nicolas. Michael was married.

"When I saw your post on expat divorce," Michael says, "I knew it wasn't just a research project. Somehow, I felt it was okay to reach out again."

He tells me how his marriage fell apart only months after he returned from his European trip. How he did everything in his power to shield his children from the unpleasantness between him and his now ex-wife. When I tell him my story, I feel like we're reading from the same script. Our values and priorities feel aligned.

"You're a wonderful, caring mother, Katia," Michael says. "I know your children will be okay in the end."

For the first time, I feel seen for who I am as a parent and as a human.

In the months that follow, Michael and I meet whenever he's in Switzerland to teach. Soon, he finds reasons to visit even when he isn't teaching. In public, we don't hold hands or show any affection; we're just two friends, exploring the town (which turns out to be to our advantage, as we keep bumping into acquaintances of mine on the street—Zurich is tiny, I find out). The first time I follow him to his hotel room, I smile timidly at the receptionist, convinced he thinks I'm a paid escort. The second and third time are even worse—now he'll think Michael is my "regular." As awkward as it feels to walk into that hotel lobby, being with Michael physically is the most natural thing in the world. We seem to know each other and what to do intuitively, as if we were lovers all our lives. I feel like I've hit the jackpot. Or is there a catch?

Only a couple of weeks into our romance, Michael sits me down to talk.

"Before this goes any further, there are certain things I need you to be aware of," he says with a somber look on his face. "As you know, I'm much older than you."

Michael is fifty-nine; I'm forty-four.

"Yes, I'm aware of that, Michael," I say playfully.

"There's something else," he says.

"What is it?"

"I have M.S."

A knot forms in my stomach.

I'm familiar with multiple sclerosis. My first boyfriend was diagnosed when we were together. He was twenty years old and it changed his life. We woke up together one morning and he told me he was seeing double. It took months to get a proper diagnosis, even as he steadily deteriorated—from the tremor in his hands and his unsteady gait to even the way he talked. Then one day, all his symptoms just disappeared. He'd gone into remission.

Michael was diagnosed several years ago, he tells me. He's fortunate to have a type of M.S. called "relapsing-remitting" and is currently doing well. He gives himself an injection three times a week to keep things stable.

"What made you think having M.S. would change anything for me?" I smile.

Eventually, Michael's spending enough time in Zurich to warrant leasing a small two-bedroom near the city center, about ten minutes from me. It has a tiny rooftop terrace and a loft where his kids can sleep when they visit. We shop for furniture together and, the day before Michael flies in, I fill his fridge with all his favorites—yogurt, berries, Stilton cheese. We have wine and cheese picnics on the floor of his apartment until a dining table and chairs get delivered. There are many things I love about Michael, but I never expected him making me laugh to be one of them. Yet, when we're together, he's witty and playful; it's a side of him I've never seen before. He introduces me to the concept of puns (he's a master), and I love how his blue eyes sparkle with mischief when he surprises me with one (even if sometimes he has to explain it to me). It's a delight to watch this grey-haired, respectable professor throw back his head, laughing, light as a feather, just because he made me laugh.

Just like spring, our love affair blossoms quickly and effortlessly. Still, we're not yet ready to share our news with the world. And by "world," I mean my family. The children are still processing my separation from their father; introducing someone new would destabilize them. Michael and I have agreed to always prioritize our children's best interests—even if it means keeping our relationship under cover much longer than we'd like.

It's easier for Michael to be open about us with his children because he's already been divorced for more than two years. The legal process for my own divorce is still ongoing—and it's not clear how much longer it will take. Like everything else in Switzerland, domestic legal matters move slowly.

A couple of days before my forty-fifth birthday, the children and I arrive in Naxos.

Organizing this getaway was stressful, mostly because I felt I had to compete with Viktor. He'd lined up a beautiful villa on another Greek island for himself and the kids and invited mutual friends to join them. He was even flying in his teenage godson from the US. When Viktor told the kids, they were over the moon. So, I felt I needed to provide something just as good or better—not only an idyllic setting but fun company. As I thought about what friends I could invite to Greece, my anxiety doubled. *Won't it feel awkward to go on vacation with a divorcée and her kids?* Then, I thought of Aliki, who's also going through a separation. Thankfully, she and her daughter agreed to come.

Michael decided to take his kids to Naxos the same week, so we booked nearby hotels.

"We may not be able to have vacations as a family yet, but it'll be nice to know we're close. Maybe you can occasionally slip away for a walk or a drink," Michael said.

With a five-year-old in tow? I thought. *Unlikely.* And yet, with a little creativity, here we are.

In a stroke of fate, the kids unanimously agree to watch *Ghostbusters* at the open-air cinema so Aliki and I can enjoy a drink at the hotel bar, where Michael will soon join us for gin and tonics. Aliki's heard a lot about him already, but this is their first time meeting.

Michael peppers Aliki with friendly questions about where she's from, and her new restaurant business, and he sneaks in the occasional question about her friendship with me. As they're chatting, Aliki's eyebrows suddenly raise and she signals with a nod that I should look toward the entrance. I turn around to find Petros and Nicolas walking right toward us.

"What happened?" I say, trying my damnedest to appear natural.

"He wanted to leave," Petros says, visibly annoyed with his little brother. "So, I had to bring him to you."

"The movie is too scary for me!" Nicolas says.

"Okay, okay, you can stay with us," I say, hoping Petros will exit as quickly as he entered—before he can start asking questions.

Naturally, Petros lingers, his eyes fixed on Michael.

"Who is this?" he asks in Greek, so Michael won't understand.

"Just someone we met here," I reply. "It's really okay, you can go back."

Petros turns to leave, and I breathe a sigh of relief. *Half*-relief. Nicolas is settling in.

"Would you like to see a magic trick?" Michael asks him.

My boy's eyes light up. "Yes, please!"

Michael takes a coin from his pocket and places it between his index and middle finger. He closes his fist and the coin disappears. A moment later he produces it from behind Nicolas's ear.

"How did you do that?!"

"Would you like me to do it again?"

Just then, Petros reappears.

"I decided I've missed too much of the movie. I'll just stay here with you," he says, looking at Michael.

"Petros, look what he can do!" Nicolas pulls his brother by the arm.

Aliki and I look at each other, trying hard not to burst out laughing. Michael, as calm as ever, continues to work his magic.

The next day, I find a moment alone with Petros, who clearly wasn't fooled.

"Michael is my *friend*," I say.

"I knew it the minute I saw him," Petros says in his usual, matter-of-fact way.

"I don't want your siblings to know yet. Please keep this to yourself, okay?"

He nods. It's a relief to not have to keep this from him anymore.

CHAPTER 23

LOSS

"People think a soul mate is your perfect fit, and
that's what everyone wants. But a true soul mate is
a mirror, the person who shows you everything that
is holding you back, the person who brings you to
your own attention so you can change your life."
— Elizabeth Gilbert, *Eat, Pray, Love*

IN MID-NOVEMBER, MICHAEL AND I arrive at a boutique
spa hotel outside Lucerne, Switzerland, where we've come to celebrate
his sixtieth birthday.

We enjoy a relaxing day—a leisurely breakfast, massages, and then
lounging by the pool with our books. We both needed this. Michael has
been working two full-time jobs, teaching at the business school and
running his own consulting company, on top of the constant back-and-
forth travel between Boston and Zurich. I've been juggling the children,
ongoing divorce negotiations, and a book. This is our chance to breathe
and disconnect from all that, to reconnect with each other.

After lunch, we drive into Lucerne to catch a movie, *Bridget Jones's
Baby*, and dinner. But as we leave the theater, Michael looks pale as a sheet.

"I'm feeling unwell," he says.

"What kind of unwell?" There's the familiar knot in my stomach.

"I'm nauseous and have pain in my right thigh. It was getting worse during the movie."

"Why didn't you say something?"

"I didn't want to scare you."

So much for that.

Michael dashes off to the restroom and when he returns, he tells me his leg is red and bruised and feels warm to the touch.

"It could be a reaction to the shot I gave myself last night," he says. "Or it could be an infection."

At "infection," I gasp. Michael had a previous infection in his leg about ten years ago and had to be hospitalized for treatment. The infection nearly killed him.

We leave the car in the parking garage and walk over to the emergency clinic. My throat is dry, and my palms are sweating, but I do my best to appear calm. Inside, I'm scared to death.

The doctor asks Michael a few standard questions about the onset and nature of his symptoms and suggests an ultrasound of the leg. Then, he calls in a colleague to assist, which doesn't reassure me. The ultrasound doesn't show anything out of the ordinary, but given Michael's symptoms, they prescribe a course of antibiotics, to be started right away.

"If you start feeling worse," they caution, "you need to go to hospital immediately."

Tears well behind my eyelids, but I have faith in the antibiotics. *Maybe we're out of the woods*, I think. We head back to the hotel, determined not to let the incident spoil our weekend.

But at 3:00 a.m., Michael taps me awake.

"I'm in a lot of pain," he whispers.

Damn.

"It's gotten worse. I'm afraid we have to go to hospital."

"Now?" I hope he's exaggerating.

Michael doesn't exaggerate.

"Yes, right now. We should also pack and check out of the hotel, just in case."

He knows we're not coming back and now so do I.

"Stay in bed," I order, as I throw on a pair of jeans and a turtleneck. I pack our bags as quickly as I can, hoping he won't notice how much my hands are shaking.

"Do you need help getting dressed?"

I hand Michael his pants and shirt from the armchair. Once he's dressed, I kneel on the floor and put his socks and shoes on for him. He doesn't protest.

I'm grateful to see someone at the front desk so I can take care of the bill and get directions to the nearest hospital. When I get behind the wheel of the car, my mouth is even drier, but my eyes are focused on the small country road. I don't enjoy driving at night, so I breathe deeply and try to steady my hands, occasionally glancing over at Michael in the passenger seat. He's completely silent.

It's a relatively short drive to Lucerne's St. Anna Clinic, thank God. Better still, there's no one in the waiting room, so Michael gets seen right away. The doctor on call quickly accesses Michael's history and sends him straight for an MRI.

"It shouldn't take longer than an hour," Michael says. He has regular MRIs. "You can go for a walk or see if you can get a drink somewhere."

"I'll wait here," I say and take my place on one of the folding chairs.

An hour and a half later, the emergency doctor phones the surgeon on call, waking him at home, and requests he come in.

Shit.

It's 5:15 a.m. on a Sunday. I'm standing in the hallway outside an emergency room. Markus, the surgeon on call, stands next to me, showing me Michael's MRI images on the flatscreen that's mounted on the wall.

"Jesus Christ," I say, a little too loudly.

"Yeah," the surgeon nods. A large portion of Michael's right thigh is covered in white.

"What *is* that?" I ask. "And how bad is it?"

"Have you heard of flesh-eating disease?" My legs start to shake.

"We're taking him into surgery now. We have to stop it from spreading."

This means emergency surgery.

I'm still wearing my jacket, but the shivering gets worse. Michael—my partner, the love of my life—lies in the next room, where he's currently being eaten alive by a monstrous bacterial infection.

I follow Markus into the room, where he introduces himself to Michael and quickly gets to the point.

"It's serious."

"Is it cellulitis?" Michael asks. The infection he had before, the one that nearly killed him.

"No," Markus replies. "It's necrotizing fasciitis."

Michael's face goes white. We stare at each other in shock.

"What are my odds?" Michael asks calmly, looking at me. He knows very well what his diagnosis means. If not caught in time, this infection kills. And even if you survive, it can maim you terribly.

"I will do my best to save your leg," Markus says, "but if I have to choose between your life and your leg, I will choose your life."

He's firm and matter of fact, but there's also a kindness about him.

"He'll be okay." Markus touches my shoulder. "Here are some forms to fill out. We have to get him prepped for surgery."

Before Markus heads for the door, I give him my number. "Will you please call me when the surgery is over?"

"I promise," he says.

Michael unlocks his phone and hands it to me, along with his wallet and reading glasses. The system moves swiftly, with Swiss precision. Two nurses wheel him toward the operating room, and I follow alongside.

In front of a set of sliding doors at 5:45 a.m., we say goodbye.

"You will always be my one true love," Michael says. The knot from my stomach suddenly lodges in my throat.

He sounds calm and in control, like I've always known him to be. Not at all like a man being rushed into emergency surgery in a fight for his life. Even now, he makes me feel safe. Tears well up again, and I barely manage to whisper "I love you" before they take him.

Minutes later, Michael's being put to sleep, not knowing whether or in what state he will wake. I must look as terrified as I am because one of the nurses stays behind and takes my hand.

"He's going to be all right."

How can this be happening? It's all I can think. We've known each other for almost twenty years, yet we've only been together for a few months. And now, suddenly, I'm his emergency contact—his only personal contact in this country. If Michael doesn't make it, I will have to call his mother, his children.

"Would you like to lie down?" the nurse asks.

I nod and she takes me to an empty room.

"You're welcome to stay here until the surgery is done." She offers a kind smile.

I lie on the bed and close my eyes, my mind spinning in every direction. Suddenly, I remember my car is still in the fifteen-minute parking zone. As I walk back toward the main entrance, my phone rings. It's barely 7:00 a.m. I don't recognize the number. It's the president of the business school where Michael teaches. Before going into surgery, Michael sent him a note explaining he won't be in to teach on Monday.

"What happened?" he asks.

I explain and he asks how I'm holding up and whether there's anything he can do for me. I nearly break down, overwhelmed by the kindness of a complete stranger. Soon, several of Michael's other friends and colleagues will find a way to reach out to me, expressing their care and offering support. I'm deeply touched to learn how loved and appreciated he is. As if I needed proof.

Back in the empty room, I pull a chair in front of the window and sit. As the morning sky grows lighter, I pray. I don't know who else to turn to but God. *Please don't take Michael away from me yet. We've barely started our journey together.*

My phone rings again and I jump up. The surgeon's name is flashing across the screen (I had saved his number, just in case). It's been nearly three hours since they took Michael into surgery.

"It went well." They're the first words I hear.

He's alive.

They removed as much of the dead tissue as they could, Markus explains. And he's hopeful Michael will recover fully.

"The next twenty-four hours will be critical," Markus says. "After a surgery like the one he's had, there's always a risk of toxic shock."

The instant we hang up, I type "toxic shock" into my phone's browser. This one can be fatal, too. It's not over.

A nurse knocks on the door and asks if I'd like to go to the recovery room and wait for Michael to wake. I follow her to the intensive care unit, walking as fast as I can. I enter to find Michael lying prone, hooked to oxygen, and surrounded by monitors. He looks battered, but he's still with me. I take his hand in mine and sit close.

Eventually, he opens his eyes and a smile forms on his face. I squeeze his hand, careful not to brush the IV needle, tears streaming down my face.

"You thought you could get rid of me that easily?" His voice is weak, but steady.

Relief washes through me.

I spend the rest of the night in that empty hospital room, not sleeping much, waiting for the critical first twenty-four hours to be over.

The next morning, Michael is in good spirits. I find him joking around with his nurses. To pass the time, he does this trick where he consciously brings his heart rate down—so low, it triggers the alarm. The nurses are *not* amused.

I drive back to Zurich on Monday afternoon, in time to pick up my youngest from school. I spend the afternoon helping him with his homework, but my mind is elsewhere. Mentally, I'm strategizing how I can spend more time with Michael while he's recovering in Lucerne—an hour drive each way. The biggest challenge is no one can know. And that means there's less support.

For the next week, I drive each of the kids to school, then head immediately to the hospital in Lucerne. I'm present for the doctor's visits, I consult nurses about his treatments, and I translate when Michael has questions for them. His room is bright and spacious, with a spectacular view of Lake Lucerne. The surgical anesthesiologist intervened to get him a private room, even though it wasn't covered by his insurance. He's not the only one whose kindness fills us with gratitude; the nurses and staff are thoughtful and compassionate. When Michael takes a nap in the afternoons, I drive back to Zurich in time to pick up Nicolas from school. The rest of my day is spent with the children, overseeing homework, and shuttling them to activities. Worrying about Michael.

When the surgeon tells us Michael's recovery will involve multiple follow-up operations and several weeks in the hospital, I'm disheartened. Not because of the drive or the logistics, but because I'm slowly running out of creative excuses. As I'm thinking this, Michael asks the doctor if he can be moved to the partner hospital in Zurich. My eyes light up; that's only two minutes by car from home, which will make it much easier to care for him. (Later, Michael will confess he'd sensed how discouraged I was by the prolonged treatment plan, and decided to leave his little cocoon in Lucerne, where he felt comfortable and, most importantly, safe in the hands of the surgeon who saved his life.) Markus signs off on the move and, the next day, we drive to Zurich by convoy—Michael in an ambulance; me following by car.

Without the long commute, we have more time together. I spend every spare minute in the hospital with Michael. His leg is attached to a machine that constantly applies suction to his wound, to speed up the healing process. We get used to its low rhythmic humming. He can't move for the first couple of weeks, so I do everything for him I can.

My favorite is helping him shave. Michael can't stand up at the bathroom sink, so I improvise with a cardboard container and a cup of water.

"Hold this under your chin," I instruct as I hand him the container. I soak a small towel in warm water and wring it out. Next, I apply shaving foam to Michael's face and chin. I dash to rinse my hand in the sink and return with a disposable razor. Slowly, carefully, I glide the razor from the cheekbone to the jaw, one smooth movement at a time.

"How am I doing?"

"Best shave ever!"

I love his enthusiasm. It belies his usual need for meticulous oversight. "Are you nervous, my general?" I tease.

Right now, Michael isn't trying to manage anything; he just lets me care for him. Although I've never played caregiver for anyone other than my children, it feels natural. Like love.

I take the small bottle of complimentary aftershave and pour a few drops into my palms, then softly tap my hands against Michael's face. He smells fresh, healthy.

When I'm with the kids in the afternoons, Michael gets to work. He resumes his consulting calls with no mention to his clients that he's doing so from a hospital bed. Whenever the nanny can stay longer after dinner, I return. I bring snacks or dessert and we lie side-by-side, watching an episode or two of *Modern Family*.

It's tougher on my weekends with the kids. I tell the older ones I'm taking care of a good friend who's in the hospital. Thankfully, they make little of it. I don't have the bandwidth to worry about whether they will share this news with their father, but if they do, he never mentions it.

Michael spends four weeks in the hospital in Zurich, where he undergoes another six operations. Five are to replace part of the (ever-present) device that makes sure his muscles and tissues are healing properly. While these procedures sound minor, they require full anesthesia due to pain. The last is reconstructive surgery, where his surgeons remove a layer of skin from the healthy left leg and graft it onto the wound in his right.

Michael gets used to the routine of surgery and I never once hear him complain. Throughout his time in the hospital, and despite being unable to move from his bed for most of it, he keeps smiling. Strangely, his traumatic event is like love bootcamp for us: it brings us even closer. We joke that, after this, we can handle anything; we're resilient. We're a good team.

And I learn a lot about myself.

I learn I'm capable of handling most things life throws my way, I can take charge and figure things out, and I have the strength and focus required to function under extreme stress. I learn I can manage on my own and I can be someone else's support.

I learn I can be a strong, reliable, and independent person—like Michael is. That I can have trust in others and allow myself to be taken care of, too. I discover I find true delight in caring for the man I love. Whether it's helping him eat when he still can't sit up, or massaging moisturizer into his dry hands—all of it brings me joy. I learn little things can bring so much pleasure, like lying side-by-side, just watching TV together.

Finally, I learn that to give that kind of support, I first have to support myself. This experience is a lonely time in that I still can't share it with anyone else in my life, not even my closest friends. To make it through, I learn to be kinder and take better care of myself by doing the things that nurture my body and spirit. I wouldn't have made it through those challenging days if I hadn't made time to sleep well, eat healthy, and get some exercise. Most of the time, I didn't feel like doing any of these things, but I committed to do them anyway.

And while I feel stronger and more capable, this has been one hell of a terrifying experience. Michael and I came together just as I was crossing the threshold to a new life and a new identity. He may have been part of my past, but he was also the essence of my future; he was my new life. After decades of feeling unseen, Michael was the one who saw me—the real me. Nearly losing him was traumatic. If he'd been taken from me, I knew I would be alone for the rest of my life, even if I was with someone else. In order to push past the terror of that possibility, I simply put it away in a little box, to be dealt with later, when I felt strong enough.

In early December, five weeks after that terrifying night in Lucerne, Michael is released from the hospital. Every two days, he has follow-up appointments with the surgeon, so he moves back to his little apartment in Seefeld not far away. I continue to care for him, driving him to and from his appointments, handling his shopping, and generally making sure his needs are met.

The nurses even teach me to change his bandages. Up to that moment, the sight of blood made me very uncomfortable. But I manage to push through, changing his bandages twice a day, and I soon find myself approaching the task joyfully. Michael tries not to move as I work, though from time to time, I catch him grimacing. I can almost feel his pain in my own body.

On Christmas Eve, Michael finally flies home to Boston. He's missed his children terribly and they're thrilled to see him, too. Having their father sick and in the hospital so far away has been scary for them. Of course, I worry about him while he's gone, but I fly out to join him a week later and we welcome the New Year together, at home with his kids. As the clock strikes midnight, I make a wish for a calmer, healthier year ahead, though I know there is more intensity to come.

And it will come even sooner than I expect.

When I return from Boston after New Year's, the kids and I take a long weekend in Berlin to visit my brother, who lives there. At midnight on Friday, Michael calls.

"Michael, I've been waiting. Why didn't you call earlier?"

"I'm at the bottom of the stairs. I fell."

As he was walking down to the living room, his damaged right leg gave in. He's in a lot of pain. And he's scared he may have ruptured the quad tendon to the knee, part of which was removed during his critical surgery in Lucerne. He's worried about potentially needing further surgery to fix it. The thought of him going back into surgery, especially with a different surgeon, in a different country, terrifies me.

But first, Michael needs to get up from the floor and make his way to a hospital.

The matter is complicated by the presence of a massive Boston snowstorm and the fact no one is nearby who can help. I plead with him to call his ex-wife, to ask her to come and assist, but he refuses. I stay on the phone as he grabs the railing and slowly manages to pull himself up. Against my pleas and his own better judgment, Michael drives himself to the nearest hospital. By the time he has the test results, it's early morning in Berlin, though I haven't slept.

As we feared, the X-ray shows Michael's tendon is torn.

He walks out of the hospital on crutches, wearing a massive leg brace, from the hip to the ankle. He's forced to leave his car and Uber home (it's stunning he drove there in the first place!). Once again, he's lost his mobility and this time, I'm on the other side of the Atlantic.

I drum up another excuse and book a flight back to Boston. Until I get there, Michael's friend Daniel arrives to fill in. He handles the shopping and cooking, but more importantly, he's present for Michael.

When Michael goes to see an orthopedic surgeon, he accesses the X-rays and makes the same diagnosis—a torn tendon. But somehow, Michael can extend his leg and hold it, which baffles the doctor. The tendon might not be torn after all. Instead of more surgery, he prescribes physiotherapy, which comes as a huge relief. I spend a few days with him in Boston, and by the time I leave, Michael's physiotherapy is making an impact. He's getting more mobile all the time.

We're both ready to have a normal life with a little less drama.

CHAPTER 24

Uncaged

"The crowning fortune of a man is to be born
to some pursuit which finds him employment
and happiness, whether it be to make baskets, or
broadswords, or canals, or statues, or songs."
— Ralph Waldo Emerson

IN EARLY JANUARY, VIKTOR AND I will meet for the last time with the mediator to finalize our divorce. Until now, my focus has been on surviving the process with my sanity intact. I haven't had much bandwidth for planning my future post-divorce. But the fog is slowly lifting, and I feel excited when I think about what lies ahead. There's also considerable anxiety. *Will I be able to earn a living and support myself and the kids? What kind of skills do I bring to the table? What kinds of jobs can I apply for? Who will even hire me after all this time?*

The obvious solution is to go back into research and try to get a job with a think tank. The field is quite limited here in Zurich, but there's a well-known center for security studies attached to the ETH, Zurich's technical university. With my qualifications and previous experience, I'd make a good candidate and get a decent salary—a *Swiss* salary. I'd just need to brush up on all that's happened in the field in the past few years. I'm not terribly excited about the prospect; I'd much rather keep writing my book (which doesn't pay) or do something related to my new, chosen field.

As I think about what to do, I remember the research I did on becoming a divorce coach. Now, that's something that excites me. When I mention it to a friend, she suggests I speak with her neighbor, who's just completed training to become a life coach. The neighbor and I meet for coffee and my interest is piqued even further. There are sessions taking place in Zurich, she says, and sends me the link to the Co-Active Training Institute (CTI).

About ten years ago, a good friend—who happens to be a coach herself—finished her certification at CTI and was genuinely enthusiastic about it. Remembering her, I decide the training program is solid.

I click the link and discover there's a training coming up in February. I fill out the contact form for more information, and a reply comes within the hour. There are spots open and they'd love to have me! I am elated and energized, so I sign up. My intention is to check out the first module just to see if I'll like it; I'm exploring.

Exploring is not something I usually do. It's both strange and exciting.

Since I made the choice to end my marriage, this is the first time I'm making an important decision about what direction to follow, trusting and investing in myself. I'm not trying to please anyone or live up to others' expectations. I'm not following someone else's agenda about what's good for me. The idea, the decision—it's mine alone.

It's also *my* money. I don't have to ask permission or justify my choices. I don't have to convince myself I'm worth it. The alimony I receive is mine to use any way I see fit. And I choose to invest in my future.

This is another decision that pushes me outside my comfort zone to try something new. Besides, attending the training aligns with my desire for lifelong learning, which is why I feel so energized about it. I'm ready to learn and expand. I feel intensely curious, and I can't remember the last time I felt this way. I'm nervous but also hopeful.

The training takes place at the Swissôtel in Oerlikon, about twenty minutes north by train. When I arrive, I take the elevator to the top floor, where I find half a dozen people gathered, getting coffee and chatting. I walk up to a pair of women who seem nice. As a shy introvert, I find unstructured social interaction—or, in English, small talk—awkward, but as the new me, I push past the awkwardness and introduce myself. The women kindly point me toward the conference room where training will take place so I can grab a name tag and choose a seat.

The room is artificially lit. There are a few windows, but it's February in Zurich, so we still need light. Chairs are arranged in a circle with two seats for the trainers, or "leaders," at the top. I select a chair, a blank name tag, and a training booklet entitled *Co-Active Coaching Fundamentals.* Most of the participants are women, but there are five men—and the group is international. There are a few Swiss, but most are foreigners from other cities—Basel, Munich, Stuttgart. It's a relief not to be the token foreigner.

As we settle into our seats, the man and woman sitting at the top of the circle introduce themselves as our leaders for this training. I'm expecting the usual going-around-the-room introductions, but instead we're asked to stand, find a partner, and take turns for three minutes telling each other about our biggest dream in life. *Dream? I'm not sure I even have one.* I set my Starbucks matcha under my chair and reluctantly stand up. *Goodbye comfort zone.*

After the icebreaker exercise, I hardly have time to get settled into my seat again when we're asked to stand up once more. We're told to pair up and take turns coaching each other on a topic of our choosing—anything we're struggling with, a situation we feel stuck in or want to change. My eyes go wide. The whole exercise feels like culture shock to my meticulous, perfectionist side. *We've hardly learned anything about coaching yet. How can we pretend to be able to coach others?*

I quiet my thoughts and decide to trust the process. After all, the organizers did call it a "hands-on, interactive training," where we would "learn by doing."

Heading home after the first day of training, I feel excited and exhausted.

On the second day, we are presented with a list of the basic "coaching competencies," as CTI calls them. They include things like "acknowledging" our clients for who they are; "championing" (encouraging, cheering them on); asking "powerful questions" (open-ended questions that make them pause and reflect); and "blurting" (sharing our intuition). Lots of terms and concepts to put in my brand-new coaching toolbox. At the end of the session, we're asked to assess which of these coaching skills we already have and which ones we'd like to develop.

I realize, to my surprise, I already have some of the qualities that make a good coach. Listening is one of my strengths, as is empathy. I'm engaged and engaging, curious and interested in people. I like to cheer them on. These are skills I've always had on a personal level, in my relationships with friends and family; it never occurred to me they'd be useful in a professional setting.

One of the most surprising things I learn is intuition—listening to it and being able to express it—is a skill that can be developed through practice. I'm not used to taking intuition seriously, so I don't know quite how to access it. I learn it's important to be able "to tune into the body." I find this difficult because I'm very much "in my head." Becoming more attuned to physical sensations and learning to listen to my body as a valuable source of information opens up a whole new world. It will take several months for my intellectual self to be convinced, even though the research is unequivocal: the body is always first to react to a stimulus; cognitive realization only follows after a significant delay.

I learn to listen more to my gut, but expressing my intuition is another matter; it contradicts the part of me that wants to please and be accepted. Saying what I see may sometimes mean hurting someone's feelings. It will take the whole six-month training for me to internalize the fact I'm not serving my clients by trying to be diplomatic instead of telling them exactly what I see.

The initial training goes by in a flash, but it's a genuine eye-opener. I discover how much I enjoy coaching—and I seem to have a knack for it. And I learn to see myself more clearly through the eyes of others. After lunch on the last day of training, we're invited to give feedback to our fellow participants. We learn the qualities our colleagues see in us, what they'd like to see more of, and one archetype or character they feel fits us. We're told not to comment on this feedback; just take it in.

When my turn comes, the shy, quiet Katia is mortified, but the rest of me is intensely curious. I have no idea how others see me. As I listen, I'm too stunned to take notes. I hear the words, "confident," "calm," "capable," "stoic," and "positive." *Positive?*

My ex-husband, the eternal optimist, has always called me a "glass-half-empty" kind of person. And I have always argued it's realism, not pessimism, and simply inherent to my Greek heritage. Strange that other people see something different in me. When the male leader of our training tosses out the word "sensual" to describe me, my face flushes. I want to disappear, but I keep listening. My training cohort recognizes my inherent playfulness, another part of me I haven't fully identified with.

When it comes to the qualities they want to see more of from me, they're unanimous: they want to see the playful side, the part of me that enjoys life to the fullest. They all agree I'm holding back a lot and need to learn to let go.

Taking in their feedback, I'm reminded of something. Almost a decade ago, I decided vitality was one of my highest personal values. Vitality is about living life fully, enjoying the good things, experiencing joy. I haven't been honoring that value as I should.

The archetype the group chooses for me is surprising, too. It's Pippi Longstocking, the red-haired, freckled, playful, unconventional, and unpredictable nine-year-old character from the famous children's book by Astrid Lindgren. The training assistant writes down my archetype, and beside it adds the words: "naughty child" and "four-year-old." *Wow,* I think. When I was four years old and still living in Cameroon, adults commonly described me as "cheeky" and "naughty." Is it that forgotten four-year-old I see in photos from that time I'm being asked to revive?

Most of all, I'm surprised by how much I've enjoyed using the unflexed parts of me, the parts I hadn't considered particularly valuable from a professional point of view: my intuition, listening skills, empathy, and compassion. This is the first time in a professional setting these qualities are being recognized as assets. And the first time I've been called to use my heart rather than my mind.

Coaching uncovers something new—or rather, something I'd forgotten I have. I'm left in a state of awe. So, naturally, I sign up for the rest of the training modules—the whole six-month program.

CHAPTER 25

End of a Marriage

"Only love can heal the wounds of the past. However,
the intensity of our woundedness often leads to a
closing of the heart, making it impossible for us
to give or receive the love that is given to us."
— bell hooks, *All About Love*

ON A THURSDAY IN JANUARY, Viktor and I are summoned
to appear in front of a judge first thing in the morning. As I get the kids
fed and ready for school, I feel tense. Nicolas resists getting dressed and
finishing his breakfast. He's notoriously *not* a morning person, but today
my tolerance is low. It's crucial we get out the door on time so I can arrive
at the courthouse early, with time to get oriented. I can't afford to make
a bad impression with the judge. I'm on the verge of losing my patience,
but I remind myself to breathe deeply and stay calm. We get out on time.

Our mediator, an experienced lawyer in her sixties, will be accompa-
nying us today, since ours is a consensual divorce. When she arrives, she
must sense my nervousness because she kindly reassures me everything
will go well. Viktor and I greet each other formally, awkwardly, and sit
down in the waiting area.

A young man comes and asks us to follow him into another room. I've
never been in a courtroom before, so I'm expecting something like you'd

see in *Suits*, the American TV show. But it's just a normal room, with a long table and chairs. The judge sits across from us; Viktor and I sit on either side of our mediator. Our mediator must have done this hundreds of times because she seems confident and relaxed, yet respectful of the process.

The judge reads through our agreement line by line, paragraph by paragraph, asking a couple of clarifying questions here and there, never contesting or asking for additional documentation.

Finally, the judge asks if we both agree with everything laid out in the decree. We both say "yes," and are asked to sign.

Altogether, the process is entirely painless (at least this final part), and within the hour, we're divorced. Our marriage has ended.

On the steps of the courthouse, Viktor suggests we go for a coffee to seal the deal. I thank the mediator and follow Viktor to a small bakery that smells of fresh butter. We sit down across from each other in a booth. There's a basket of pastries on the table. I order a cappuccino and take a croissant from the basket. Viktor orders tea and a sandwich. Perfectly ordinary, except for the awkward silence. I can think of nothing I want to say to him right now. Apparently, neither can he. We've said so much to each other in the past two years that there's nothing left.

We've known each other for twenty-two years, nineteen of which we spent married. Yet, I feel like an introvert sitting across from a stranger.

"Now that it's all behind us," Viktor says, "maybe we can start over?"

I look at him, confused. "What do you mean, start over?"

"I know you were unhappy for a very long time. So, I was hoping that, now that you've gotten what you wanted, we could . . . try again. Maybe go on a date. Is that possible?" he says with a shy half-smile.

I look at my now ex-husband, not sure what he's saying. "What do you mean, now that I got what I wanted?"

Now I've asserted my independence? Become autonomous and separate from him? Now I'm making my own decisions? In Viktor's mind, those things were simply a solution to my unhappiness, as though divorce was yet another concession he made for me, to make me happy. I can't blame him; I've been holding him responsible for my happiness—or rather my *un*happiness—for the entirety of our relationship.

"That's a *very* expensive date," I joke. "I don't think it's a good idea."

Viktor seems surprised.

I just want to be free. Divorce has been a torturous, unpleasant, anxiety-filled process—and it's finally over. The only thing that still binds us to each other—and always will—is our children.

CHAPTER 26

Fulfillment

"Every living organism is fulfilled when it
follows the right path for its own nature."
— Marcus Aurelius, *Meditations*

MICHAEL AND I DECIDE THAT, after almost a year of us being
together, it's time to let our families know. Keeping our relationship under
wraps was hard. It wasn't a choice we made lightly; protecting our kids
was non-negotiable. Yet lately, the secrecy has started weighing on us. We
crave a life without secrets, where we can share our joy with those we love.

We choose a weekend in March when my kids are with me for the big
reveal. I invite Michael to a dinner with my brother and his family who
are visiting (Michalis and his wife are already in the loop). Petros knows,
of course, but I'm nervous about the other two. Will Margarita feel torn
between her dad and wanting the best for me? Will Nicolas remember
meeting Michael last summer?

My heart is pounding as we break the news. But with Michalis cracking
jokes and gently guiding the conversation, everyone seems to take it in
stride. A wave of relief washes over me. No more hiding; now we're building
something new, together.

The first weekend of April, I attend the second training module, which
has been given the lofty title, "Fulfillment." The word itself feels a bit empty

to me, maybe even cheesy. I half expect the weekend to be full of fluffy platitudes about leading "a meaningful life."

I arrive at the hotel and pick up a matcha at the Starbucks downstairs with five minutes to spare before training starts. There are a couple of new participants, but one of the leaders, a German woman named Victoria, was with us the last time. She and the other leader, Chris—he's new to me—have great chemistry, as though they're performing a dance. As they go back and forth introducing themselves and welcoming us, it all feels seamless and natural.

We go over what they call "the agreements"—aka "designing the alliance" in co-active speak. It's about confirming a set of ground rules.

"What do we need to make this a safe space for learning and growth for all of us?" Victoria asks. Everyone's feeling hesitant to speak up first, so she volunteers an answer.

"Rule number one: nobody gets to be wrong—or right." The principle of non-judgment.

"Confidentiality," someone says.

"Honest and direct feedback."

"Mutual support."

Chris adds the last agreement: "Beginner's mind. We're all the same here. We leave our expertise at the door."

I breathe a sigh of relief. I don't need to prove anything. I don't need to *do*; I just need to *be*.

The leaders explain fulfillment comes from leading a life aligned with our values and purpose, which they see as a radical, courageous act. *Sounds a little touchy-feely to me*, I think. *But go on.*

"Now," Chris says, "we're going to do a series of visualizations to help you get in touch with your life purpose."

I've never done a visualization, so I'm nervous about understanding what I'm supposed to do and whether I'll do it "right." Life purpose sounds like a huge, scary concept. *How do I even begin to talk about it, much less visualize it? Besides, isn't visualization a bit of a woo-woo thing to do?* (Later, I will learn this is my Saboteur speaking—the voice of my inner critic).

I take another deep breath. Only a few minutes ago, I agreed to leave my biases and preconceptions at the door. So, I give myself permission to be a beginner and close my eyes, listening to the sound of Chris's voice.

"You are getting into a rocket ship. You are on your way to an uninhabited planet. You can create this planet any way you want; you have the power to do that. When you land, what is it you're going to make happen? What's the impact you want to have?" Chris pauses so we can take notes. I jot down a few words: "home," "warmth," "connection—to myself and others," "belonging."

After a few minutes, Victoria speaks.

"Now, imagine that you're on a stage in front of a large group of people whom you're about to address. You will have thirty seconds to make an impact, to potentially transform their lives. What message will you share?"

I can't think of a message. What keeps coming up for me is I want to be that person at the front of the room. I want to inspire and lead others. This is so unlike me. I prefer to be in the background, to listen rather than speak. To support rather than lead.

I write in my notebook: "Inspire and lead through change. Not be the person in the back of the room anymore."

The final visualization is short.

"You have been given a billboard and can display any message you want on it," Chris says. "Thousands of people will see your message every day. What message do you choose?"

I think about Gandhi's words, "Be the change you wish to see in the world." And Nike's motto: "Just Do It." In my notebook, I write, "Just Be."

Afterward, we debrief our visualizations with a partner, then work on what the leaders call our "life purpose statements." Again, life purpose sounds a bit grand and, honestly, a little presumptuous. *I've never had a life purpose, much less made a* statement *about it,* I think. But I catch myself. *I'm doing it again. My biases and skepticism don't belong here; they're not part of the learning process. I'm here to explore new things.*

Even daring to think about a life purpose is powerful. I've never thought of my work in terms of what makes it meaningful or purposeful—how

I'm contributing to others, my community, or the world around me. But as I think it through, I notice a hunger for purpose and meaning within me. That hunger is what brought me to this training. It's a desire to give rather than achieve. That certainly puts things into perspective.

My head is already buzzing and it's not even lunch time.

After the break, we move on to values. In the past, the word "values" often put me on the defensive, since "we have very different values" was a constant refrain in my marriage. But if discovering life purpose was powerful, discovering values is transformative. I knew what they were, but I'd never taken the time to fully articulate my own.

Next, we talk about *resonance*.

"There's a feeling of wholeness, aliveness, and motivation that comes when our life is aligned with our sense of purpose and values," Victoria says. "Conversely, there's a sense of underlying *dissonance* when our values are not honored. We feel frustration, boredom, indifference, anger, or resignation."

A lightbulb goes off.

For the last several years, I've felt like everything was *off* somehow. I grew frustrated, angry, and resentful with my then husband and our life circumstances (living in a place that didn't feel like home to me), but the truth is I felt that way mostly because I had not been honoring *my own* core values.

In my notebook, I make a list of the core values I want to honor. Freedom, independence, integrity, kindness, and tolerance. *How did I manage to stray so far?*

It's eye-opening. Recognizing the underlying dissonance feels liberating. I am suddenly lighter. Everything makes more sense. I don't *lack* values; I just chose to lead a life that didn't reflect them. And it's no wonder, since I'd never consciously articulated them until now.

I'm not done. There are other values I want to honor in my life: vitality, daring, confidence, positivity.

When Victoria and Chris describe the Saboteur, I get it. It's a name for the voice of the inner critic—the self-judgment and limiting beliefs that hold us back. My Saboteur has always been particularly vocal. And it's kept me in my cage for most of my adult life.

Learning to recognize and give it a name is powerful. Making the Saboteur conscious allows me to disconnect from it, to see it as separate from my true essence. I know I'll never get rid of my inner critic (who does?), but simply recognizing it lowers the volume. And that brings me closer to the value of freedom I want to honor. It's like reaching out from the inside to open my own cage.

On Saturday evening, our homework is to coach a practice client. We're told to avoid coaching a friend, but I'm terrified of attempting this with a complete stranger. Besides, choosing a friend means there's less work in finding someone to practice with.

When I ask my friend Bianca if she'll be my guinea pig, she enthusiastically accepts. Bianca is bright and witty, and more importantly, a kind soul. She's also extremely creative and talented. Bianca's an expat, like me, originally from Verona, like Shakespeare's *Romeo and Juliet*. We met when our boys started kindergarten in the same class, and we instantly connected over our love of warm weather, good food, and our distaste for the restrictions that come with Swiss precision.

Bianca arrives and I make tea for us before we move up to my office for more privacy.

"What would you like to be coached on, Bianca?"

She sits up against the couch and looks straight into my eyes. "Katia, I love my children to death. I love taking care of them. I'm delighted to watch them grow." Bianca pauses, takes a sip of her tea. "But . . . how should I say this, there has to be *more*. I know it sounds terrible, but I can't just be a stay-at-home mom. I'll go insane!"

"What's important for you about this idea of *more*?" (This is a classic Fulfillment question I've just learned, used to help align the client with their values.)

Bianca shifts in her seat, uncrossing her legs, and crossing them again.

"Don't get me wrong," she says. "I have a lot of respect for all the moms out there. Raising kids is a tough job. At the same time, I feel like I have so much more to give, so much that's sitting inside me. And I crave adult conversation! I loved being a professional—being able to get out of the house, interact with real people, to feel like I was creating something."

"What would you love to be doing?" I ask. "What would energize you? What would bring you joy? Think big!"

As we brainstorm ideas, suddenly Bianca's eyes light up.

"I would love to start a blog!"

I get curious. "Wow! What would it be about?"

We brainstorm again, thinking about the topics Bianca finds exciting.

During training, they instructed us to be attentive beyond our clients' actual words. To try and sense their whole presence, including their body language. To take in how they sit, how they move, how fast or slowly they speak, whether their pace or tone of voice changes. As my friend talks about blogging, I notice a shift in her energy. She seems lighter, bubblier. Her eyes sparkle. She talks faster, gesturing with her hands in classic Italian fashion.

"These are all such great ideas. What will you do, Bianca?"

My friend commits to research different blogging platforms and how to get started. I'm excited for her and inspired by the energy we have created together. I understand what our trainers meant when they said the power of coaching is in the relationship—it's not what I do as a coach or what the client does on their own, it's what we make possible together.

Still, a small part of me remains skeptical. How can such a big shift really happen from only an hour of coaching (especially when I'm not technically a coach yet)? I'll need to learn to trust the process.

Two weeks later, I receive an email from Bianca with the subject, "IT'S LIVE!"

I open it to find a link to her new blog, where she writes about her adventures around Zurich, in search of the perfect cup of coffee. Bianca is Italian, after all. Her first post is already live, and she's set up social media accounts to go with the blog. From our session together I know she has the expertise to handle the technical aspects of her new platform. And I admire her courage to take on the challenge of creating content, something she hasn't done before.

As I read Bianca's post, I get goosebumps. All this energy and creativity has been brewing inside her, marinating, waiting to be activated. It's all there. My job was simply providing the safe space she needed to explore a new possibility.

The next day in training, as we debrief our coaching sessions with the group, I share my experience and how I learned small shifts can make a big difference, just by providing a safe space for something new to take root and blossom. Privately, I'm astonished by how rewarding the experience was, in a way that's completely new for me. I was able to make a direct impact on someone's life. In contrast to my previous work, where intellect, analytical ability, and subject matter expertise were what brought results (and ensured I got paid), the coaching exercise required only my presence, curiosity, and intuition. In fact, it's only by letting go of the need to be the expert and getting out of my head that I get results. For the first time, I accomplished something by leaning into my stated values, like service, learning, and growth.

A different shift happens when I go through what's called the "Process" module, the fourth in the co-active coaching training sequence. For a while afterward, the experience leaves me feeling like I've been run over by a bus—physically and emotionally. What I don't know yet is how transformational it will be.

Process coaching is all about shining a light on the client's internal experience. We use it when a client appears to be disconnected from their emotions, or what the coaching world calls being "flat." Process can also be used in situations where a client becomes too emotionally overwhelmed or stuck. The idea is for the coach to learn to fully and mindfully *be with* the client, exactly where they are in the moment, supporting them in simply slowing down and connecting to whatever is present—even when emotions are charged, messy, unpleasant, or scary. Process work is about the heart rather than the head; about feeling rather than thinking; experiencing rather than explaining. It's deep, powerful work.

This time, our sessions take place in a windowless conference room on the first floor—not very motivating, given the beautiful June weather outside. Like all the other trainings, this one is interactive and hands-on. Our leaders this time are both men and brilliant coaches. Enrique is Spanish and, true to his culture, lively, buoyant, and expressive. Robert seems grounded and measured—not unusual for a Brit—but his eyes are kind. Robert is also more assertive and in-your-face than I'm used to (or comfortable with). Even so, Enrique and Robert's different energies mesh well. I find their "dance" as leaders to be natural and fluid.

During our first demo coaching session led by Robert, he challenges his "client," a woman from the group, to quit a job she hates. She's shaken and bursts into tears. *I'm certainly not volunteering for any of these demos*, I think.

On the second day, I pair up with a fellow student for an exercise. One of us will be the coach and use the tools of process coaching to help the other connect with their emotions. As the client, we're asked to choose a topic that's solid and coachable—not too trivial, not too dramatic. Martin is German, from Hamburg, and he's been with us since the first module, flying in each time for the training. I can see a kind soul shining through his eyes, even if it's wrapped in Germanic awkwardness.

Martin takes the first turn as the client and I feel good about our session.

When it's my turn as the client, I tell Martin how my mother has often discouraged me from doing things, especially things that fall outside my comfort zone, and the impact it's had on me.

"Ever since I can remember, my mother has been the voice of caution in the family—and in my life. This created a certain dynamic between us. Every time a new endeavor was on the table for me—a big trip, a new boyfriend, a new business idea—my mom would play devil's advocate and list all the reasons why I shouldn't embrace it. She could make a persuasive case, including an exhaustive list of all potential risks and worst-case scenarios.

"Rationally, I understand it all came from her desire to protect me. But what it actually did was hold me ba—"

"You're in your head, Katia," Martin interrupts.

This is a classic coaching comment, and it gets on my nerves. *Of course,*

I'm in my head. I'm telling a story. I need to get the words out. I'm not sure how to get out of my head. What's that even like? I say none of this to Martin, of course. I'm far too polite.

"What's here now, Katia?" he asks. (Coach speak for "what are you feeling right now?")

"Well, whenever I would assert myself and go forward," I continue, "despite my mother's view that I shouldn't, she would tell me I was being selfish. So, because I was persistent and determined, I inevitably took on the role of 'the selfish one' in my family. At some point I got tired of fighting the label and decided to embrace it. But deep down, I felt I was less worthy because of it."

Martin interrupts me again, repeating his question. "What's here now, Katia?"

What's here, I think, *is I'm irritated by your question. And confused. Haven't I been describing perfectly well how I feel?*

Martin smiles and tells me he needs me to be *in* my emotions, not to talk *about* them.

"Close your eyes for me," he says. "What are you feeling in your body— right now?"

I close my eyes and take a deep breath. *I'm not good at this.* Trying to connect to my body's sensations has been the hardest part of this training for me. But to my surprise, the signals are loud and clear.

"I feel like there's this huge weight sitting on my chest. It's preventing me from breathing." As I say this, I feel my head getting warm and tears welling in my eyes. A massive wave of sorrow suddenly washes through me. "I feel sad," I say.

"Tell me about the sadness."

"It's crushing. Overpowering. It just sits here, on my chest. It says I'm not good enough. No matter what I do, I'll never be enough. My children, my partner; they have no idea who I really am. I've managed to fool everyone. If they knew, they'd leave me. If I were them, I'd leave me, too."

I'm not just talking about feelings of inadequacy, I'm living them, experiencing them. I'm feeling deep sorrow but also shock. It has never occurred to me in all these years that not only do I not love myself—I don't even like me. Tears are streaming down my face.

Martin looks at me with kind eyes. He's tearing up now, too. For several seconds, we say nothing. Then he speaks.

"What do you need to hear, Katia? What would you want your mother to tell you? Imagine you are her and speak as her." He leans forward to hear me through the heaving sobs.

"You are enough," I croak. "I love you. Just the way you are. Unconditionally."

"You *are* enough, Katia," he says softly. Then, Martin, the awkward German, asks shyly if I'd like a hug. I nod through my tears.

What began as an investigation into my relationship with my mother ends up being about my relationship with myself. I'm stunned by it, but it all makes sense.

I've learned through training I haven't been honoring my values, but I didn't realize the impact it had on how I view myself. I don't like the person I've become. I see myself through my ex-husband's eyes—as selfish and capricious, undeserving of love or trust. I've embraced those labels, too. Deep down, I've believed it was *who I am.*

Until I met Michael, there was no one to tell me otherwise. Still, even when he tries to convince me the person he sees is kind, loyal, and caring, I don't believe him. And I've been secretly terrified that one day he'll discover I'm not worth his love.

I'm lost in my own thoughts until the leaders call everyone back together.

On Sunday evening, I'm not myself. And I'm not very present for Michael either, though he doesn't mention it. He just gives me the space I need.

I spend the next week in a daze, trying to make sense of what happened. I talk to Michael and a couple of friends. One of my coaching friends tells me not feeling worthy is a common feeling, almost universal. I'm not sure that comforts me. The depth of the sadness I feel doesn't make sense.

But then it occurs to me, what I'm experiencing is grief. Grief for all the years I've felt my mother's love—and later Viktor's—was conditional.

And for my inability to love myself. Grief like this is *physical*, it goes deep into the body. At least I'm making progress in body awareness.

Thursday evening, the kids are with their dad, and Michael and I are having a drink together. Suddenly, I start to feel dizzy—*very* dizzy. The vertigo isn't new; it's been going on for a few months. But since all my medical checkups confirm I'm perfectly healthy, we attributed it to the stress of divorce. Maybe it was just a sign my body was releasing stress.

But when the vertigo hits me again that Thursday evening, it's ten times as bad as before. The room starts spinning and so does my stomach.

"I'll go lie in bed for a while," I tell Michael. "Hopefully, it will go away."

He offers to help me, but I tell him I'm fine, so he stays behind to clean up dinner.

Lying down only makes the spinning worse. Almost immediately, I have to make my way to the bathroom, clinging to the walls for support. Thankfully, I make it there before the vomiting starts—although it doesn't stop for a long time. I'm crouched on the bathroom floor, terrified, when Michael comes up to check on me.

"I'm taking you to the nearest emergency room." I don't argue.

When we arrive, a doctor puts an IV in my arm and administers something for the nausea. I take deep breaths and wait for it to take effect. Several tests are run, but all come back negative. There's nothing wrong with me, I'm told. So, I can go home. At least the meds are effective; my dizziness subsides.

Michael and I spend a calm weekend at home. He forces me to rest—no work, no errands. It's a few days before I make a connection between the intensity of this vertigo episode and what happened in the Process training module. My body is processing grief.

Slowly, things shift. As I go through the grief, it turns into insight, and insight into energy. I start to feel relief, lightness, acceptance, and release. It's like I've given myself permission to be kind to myself, to experience joy, to love who I am—without labels and without conditions. I feel calmer and more grounded. Maybe Michael is right when he tells me I'm not the selfish, unlovable person I've always thought I was.

Miraculously, my vertigo attacks stop.

For the final training module, the CTI leaders take us through a series of closing rituals. What was initially a group of strangers has somehow become so close. It feels weird we'll soon be saying goodbye to each other.

On Saturday evening, the night before our final day, we're told to prepare to stand in front of the group and tell the story of our journey as coaches, but from the *future*. We'll have ten minutes to talk about what brought us to coaching, what our coaching path has been so far, and what the future looks like for us—as if it's already occurred.

The kids are at their dad's for the weekend, so I give myself half an hour before bed to reflect and prepare some notes. I know in my soul this training has been transformative, but I struggle to articulate for myself the ways in which I've changed. So, how can I explain it to others?

As I think about the exercise, I alternate between excitement, frustration, and self-judgment. It's a battle between my wise Inner Leader and my army of Saboteurs. But I keep going, and soon, I'm truly moved by what I see unfolding.

Over the past six months, I've become more aware of what drives me—my thoughts and emotions, my patterns of behavior. I've also gotten better at noticing what holds me back—my self-sabotaging thoughts— seeing how they taint my experiences and disempower me. And for the first time in my life, I'm noticing the impact I have on others. My growth is shaping my interactions and my relationships for the better. Even the quality of my conversations has changed. I'm more present, more curious. I don't need to fix anyone or find solutions; I ask questions instead. I'm more comfortable with silence.

As I reflect, the visualizing-the-future part of the exercise becomes easier—and more exciting. Discovering coaching has allowed me to envision the possibility of a completely new career. A new identity. I'm learning I have the "soft skills," like empathy and listening, that I never thought could be valuable in a professional setting. Beyond feeling qualified, I feel compelled—as though I have a calling, a purpose. I feel passionate, driven by a desire to serve and make a difference. This passion empowers me and fuels the momentum to keep taking responsibility for my life and my own choices.

For the first time, I see new possibilities in place of prescribed paths. I know I can become an entrepreneur and create work of my own—fulfilling, meaningful work.

The next day, we are asked to push our chairs out of the way and line them against the wall of the conference room. Then, we're invited to form a circle. We will take turns sharing our stories from the center of the circle, while wrapped in a collective embrace.

"Who will go first?"

My heart is racing. I can't bring myself to raise my hand. Someone steps forward and begins. I'm so nervous I struggle to focus on what he's saying. Several others share their journeys before I finally volunteer. My palms are sweaty, and I feel the blood rushing to my head. It's one thing to daydream on my own and another to stand before a room full of people and talk about my dreams. My inner critic harps on about how silly my dream is and how ridiculous I look, but I ground myself and begin.

I tell the group how a series of coincidences inevitably led me here. How, after the first module, I was hooked. And how life-changing it was to discover my values and align with a purpose.

Then I talk about the shift.

"Process taught me that if my purpose is to help people change their lives, I have to change myself first. It challenged my core beliefs. It made me uncomfortable and sick, literally. Then, it transformed me. Transformation? Not such a fun process."

I hear laughter around the room. I look at my colleagues' faces and see them smiling and nodding. They know what I'm talking about. My hands are shaking a little less now.

"But transformation, however painful, has led me to a new beginning. A new sense of self."

My tribe is the globally mobile—other nomads, expat families, and expat partners. I work with them as they navigate big life transitions. I help them make moves and settle into new places, creating a home in the process. I support them when they decide to change careers or to reinvent themselves. I'm there when their relationships and marriages break down and they're far from home and family support."

As I close my talk, I feel emotional. *I made it.*

There's something else I'm particularly grateful for, though I don't mention it in my talk. It's how well Michael and I have fared through the past six months. Going through the program, I'd occasionally hear others talk about people who decided to end their relationships after this kind of training. Apparently, even one of our leaders did that. Self-development and transformation can be disruptive and scary to those who love you and fear losing the version of you they know. The uncertainty of a powerful transition can be stressful and disruptive.

Yet, Michael has been stable and supportive throughout. He never got jealous or possessive about the thought of me sharing intimate details of my life with complete strangers, many of whom were men. There was never so much as a hint of insecurity in him. He has faith in us—and in me. He's my secure base. He makes me feel safe, while at the same time pushing me to go out, show up, and explore. As I think of him, I feel overwhelmed with gratitude—and filled with hope.

CHAPTER 27

Glimpse of a New Life

"Character—the willingness to accept
responsibility for one's own life—is the
source from which self-respect springs."
— Joan Didion, *Vogue* 1961

ON A FRIDAY EVENING IN late June, we're sitting on the couch
in Michael's apartment in Seefeld. It's thirty degrees Celsius outside and
we've opened all the windows to let in the breeze. Michael is feeding me
perfect little crackers with Saint-André cheese—my favorite. I'm spending
the weekend at his place, which always feels like a weekend getaway despite
being so close to home. But this weekend, we're here to work: Michael
is moving in with the kids and me. We're packing up his few personal
belongings—kitchenware, clothing, toiletries.

"I was going to wait for your birthday to give you this," Michael says,
"but I've decided we need something to look forward to." He pulls a red
envelope out of his pocket and hands it to me.

"An early birthday card?" I ask.

"Just open it."

I tear open the envelope to find a card depicting a bright red wind-
flower against a pastel green background. Inside the card, Michael has
written a poem.

Balanis, beloved
Grenevan dryads
Descended from
'Men of the Oaks'
Queen of my heart.
Receive this
Shimmering shard
Of Grecian summer
Carry it always
*To lighten your way.**

At the bottom of the poem is an arrow pointing down.

"It's beautiful. Did you write it?"

He smiles, which I know means he did. I look back to the poem.

Balanis, the Ancient Greek word for acorn, the nut of the oaks. Men of the Oaks, does he mean the Greeks?

"What's the arrow pointing to?" I ask.

"The arrow is pointing to something else that I need to give you in order for you to better understand the meaning of the poem," Michael says cryptically. He reaches into his pocket again and takes out a small wooden orange box and hands it to me.

"Open it."

Inside the box is a bright yellow oval-shaped stone the size of my pinky nail, set on a platinum band, held together by four delicate prongs. The stone is framed by two finely crafted oak leaves.

"It's the most beautiful ring I've ever seen," I whisper, stunned.

"The oak leaves are a symbol of your home country. The stone is a yellow sapphire. It symbolizes the sun. And I know how much this Greek girl needs sun," he says, smiling. "I thought you needed something to remind you of Greek summers, to help you make it through the dark Zurich winters.

---

*   Michael Watkins, "Balanis" (2017).

"This is your ring of power!" he says enthusiastically, as if I'm a character in J. R. R. Tolkien's literary imagination. "You can charge it up in the sun!"

I turn the ring slowly between my thumb and index finger, watching as the evening light reflects in the sapphire's facets.

"I will carry it always to lighten my way."

Michael takes the ring from my hand and gently places it on my left ring finger. He looks me in the eyes.

"Will you marry me?"

My eyes well with tears.

"Of course, I'll marry you." I take Michael's face in my hands and kiss him.

"I'm sorry," he says. "I wanted it to be more romantic, but I really couldn't wait."

"And that's what makes it so romantic, silly."

We embrace, dreaming of our own "big fat Greek wedding," perhaps on an island with all our friends and family around us.

"How would you feel about getting married in a Greek church?" I ask.

"Of course, I would be okay with that. I'm agnostic, not an atheist!" Michael laughs. "I want all our children to be there."

"Mine will need some time to adjust to the idea of you before I can tell them that we're getting married."

We agree not to plan anything before next year.

"In sickness and in health," I say.

"We've done the 'in sickness' part already, haven't we?" he says, chuckling.

"Oh yeah." I sigh and snuggle into him. I feel safe, held.

Being with Michael is effortless, uncomplicated. I can be myself when I'm with him—playful and cheeky, strong-willed and temperamental, sensual, curious, flawed, and vulnerable. I don't have to tone it down or hide certain aspects.

"You got the short end of the stick," I tease. "I used to be much more docile and easygoing."

"I find the powerful you irresistible," Michael says, smiling. "So, bring it on!"

Being with Michael is *my* choice, not the prescribed or the "right" choice. And I make it, fully aware of the downsides (the age difference, the health complications), the obstacles to overcome (the physical distance), the potential disapproval of family and friends. I know my mother would have preferred I wait, be alone for a while after the divorce, evaluate my options, meet someone younger perhaps. But I met someone who makes me a better person (and I believe I do the same for him). I met someone who saw me for who I truly am. So, why wait?

A week later over Sunday brunch, I tell the kids that Michael will be moving in with us.

"He's only in Europe two weeks a month and a lot of that time he has to teach in Lausanne, so he won't be here all that much."

"Will he sleep in your bed?" This is my youngest son's immediate concern.

"I'm afraid so, my boy," I say, softly. "But only for part of the time."

"Where will his stuff go?" My daughter, ever the practical one. "Where will we put his furniture?"

"He won't be bringing much furniture. But he *is* bringing his electric guitar. I'm sure he wouldn't mind letting you try it." I know that will get her attention. Margarita has been begging us to let her switch from classical to electric guitar.

As we talk, Petros says little.

Even as I make the announcement, two conflicting voices rattle on inside me. One is critical and driven by guilt. *Will the children be okay having to share me with someone else? Will they feel abandoned by me? Will they reject me?* The other voice tells me I deserve to be happy. I've sacrificed enough.

Viktor and I have been separated for more than two years. And Michael and I have worked hard to make sure our children are protected as much as possible from the upheaval of our respective divorces. We've taken the time to allow them to adjust to the new reality.

Back when I was agonizing over whether to separate from Viktor, my therapist asked me what I wanted my children to learn from it. And

I realized I didn't want them to think my relationship with their father, what it had become, was the model of a happy marriage.

I come from a line of self-sacrificing women. My maternal grandmother selflessly placed everyone's needs above her own. My paternal grandmother, after losing a husband she didn't even love at a young age, decided never to remarry, never even to have another relationship so my father—already sixteen years old—wouldn't be hurt. My mother gave up her own education and career dreams to raise my brother and me.

Now, my choice is either to model the ideal of self-sacrifice or break the chain, claim my right to be happy, and give my children permission to seek the happiness they deserve for themselves. I think especially about my daughter and how much I want her to feel empowered and deserving. I trust watching me ask for what I need will not break my children but will set them free.

It's a January afternoon and the snow is at least thirty centimeters deep. I tighten my arm around Sean, my soon-to-be stepson, and my protection against wiping out. I'm wearing thigh-high purple stiletto boots, a conservative short white dress, and I'm carrying a bouquet of white roses. Michael's two other children, Chloe and Adam, are right behind us. Michael is parking the car.

I woke up this morning surprised my head was no longer pounding, my nose no longer congested from the cold Michael and I had for days. Maybe it's all the Theraflu I've ingested, but my body seems to be rallying for today.

Sean and I walk slowly, carefully up the icy steps to the entrance of Cambridge City Hall. I hate the cold. And I hate snow with a vengeance. But today, I barely notice the sharp breeze prickling against my exposed skin. We were supposed to be married yesterday but all public buildings were closed due to the snowstorm. Thankfully, we were able to reschedule and got the last available appointment for today.

Inside the main entrance, people are waiting for us—two of Michael's close friends from college, my dear friend Lori, and my host family from the Harvard years. Michael's friends flew down from Toronto, and Lori drove through the snowstorm from her home in Westport, Connecticut.

"Why rush?" my mother asked. "Can't you just stay together without getting married?"

But instead of feeling frivolous, irresponsible, or thoughtless, I feel grounded. My marriage to Michael is as intentional as it gets. I choose him—and he chooses me. I choose to spend the rest of my life with him. I choose to close all other doors. Yet, my choice is liberating. Michael and I make each other better. He doesn't try to force me into a mold of what's acceptable or desirable to him. He sees me, the essence of me. He honors and loves who I am. As I honor and love him. Our commitment isn't restrictive; I feel free and whole in our relationship.

Michael walks in the door, handsome in his dark gray suit, purple tie, and pocket square—to match my boots. He convinced me to buy them. We were shopping online for my dress and shoes, and they instantly caught my eye.

"They're so you," he said, "cheeky and playful. They'll go perfectly with your wedding dress."

When our eyes meet, Michael's face lights up. He does this thing sometimes where he just stands there, looking at me with the biggest smile on his face. The first few times he did it, I got annoyed, thinking he wasn't paying attention to what I was saying. Then, I realized he was just adoring me, savoring the moment. He's doing it now.

"Let's do this!" Michael says. He takes my hand as I wobble up the stairs to the State Room where the Justice of the Peace will officiate our nuptials.

There's delightful symbolism in getting married in Cambridge—the place where we first met, twenty-two years ago. But it's also the only place we *could* get married. Our romantic idea of a church wedding on a Greek island was crushed pretty quickly. For that dream to happen, we learned we'd need to get our respective divorce decrees translated into Greek and submitted to the Holy Archdiocese of Athens (the relevant Orthodox Church authority), so they could issue a Church-approved divorce certificate.

In order to tie the knot in Switzerland as a non-citizen, I would have to obtain a fresh copy of my forty-seven-year-old birth certificate from the authorities in Cameroon.

When I relayed the tangle of bureaucratic red tape to Michael, he had the solution.

"We can elope to Cambridge!" he said. "It will be romantic."

In a rather humorous twist, when Michael called Cambridge City Hall to ask about the requirements, he was told there were none. "Not even ID? Don't you need proof that we're not already married to other people?" he asked.

The civil servant was matter of fact. "If you shouldn't be getting married," she said, "that's your problem, not ours."

Our courthouse ceremony feels at once foreign and familiar. In Greece, marriage is a sacrament, all liturgy and Byzantine psalms. No one asks whether you *want* to marry; if you both show up, they assume you do. Here, I feel like a character in a Hollywood movie, complete with "I now pronounce you husband and wife," and "you may kiss the bride."

By the end, I can barely hold back my tears.

PART THREE

CHAPTER 28

Prepare for Launch

"Give a girl the right shoes, and she can conquer the world."
— Marilyn Monroe

JUST OVER A YEAR after our divorce becomes final, Viktor tells me he needs to reduce his child support payments. He has a new job in Germany—another well-paid C-level executive position—but says he can't afford the payments due to German tax laws. As if that has any impact on what's required to meet the children's needs. I remind Viktor he was recently relieved of alimony payments (since I married Michael) and ask him to honor our barely one-year-old divorce agreement. His response is to file a lawsuit against me.

I don't say a word to the children, of course. How would it make them feel?

I try to compartmentalize, to shelter us from the ugliness of continued domestic legal drama, though I don't always manage. I'm angry. Why should I be forced to waste hours of my life digging out and scanning bills, receipts, policies, and justifications for the kids' expenses?

The solo silver lining is my lawyer: she's brilliant, steadfast, and confident. Having her on my side gives me peace of mind.

Still, the tension, the anxiety, the anger—all that negative energy is taking a toll on my body, which is tensing for battle. Most days, I wake up with an aching neck and shoulders. Sometimes, even simple things, like turning my head or lifting an arm, are painful. My migraines return. Yoga and physiotherapy help, but only to a certain extent. I download an app and commit ten minutes every day to meditation. I don't notice a difference at first, but I keep going and, after a few months, I feel more grounded.

As much as I can, I turn my focus to the publication of my book.

After signing the contract, the publisher sent a detailed schedule with milestones and dates. I make the delivery deadline and, to my surprise, manage to stay on track with the schedule. I work closely with an editor to streamline and polish the manuscript and select the cover design. I post the designer's options to my Facebook page and ask friends to vote on their preference: a dark blue background with white letters and neon accents is the favorite. Elegant and simple.

When the team presents me with a twelve-month marketing plan for the book's promotion, it starts to feel real. Multiple times a day, I pinch myself. *Holy shit!* I think. *My dream is actually happening.* There will be a press release, interviews, podcasts, and launch parties—one for each edition of the book. I'll be in London in June for the UK edition, and New York City in September for the US launch.

The publisher negotiates a deal with a global relocation company who has agreed to co-sponsor my UK launch and do some joint promotion. We arrange a meeting with their CEO and our missions and philosophies—supporting worldwide expats on their journeys—align. The CEO writes the foreword to my book, and we produce a couple of articles together. I'm touched by and grateful for all the positive feedback the book receives.

Finally, the big day arrives.

On a Friday morning in mid-June, Michael, the kids, and I take a plane to London. Michael comments on the grin I'm wearing for most of the flight. My body is tingling. And why shouldn't it be? In many ways, this book is my fourth baby coming to life, and I have my other three and my love with me to share the moment. It doesn't get any better.

Like me, the kids are bouncy, restless. Nicolas has a thousand questions:

"How many people will be there? Will you give a speech? Will you talk about us?" I smile.

Margarita's hair is in two French braids. The boys are wearing white button-down shirts (Petros hates dressing up, so this is a big deal). I've taken them out of school. It was important to have them here with me on this day; I want them to witness me making my dream a reality. I want them to see what happens when you believe in something and work hard to achieve it. I want them to be proud of me.

We drop off our things at the Airbnb close to Covent Garden, and Michael and I change for the event before walking over to the venue. I had my hair done earlier this morning, too, and my dress and shoes are brand new. I wanted my clothing to complement the book, so I bought a dark blue sheath dress, softly tailored, and cut just above the knee. I smile as I put on the dazzling, neon pink suede stilettos I chose. When I saw them in the store, it was love at first sight, though I hesitated to buy them.

"Perhaps I should go for something more sensible," I said to Michael. "I want to be taken seriously. I don't want anyone to think I'm a flake."

"No one can possibly think you're a flake, darling," he said. "Get the damn shoes!"

The book party takes place at the Hospital Club, a seven-story brownstone that once held St. Paul's Hospital before it was restored at the beginning of the century. It's a members' club for creatives, musicians, filmmakers, designers, and writers whose aim is "to inspire diverse thinkers, makers, and doers through innovation and culture." Michael tells me the club was founded by Microsoft billionaire co-founder Paul Allen and Dave Stewart of Eurythmics. What a fitting place for a book launch.

We give our names at the entrance and head toward the elevator. I remove my ballerina flats and slide on the vertiginous pink stilettos. I touch up my lipstick and smile at my daughter's playful eye roll. When the doors open, I walk out first. I straighten my back, take a deep breath, and feel my lungs expand. *Show time.*

I love the vibe of this place. The furniture is a blend of colorful '70s vintage with modern touches. There are shiny aluminum panels on the walls instead of mirrors, grey crushed velvet armchairs, orange leather sofas, and retro hanging lights. We're greeted by two publicists and the director of the publishing house—our first in-person meeting. Everyone is smiling and friendly. They offer refreshments to the children. People start pouring in—guests from the relocation industry, some HR clients, and a couple of journalists. Two London-based friends I haven't seen in years turn up, too. It's Friday afternoon and everyone is feeling festive, relaxed.

Everyone except for me.

I'm nervous about speaking in front of all these people. I've rehearsed my talk so many times I know it by heart and still, my hands are shaking as I clutch my notecards. I excuse myself to the restroom to have a moment alone. I've read power-posing, adopting an expansive body posture, helps with confidence, so I stand tall in front of the mirror, planting my legs firmly on the ground, and opening my arms wide. I think about how far I've come—from the resentful, annoyed, languishing Katia of Vienna who felt trapped, to the confident woman of today who's reinvented her career and is about to tell the world how she did it. I take another deep breath and head back.

Multiple copies of my book are stacked on a side table and lined up on shelves along the wall. Two massive zebra-print armchairs take up the middle of the space. Behind them, there's a screen on which my book cover is projected. Left and right of the chairs are promotional posters.

I'm introduced to the room by the European CEO of the relocation company.

"As you will hear today, Katia's book fits perfectly with our philosophy, which is why we're delighted to be collaborating with her on this project," he says, casting a big smile in my direction. *Funny how I don't mind the word "project" now, in the context of my book*, I think.

His words are kind, respectful, and admiring. As he hands me the microphone, my heart is full. It's also pounding like crazy. My palms are still sweaty. My mouth is dry. I look at my children sitting in the front row and think, for them, I'd go through the whole struggle again if I had to. My hands are still shaking as I look at my first notecard and begin. I tell the story of how I came to write this book (I never get to the second card; I just hold them in my hands like a prop).

When I talk about how unhappy I was in Vienna, it suddenly occurs to me I haven't ever told my children this. I watch their faces closely. They seem surprised.

I discuss my mission, to support expats in their journeys, and my dream that the book will make a difference in their lives. The Q&A goes well. I feel confident and knowledgeable; this is my topic.

By the time my talk is finished, I feel awake and energized. I look over to Michael standing at the back of the room; his eyes are filled with adoration, and he has a big smile on his face.

"I'm proud of you," he mouths, as people come up to the stage to talk to me.

The week after the launch, the book receives a few really good reviews. But the highlight for me is it's chosen by the *Financial Times* (*holy crap!*) to be featured on their "*FT* Business Book of the Month" list—another major "pinch me" moment. Promoting the book takes over most of my time through the summer and into fall. I'm featured in interviews and podcasts, published in online magazines, and invited to be one of the keynote speakers at a major relocation industry conference.

Michael suggests I hire a company to help me with my digital marketing strategy. In our launch meeting, they ask all sorts of questions about my business: *Who's your target audience? What are your primary business goals (to sell books? to get coaching clients? to become a recognized expert in your field?)? Do you have a website?* It's a steep curve but I learn a ton in a short time—about market positioning, audience demographics, key brand messages, content strategy, and other fancy terms. Soon, I'm set up with a new website and a brand strategy.

I contact our tax advisor and ask him to guide me through the process of setting up a business in Switzerland. It's straightforward and my sole proprietorship is up and running in only a few days. I'm the daughter of an entrepreneur, yet it took me until my mid-forties to build something of my own. I think about how different it was for my father, who built his business from nothing. I have a tax advisor, marketing consultants, a publisher, and unlimited, publicly available resources on how to set up a business. Still, I know he would be proud.

True to my values, I want to learn everything I can. I sign up for courses on entrepreneurship, digital marketing, and money mindset. I read a lot. I get more and more comfortable with calling myself an entrepreneur. In fact, secretly, I feel kind of cool. More importantly, I'm learning and growing in the process. Most mornings I wake up with butterflies, the excitement and energy of creating something new rushing through my body. I want to share my message with the world, to help people like me and make a difference.

In July, Michael and I have our "Big Fat Greek Wedding Party" on Tinos, an island on the Aegean we've grown to love. We manage to gather eighty of our dearest friends and family from all different phases of our lives. Our children are there. My mother and cousins are there. People fly in from different parts of the world. We book a sweet little seaside boutique hotel just outside of Tinos. When we arrive, the owner welcomes us with a warm hug and a glass of *raki*, a Greek island spirit. The hotel is as spectacular as its photos; built as a collection of whitewashed sugar cube houses with pastel blue doors and window frames. Besides the ever-present white, the interiors are appointed in neutral shades of cream, ivory, and tan. The design is simple and tasteful, and the personnel treat us like celebrities.

Our party takes place over a three-day weekend, culminating in a special ceremony on Saturday evening. Michael and I may be married already, but we haven't given up our dream. We've asked our dear friends David and Lori to officiate a marriage ceremony they create especially for us.

On Saturday, shortly after 8:00 p.m., Michael and I stand on a large stone-paved terrace overlooking the bay and facing our friends, all dressed up and festive, gathered here to celebrate us. David and Lori and a few of our closest friends each say a few words about marriage, about each of us, and about how they know we belong together. I keep dabbing at my overly made-up eyes, trying to prevent all the makeup artist's work from going to waste.

Then, Michael and I take turns reading the vows we've written. Behind us, the Aegean shimmers in the evening sun, the light bathing us in shades of orange and pink.

"I love that you're no longer a graduate student," Michael says, "and that Harvard University's statute of limitations on fraternization has expired, so that I could marry you with a clear conscience."

Everyone bursts into laughter.

The party is wild. There's a lot of laughing and dancing and red and green shots of alcohol of undefined origin passed around. There are people thrown into the swimming pool—including the married couple. Even my oldest son is seen dancing (I've never seen him dance before!). The next day, many of our (hungover) guests tell us how wonderful our friends are and thank us for introducing them to our tribe.

It's three minutes to 6:00 p.m. and I'm about to go on stage to present my book. This is my second book launch event, this time in New York. The book came out in North America last week.

I feel glamorous. I always feel glamorous when I'm wearing stilettos—four-inch, animal print suede pumps, to be precise. I bought them the day before; they just called out to me. And good fortune! As I was walking down the street, I spotted a matching clutch—animal print with a red clasp—in the window of a vintage shop. But I digress.

I adjust my sleeveless little black dress, making sure my bra straps aren't visible. If someone had told me a year ago I'd be traveling to places like London and New York to talk about my book, I'd have laughed at them. My heart is racing, but my mouth isn't dry this time. There's no impending disaster here—it's my night.

I watch the audience take their seats in the common area of the coworking space, where my American publicist has booked the event.

An image of the book is projected on a white screen facing the audience. In one corner at the back of the room, there's a big round table with two stacks of my book and another holding agendas printed with the publisher's logo. The space is modern, even industrial, with wooden floors, big round steel pillars, and colorful tilework.

There are about twenty people in the audience. Some are friends, old and new, that live in New York or who have come in from near (Pennsylvania, Connecticut) and far (Montreal, Zurich). Others, I don't recognize, but we're all expats. Many seem to know each other. I reached out to my expat network ahead of the event and asked for their support to spread the word. Their response was immediate. My heart is full of gratitude for the kindness of this community. Everyone seems relaxed, comfortable, smiling as they take their seats. My publicist's idea to start with drinks and finger food seems to have worked perfectly. I glance at Michael, ready with phone in hand to record my speech. He has a wide grin on his face. My rock.

I fill my chest with air and walk to the middle of my "stage."

In London, I talked about myself. I told my story, how my personal struggles led me to discover my passion: helping other expats. In New York, I start with my audience. I describe their common struggles, their fears and emotions. I watch them sit up in their seats, some nodding in agreement. I talk about intention, conscious choice, and the difference between a victim mindset and a mindset of possibility. My fingertips are tingling, and my chest feels warm and light. When I eventually talk about myself, there's less of my story and more of my passion—my "why," my vision for the work I do.

The Q&A lasts nearly as long as my talk; the audience is engaged. The room is upbeat and curious, and everyone's questions and comments are honest, real. Afterward, as Michael and I walk back to our hotel in SoHo, I'm bouncing on my feet and talking up a storm, feeling a warm energy radiating through my whole body. My brain is exploding with inspiration and possibility, and my heart is filled with gratitude.

In the days following the New York event, I receive several lovely notes from people who'd attended, thanking me for the invitation and for their signed copy of the book. One email stands out: from Celia, a woman I met for the first time at the launch. She says she's reading the book now and loving it. She calls it "The Moving Bible."

> *I was reading Julia's story* [an expat partner who struggles to maintain her career while following her husband abroad] *in your book, and it made me think of my own journey. My partner, my family, not even my therapist could understand what I was going through—the struggle to adapt, to create home for our family, and to pursue a career at the same time. I was on my own.*

> *It's so comforting to know that someone gets it, Katia. Your chapter on expat partners blew my mind. It really helped me understand that I've been putting myself last all these years, and how unhealthy that is. It guided me to think through what I need to do, starting right away, to reconnect with my identity and build a future for myself.*

Reading Celia's letter, tears of gratitude fill my eyes. This was always my secret wish, my vision for the book: to help people feel seen and understood on the one hand, and to energize and encourage them to take responsibility for their lives on the other. As Celia continues reading the book, she sends several more messages. We discuss concepts and exchange experiences. She tells me how grateful she is I accompanied her through the reading of my book. I'm grateful myself for the gift of her feedback.

The fall is dedicated to book promotion—writing articles, getting interviewed for podcasts, and speaking at conferences and expat fairs. All the while, I continue to build my coaching business. A friend and fellow coach recommends I hire a business coach to guide me through the process. The investment stings but it makes me even more dedicated.

Sylvia, a former sales exec, is down to earth and spiritual at the same time. Working with her changes how I approach my work. She teaches me about marketing and selling—how to understand my ideal client, communicate a clear message, create my coaching offer, and close the deal. Beyond the mechanics, Sylvia believes mindset is at the foundation of success. I learn about maintaining positivity through daily rituals like affirmations, visualization, and gratitude journaling. These are all new habits I build into my life with delight. Every day I complete my new morning ritual and put a big red "X" on the calendar, I feel myself moving forward. And as I work on my mindset, I gradually start to build—or rather rebuild—my confidence. This work motivates me to read, listen, watch, and learn more about coaching.

Eventually, I find my own voice, just as I did with writing. I synthesize the many perspectives I find useful and incorporate them into my own coaching style.

CHAPTER 29

Tango

"Dance, when you're broken open.
Dance, if you've torn the bandage off.
Dance in the middle of the fighting.
Dance in your blood.
Dance when you're perfectly free."
— Rumi, "The Turn"

IN FEBRUARY, I HEAD TO A RESORT HOTEL on Lanzarote, one of the Canary Islands off the coast of southern Morocco. From the air, the island looks like a big, jagged piece of rock emerging from the sea. Cliffs and craters pepper the wild, dry landscape, colored in various shades of red, orange, and anthracite. In the taxi on the way to my hotel, the colors stand out even more starkly against a sea of white, flat-roofed houses. The combination of white walls and pastel-green and blue shutters reminds me of a Greek island. Except for all the palm trees.

The second I step out of the taxi I'm hit by the saltiness and tropical humidity. The sprawling resort is built on a hillside that slopes down to the sea, with its rooms, restaurants, and many swimming pools dispersed across different levels. I usually prefer smaller, more intimate hotels (not least because I lose my way easily), but this one makes up for its massive size in sheer luxuriousness. It's well cared for and stylishly decorated in warm tones and natural materials—stone, terracotta, and wood.

After getting settled into my room, I head back to the lobby where the concierge provides detailed instructions and a map through the maze. With it, I find my way up to the raised terrace where yoga classes take place. The platform stands high above a long stretch of white sand beach and gives the illusion we're floating over the brilliant turquoise water.

This yoga retreat was a last-minute thing. Michael and I felt we needed a break from the winter cold and, especially, from the stress of the past few months. We know someone who organizes retreats in beautiful places, and this one on Lanzarote coincided with our schedules, so we jumped at the opportunity. Michael will meet me here after a few days, once he finishes a teaching commitment.

I almost didn't get on the plane. I woke up this morning in severe pain, unable to turn my head. My neck was blocked again and even breathing was painful, as if all the muscles around my chest were tightly clenched. It felt like every muscle and tendon in my body was being pulled in all directions by invisible strings. Every move I make tenses the strings and sends shooting pain down my neck, shoulders, and lower back.

"I've never felt pain this intense before," I told Michael this morning. I was trying hard to keep my breathing as shallow as possible, to minimize the pain. "I don't think I can make it through the trip."

I thought I was done with this kind of pain. Once the stressful divorce process was over, I was sure my anxiety level would finally go down, that I'd be done fighting and arguing, that things would settle into a new normal. That hasn't happened yet.

"You *need* to go." Michael was insistent. "You need this retreat. I'm making you go."

I knew he was right. All my energy has been devoured in the latest legal battle with Viktor, and the Swiss legal system is moving at a glacial pace. *I need to just* be *for a change. No to-dos, no expectations; just take time for myself in peace and quiet.*

Standing on the terrace, a warm breeze embraces me. I breathe it in deep.

Several mats are lined along the wooden floor in rows of three. Three women are here already, chatting to each other. I approach and address the one who seems to be the yoga teacher.

"Hi, I'm Katia."

"Welcome, Katia. I'm Christina." Her accent is South African.

Christina is about my height, with piercing blue eyes accented by dark eyeliner, and a mane of unruly dark blond curls. Her body is the body of yoga teacher: slender but not skinny, with defined arms and legs.

"Thanks, Christina. I just wanted to let you know I may not be able to stay through the full class," I explain, ever the dutiful student. "I'm in a lot of pain today."

Christina looks at me with large compassionate eyes, as if she's known me for years.

"Honey, your body will tell you what you should do. Listen to it. There's nothing you *have* to do here. If all you can do is just sit on your mat and breathe, that's fine."

I have permission to just be. So, I sit down on my mat and breathe, waiting as everyone settles in.

"Place your right hand on your heart," Christina says in a soft voice. "Now, place your left hand over your right. Breathe into your heart."

I inhale deeply and hold it.

"Exhale into the base of your spine. Now, imagine a white light entering your body through the crown of your head and coming out through the base of your spine."

I can do this, I think, chuckling to myself. *As long as I don't have to move.* We sit this way for a while.

Next are sun salutations. I'm an advanced yogi, so I'm used to moving into and through the postures. But when it's time for the low plank—or *chaturanga* in Sanskrit—the pain in my shoulders brings me to a stop. I shift into the beginner version, placing my knees down and using my arms to lower my chest to the floor. I hold the posture and breathe. *I can do this.*

I try the transition into cobra pose, which requires me to press into the floor with my hands, straighten my arms, and arch my back while pushing out my chest. My lower back is on fire, so I place my knees on the mat and slowly curl my body over into child's pose, releasing and stretching the back muscles in the process. Christina notices and comes over, placing the palms of her hands on my lower back, pushing down to help me stretch even more deeply. The sensation brings welcome relief.

After class, despite its difficultly for me, I feel lighter than I've felt in months.

Early the next morning, I attend a second yoga class, and afterward, have a breakfast of green tea and poached eggs with Christina. We eat overlooking one of the smaller pools, surrounded by thriving palm trees. There's a little boy in yellow swim trunks at the shallow end of the pool. He's face down in the water and a man, probably his father, has the palm of his hand on the boy's belly, holding him up so he floats. He must be learning how to swim.

I tell Christina about meeting Viktor, about our family, our life together, our divorce and all the pain that goes with it. I tell her about my anger and my anxiety about the future. She's at least a decade younger than I am but exudes a deep, unpretentious wisdom that belies her age.

"Everyone is our teacher," she says. "Even the ones who hurt us the most." She pauses. "Especially the ones who hurt us the most. What's your ex-husband teaching you here? In what ways is he making you better, wiser?"

I know hardship leads to growth but being grateful for the one who's making me miserable? *Feels like a stretch*, I think. But I like the way she's framing it.

"He's teaching me how strong I am," I say. "And how determined. Especially when fighting for what I love, for what's important to me. And that I won't take anyone's bullshit."

Christina has a broad smile.

"You're a lioness, my friend. He'd better not mess with you." We laugh.

"But you also need to be kinder to yourself," she continues. "Take some distance, put things into perspective. Your body . . . it's sending you signals to slow down. Be gentle with it. When the pain comes, don't resist it. *Be* with it, listen, breathe into the pain, make the necessary adjustments.

You've got this. You don't have to constantly push yourself. You don't have to be on the go all the time. You don't have to do multiple *chaturangas* every day, all day. Allow yourself to soften. Allow your heart to open. Take time to breathe and recharge and take care of your body and soul. You're not weak if you do that; you're powerful and in control."

"I don't know how to thank you, Christina. This was exactly what I needed to hear."

"Nothing is permanent, sweetie. This too shall pass." She smiles again.

I look around us. We're the only ones on the terrace now except for the servers, who are setting up for lunch.

"Is therapy part of the package on this retreat?" I laugh. "If so, I'm getting a much better deal than I thought!"

Back in my room, I step out on the balcony and lie down in a bamboo lounge chair. Beyond the sprawling hotel facilities is an endless blue ocean. The midday sun shines straight down on the water so it seems to catch fire. I stare at the glittering surface a while, then close my eyes. My body, thirsty for sunshine and warmth after the Swiss winter, soaks it all in. I'm still in pain, but it's lessened. It no longer feels as if every part of my body is being pulled in different directions. I'm overcome with a wave of gratitude—for this beautiful place, for the opportunity to nurture my body and soul, and for the clarity I'm gaining. I'm used to talking about my issues with Viktor with the same people—Michael, my mom, my closest friends. I know their perspectives, and it's a relief to know they're on my side. Still, their perspectives are unchanging. Talking to Christina has been different, and that's refreshing.

After a while, I walk back inside, sit down at the desk, and open my journal. I write, remembering Christina's words.

I listen to my body and treat it with kindness.

I take care of myself.

I breathe deeply and fully.

I allow my heart to be open, unblocked by the anger, resentment, and negative energy that only makes me sick.

Everyone is my teacher. I look for the lesson in everything that happens to me. I look for how it makes me a kinder, better, wiser person.

Then, I continue with my own thoughts.

Viktor is teaching me that I'm more resilient than I thought, that I have reserves, even after having gone through this divorce. He's teaching me to compartmentalize, to focus on my goals, to stay positive no matter what. He's teaching me compassion—for others and for myself. He's teaching me perseverance, patience, and gratitude for all that I have in my life and for the person I've become.

By the third day of the retreat, I'm sore all over—my shoulders, my lower arms, and, *oh my God*, my hamstrings. During morning classes, the first forward bends of the day are agony. But I'm now able to make it through the sun salutations, and even manage to do a few real *chaturangas* without wincing.

Halfway through the practice, Christina asks us to go into a seated twist.

I sit still. I know from the previous two days my body will refuse this posture. The blockage in my chest and the pain in my neck are too intense. Christina walks toward me.

"I can't do this. It hurts too much." I look up at her plaintively from the mat.

"Just try. You're warmed up now. Just see how far you can go without pushing it."

This won't work, I think. But I nod to Christina.

Slowly, I cross my right leg over the left. To my surprise, I'm able to push my shoulders back a little more. My chest feels open enough. I turn to the right and hook my left elbow on the outside of my right thigh. I turn my gaze over my right shoulder, waiting for the familiar pain to shoot through me. It doesn't! As I breathe into my newfound range of motion, I imagine what it would be like to let go of my anger toward Viktor.

"Allow your heart to open." I hear Christina's voice and with my eyes closed, I visualize my heart opening to compassion and gratitude, instead of shutting down with resentment and pain. The tension in my muscles relaxes even more.

Yoga allows me to relate to my body, to be present with what's here in every moment—like this twist. I feel the impact on my mood, my mindset. I'm calmer, less irritable, and more centered. It helps that, for the first time in a while, I have time for a set of daily rituals. I meditate. I read affirmations. I take walks. I start a gratitude journal. I spend a lot of time alone in my room, sitting on my little balcony overlooking the alabaster sand and blue waves, reading or writing in my journal.

For a person who's always dreaded—and avoided at all costs—being alone, I am thankful for the gift of space and solitude.

I'm full of gratitude for the person I'm becoming. I respect and appreciate the work it took to get here. I feel empowered to make my own choices and lead my life with purpose, honoring my own values rather than what others expect of me. I'm taking back my power. I'm grateful for the relationship I have with my children, that I can be a secure base for them, that they can feel safe and nurtured with me, even if we don't always agree. I'm grateful to have a partner who loves me unconditionally, shares my values, and supports me with such enthusiasm.

I want to hold on to this energy, to take it home with me. I'll have to keep reminding myself when I get overwhelmed, it's a sign I need to slow down. I'll still be able to take care of my loved ones, but I'll do it in a more sustainable way, aligned with my energy and my own needs.

On my fourth morning in Lanzarote, Michael arrives. I see him from across the hotel lobby, stepping out of the taxi, and I run toward him, throwing my arms around him.

"You'll never guess!" I say, before he can even speak.

Michael looks disoriented. He didn't see me coming.

"What happened?"

"I'm no longer in pain! Isn't that awesome?"

"My love, that's wonderful!"

"I can do twists and sun salutations and back bends . . . isn't that just the best?"

The pain doesn't come back. My heart is calmer, more peaceful—and I'm blown away by the connection between my mind and body.

"You've come a long way, my love," Michael says. We're out on the balcony now, enjoying the evening sun before we head out to dinner, just the two of us. We need some time to connect and catch up.

"You've worked hard to get here, to be the woman you are today."

"You were a big part of this," I say. "You saw me, the real me—as a parent, a professional, a partner, a woman—and that made all the difference. I've been able to reclaim the identity I'd lost for so many years, to rebuild it. I've shed my victim mindset. I've taken charge of my life. And now I'm learning to let go of whatever resentment is still there, to gain perspective, to keep moving forward. I don't know that I would have done all that without you."

"It's all you. It was all there already," Michael says, smiling. "I only helped a little bit on the margin."

"We could argue about this for hours," I joke.

"Do you think your experience could help others in similar situations? Would you be willing to share it?" he asks.

"You mean write about it?"

"Yes. Write your story and show how you regained your identity. How you got out of the 'expat cage,'" he says, referring to an article I published about how expat partners often give away their power voluntarily. I wrote it while still in the expat cage myself and it seemed to hit a nerve.

"A memoir?"

"Yes, a memoir," he says.

Over dinner, we brainstorm an outline for the book. I make notes on my phone. I love how our creativity explodes when we're away from home, both relaxed and calm, no lengthy to-do lists to complete. Whether we talk about my work or his, we are full of ideas; we dream; we set goals and make plans; we see new opportunities, new possibilities. We interrupt each other, complete each other's sentences, feed off each other's ideas. It's like a tango—a powerful, intense, passionate, graceful dance.

A dance I've never had with anyone until Michael.

CHAPTER 30

Mérite D'être Célébré*

"J'ai été prisonnière de moi-même toute ma vie."†
— Brigitte Bardot

MY FATHER PASSED AWAY more than a decade ago and I have missed him every day since.

Whenever I'm struggling, I try to think of what he would have done in my position. I imagine how different things would be if he were still here to have my back. After all, he was my fiercest defender. And now, after things have been going so well—I've found love and purpose and a new, deeper sense of identity—I wish he were here to share in it.

I think of how incredibly proud he would be of his grandchildren. I talk about him often to Nicolas, who never met him but who reminds me most of my dad. I want to ensure all my children know about their grandfather and remember him.

Thinking of his absence from my children's lives brings to mind the period of his absence in my own. It's difficult to remember what I felt about it at the time; I was so young. So, I ask my mother about it on one of our regular morning calls.

---

* Worth celebrating.
† I've been a prisoner of myself my whole life.

"Do you remember how I felt about being so far from Babás after we moved away from Douala?"

"What makes you ask that?" she asks, surprise in her voice.

"I've just been thinking about it. Wondering."

She's silent for a moment.

"You were so *good*. You never complained," she says. "But then again, I made sure you and your brother were embraced. You were surrounded by so many people and so much love. We didn't let you miss him."

My chest tightens at her words. An image flashes through my mind: four-year-old me, suffocating in this tight embrace. She's right. We had a busy house with a lot of family and friends around. Some would come and stay for weeks at a time. We were never alone with our feelings for even a moment.

When we hang up, I call my aunt and ask her the same.

"You were such a happy camper," she says, without hesitation.

"But didn't I ever ask for Babás? Didn't I ask to talk to him at least?"

"Nope." She says it with conviction. "That's how these things work. Out of sight, out of mind."

Her words sting. I feel the blood rushing to my face. *Did I really not miss my own father?*

I want to tell her I did miss him, very much, but no words come. I make an excuse to hang up, and afterward, burst into sobs. A deep sadness washes over me that lasts for several weeks. It comes and goes like a wave, without warning or logic, without explanation. I drag myself out of bed in the mornings. My limbs feel heavy. My heart feels heavy. On most days, I force myself to eat so my children won't worry. But every time I see food, my throat feels constricted and my stomach knots. I spend my days holding back tears until I have a moment alone. Then, I lock myself in the bathroom and cry.

"Of course you missed your father," my therapist says. "Your father was the center of your universe and suddenly he wasn't there anymore. It's possible you experienced this as abandonment."

"Then why don't I remember feeling sad or homesick for him?" I ask.

"Maybe it was all too much. Abandonment is one of the scariest experiences a child can have. It feels like you're going to die. That emotion may have been so painful that you shut it down, pushed it out of your awareness."

I think about my clients. When they're feeling overwhelmed, I point out how many transitions they are going through at the same time, like moving to a new country and starting a new job, or getting a divorce and moving out of their home. For most, this comes as a revelation.

I think about my own transitions. At the age of four, I lost the only home I'd known and was moved to a new country, forced to experience a completely new culture and new way of life. As this was happening, I lost one of the two most important people in my life.

I was alone.

"What you're experiencing is grief," my therapist says. Grief. Such a small word, yet it covers so much ground.

"But it's been forty-four years! Isn't there a statute of limitations for grief?" I'm still trying to make sense of this in my head.

"You didn't get to grieve when you were separated from your father, so you're grieving now." She says it as if it's the most logical thing in the world.

I lean back in my chair and cross my arms over my chest. I can feel my brow furrowing.

"Of course you're grieving, Katia. The four-year-old you *had* to be devastated when you were suddenly separated from your father. Perhaps you also felt that you weren't allowed to express what you were experiencing. Maybe you thought that if you missed your dad or felt sad, you'd hurt your mother's feelings or those of all the well-meaning adults around you.

"How did your family respond to negative emotions?"

I'm not sure.

"Perhaps you thought that if you were 'good' and didn't cause any trouble, your father would come back. *Good* kids don't ask for things," she says. "What matters is that you still carry unprocessed grief."

I close the Zoom call with my therapist and open a new tab on my web browser and search: "effects of parent-child separation." No surprise: there are tens of thousands of results.

An article from *Psychology Today* catches my attention with its sub-title: "The child has lost its lifeline, and often its sense of self." Is this what happened to me?

I read on. "Studies have shown that if a child suddenly loses a parent, either through death, abandonment, or a prolonged separation, the child experiences intense fear, panic, grief (a combination of sadness and loss), depression, helplessness, and hopelessness."* My therapist was right. I *must* have felt at least some of these emotions. I *must* have been in distress.

There's more: "Children actually blame themselves for a parent's disappearance. The child naturally concludes: 'I must have done something wrong, otherwise my parent wouldn't have left. I must be bad.'"

Wow, I think.

My muscles tense and heat rushes through my body. I want to take that confused, scared four-year-old girl in my arms and tell her it's not her fault her father isn't there. I feel a lump in my throat. My chest tightens again.

I read on. "Other studies show that if a child is separated from a parent, eventually they can also react with detachment, indifference, or even anger towards the parent who 'abandoned' them." There are negative impacts in their lives as adults, especially in relationships, how secure they feel, and their ability to trust others.

Until this moment, it had never occurred to me I might have abandonment issues.

My mind may have blocked painful memories, but my body remembers. My grief is physical. It shows up as a weight on my chest, constriction in my throat, and my stomach in knots. It shows up as extreme vertigo, forcing me to cling to physical walls for some sense of internal equanimity. It shows up as debilitating back pain and a lack of desire for food, as though my grief were more powerful than the body's impulse for survival, for life.

I know by the way Michael looks at me that he worries. He notices I've lost weight, which always makes him uneasy. He knows my patterns. So,

---

* Meri Wallace, "The Effect of Separating Children From Their Parents," *Psychology Today*, June 15, 2018.

when the children are with their dad, he takes me out to dinner to my favorite restaurants, buys me ice cream, and big buckets of popcorn at the movies. He helps me put together the pieces of my puzzle.

Michael and I are clearing the dishes after dinner.

"So, that's what my mother and aunt meant when they said that I was 'good.'" I've been mulling over their words for days. "I wasn't sad. I didn't complain. And then I took it to the next level. I became 'good' at everything. I was well behaved, I was the best in class, I tried to please everyone. I was the Good Girl."

I got used to playing the role. I internalized it, and at times, even rebelled from it. But the Good Girl is who I *became*. It's not who I really *am*.

"It was a survival strategy, my love," Michael says. "Who knows what went through your little head? Maybe, like the studies say, you thought it was your fault that your father didn't follow you to Greece. Maybe you thought that if you were really good at everything, he would come back sooner."

"And somehow even that wasn't enough," I say. "I was also the 'selfish' one. Never self-sacrificing enough."

Michael takes me in his arms.

"I always thought I had a normal childhood," I whisper. It's a lot to take in.

Over the next few weeks, the emotions come over me in waves. They show up during my morning meditation, in the middle of yoga class, or when I'm making dinner. They start in my stomach, then climb up to my chest and throat. When the tears flow, there's nothing I can do to stop them—not that I want to.

Several weeks later, something finally shifts. The heaviness gives way to a sort of release. All cried out, less weighed down, I'm ready to look at my life, my past. Michael is my sounding board. He helps me understand and, through his unconditional love and support, accept what I discover.

Michael and I are at a table in one of my dad's favorite cafés on the Avenue des Champs Elysées in Paris, sipping Kir Royal, a French cocktail of champagne and *crème de cassis* (blackcurrant liqueur). It's a warm fall evening—Parisian Indian summer. The last rays of sunlight make the bright red liquid in our champagne flutes sparkle. I take a sip and let the smooth, syrupy fluid slide down my throat, feeling the bubbles tickle.

It was Michael's idea to come to Paris.

"It could be a sort of pilgrimage to your father. Wasn't Paris his favorite city in the world?"

With the October holiday coming up and the kids due to be with their dad for a week, it sounded feasible. And, given the emotional roller-coaster of the past few weeks, I was drawn to the idea. Such a pilgrimage might be cathartic.

We took the TGV—the French high-speed train—from Zurich (it's only a four-hour ride), and Michael booked a stylish boutique hotel in the Marais district, the old Jewish quarter, now full of trendy restaurants, cafés, and shops.

After we get settled into the hotel, Michael looks at me. "I want you to take me to all of your dad's favorite places."

We take the metro to Etoile and walk toward the Avenue des Champs Elysées. My parents, but especially my dad, spent a lot of time in this part of town. The little studio he owned and cherished was here—his jewel. He felt at home in Paris. Selling the studio a month ago wasn't an easy decision. But we didn't make enough use of it to justify the high fixed costs. Still, it felt like severing a bond.

We walk in the direction of Place de la Concorde. I show Michael the pizza restaurant where Babás liked to have dinner. We go past the Monoprix supermarket where he shopped and the movie theater where he passed time on lonely afternoons.

My father knew where to go for a good lamb fillet, *à volonté* (all you can eat). He knew the best bakery for croissants and *pains au chocolat*, or the high-end *traiteur*, where, on special occasions, he treated himself to foie gras and obscenely expensive smoked salmon. My father was unapologetic about his expensive tastes; he'd earned the right to them, he said. And he prided himself on having transmitted those tastes to his children. Even as a young child, I knew which brands of champagne were worthy of a proper celebration.

As we explore my father's old haunts, it occurs to me most of the times he was in Paris, he was there alone. That fact didn't seem to bother him; in fact, he sought it out. How different we were in that respect.

"All my life, I hated being alone," I say to Michael. "It made me miserable. I wouldn't know what to do with myself."

I think back to my first days at Cambridge, the lonely weekends I spent walking around the city, browsing bookstores for hours, sitting in cafés by myself, just so I could be near other people. My mind skips forward to the first few months after moving to Paris with Viktor, when he traveled nonstop for work. The incredibly long weeks I endured while he was away. My shoulders tense just remembering.

I tell Michael I've been reading about abandonment.

"Apparently, people with childhood abandonment issues have lower self-confidence, feel jealous more often, have a harder time trusting others, and a harder time being alone when a relationship ends. They just grab on to the next one quickly, even if it's the wrong relationship."

"Do you feel that applies to you?" Michael's face is sincere.

"For sure. I put so much energy into avoiding solitude. I went from one relationship to the next. I always had a backup plan, a waitlist of potential candidates in case things fell apart."

"Perhaps you anticipated the abandonment, so you prepared for it," he says and pauses for a moment. "You did what you needed to do to survive, my love. You were trying to fill the void your father left."

"But isn't it ironic that I married men who constantly leave?"

"Maybe that's what's familiar to you. There's comfort in familiarity."

Michael knows me; he knows my patterns. But being this vulnerable makes me worry he might judge me, like I've judged myself for years. For most of my adult life, I've carried the labels given to me—by my family, by Viktor—without question. I was my father's daughter: flirty, frivolous, fickle, selfish. I took those words as a description of my nature, even when they didn't feel good or right. Now, Michael tells me I'm giving, not selfish; loyal, not fickle. My coping mechanisms were never my true essence. I want to believe that.

Michael gives me an opening, an invitation to live in the light, to change the narrative. I want to take it with every ounce of my being—to lead a life of integrity and openness, with him. So, for a moment, I forget about my fears. I share all my stories with him, the ones I had kept to myself until now because they might make me look bad, untrustworthy, or unfaithful. I empty the closet of all its skeletons. I do it because I trust in Michael's love for who I am, not for what I've done. The more I share, the lighter I feel.

"That's not who I am anymore."

"That's not who you are, period," Michael says. "You were never that person, Katia. That was not your essence; that was survival. Deep down, you're still that little girl who's worthy of being adored, unconditionally." The way my father adored me.

We spend four days in Paris, talking like this. And I continue piecing together a deeper understanding of my life.

From a young age, I began disconnecting with the parts of me, especially the difficult emotions, that didn't comply with the image of the "good girl," someone lovable and worthy. Becoming "good" meant abandoning the playful, wilder, freer parts of myself. Being "good" became a cage, a prison built of others' expectations and opinions. But I closed and locked the door with my own false beliefs about myself. Now I understand where my secret urge to rebel, provoke, and deviate came from. Getting a tattoo at thirty-six, wearing a dragon ring to a formal work dinner, taking pole dancing classes—my wild side needed a voice. She would not be restricted or controlled, not even by me.

Slowly, I'm reconnecting with the Katia who was left behind. She's both new and familiar. There's a picture in an old photo album of me at four years old, sitting on the floor at my aunt's home in Cameroon, pretending to talk on the phone, a naughty smirk on my face. I remember looking at that picture when I was older and hearing my mother remark, "what a character."

"You had to get your way," she said. "Just like your father."

But when I think back to that photo, it isn't defiance on my face I see, but spiritedness. I see a bold, sparkling, fiery, and fearless little girl—playful and curious, not unlike my own daughter. And those qualities were never "bad" or difficult, but simply true—intrinsic to my soul's essence.

I think my father would agree.

EPILOGUE

Letter to a Little Girl

DEAREST,

I'm sorry it took me so long to write. You see, for the longest time, I had no idea how you felt. I didn't know I could help.

But now I see you, little girl. I hear you. I get you. I get how scared you must have felt—that the people you love would disappear from your life, again. And that you'd end up alone, again. But scared is not who you are. Your fear doesn't define you—even as it takes over your little soul and grows roots in your body for years to come. You're so much more.

You're a force of nature, little girl. You're vibrant and you're playful and even cheeky sometimes. You like to break the rules, but only a little bit, to test the waters. And you're a force of love. Limitless, abundant, overwhelming love. It flows from you, through you, and out to "your" people. It wraps itself around them gently, protectively, a soft but impenetrable shield. You were born radiant, little one, and you're unstoppable.

Except when you stop yourself.

Because you see, my love, you learned early on to put limits and constraints and "containers" around who you are, only allowing part of you to come out. The "good" part. You were still a child when you were told not to shine too brightly because it hurt others. Growing up, you were

257

told again and again to "tone it down," "keep it down," by people you loved and whom you knew—you thought—loved you. *They must mean well*, you assumed.

So that's what you did. You tried not to take up too much space—with your voice, or your needs. You worked hard to fit yourself into all those boxes you were checking, triumphantly, one after the other, not once pausing to ask yourself what *you* truly want (did anyone ask you?), or what your heart desires.

In fact, that's another thing you stopped doing early: allowing yourself to desire (truly desire, with your whole being, body, and soul), because when you did, you were censored, shut down. So, you stopped desiring. And you put all your focus into being perfect, flawless, successful, so at the end of the day, you would be loved.

When you deviated from that perfection, because for a moment you succumbed to the need to feel free, you beat yourself up with such cruelty. You felt like the worst, least kind, most unlovable person in the world. The kind of person that deserved to be left alone for the rest of her life.

Listen. I get all that. I get you're scared. Being alone is a scary thing when you're little. I understand why you felt like you had to work hard to make sure that didn't happen. And I'm here to tell you don't need to work that hard anymore. You can rest now.

You don't need to be high-functioning and on top of things to be loved, because you are worthy of being loved just for who you are. Just as you love your children—unconditionally. It's your birthright to be loved.

So, you can let go now, my love. I got you.

It's ok. You'll be ok. I won't let anything happen to us.

Acknowledgments

WHEN I STARTED WRITING THIS BOOK, I knew that a memoir is not just about what happened; it's also (mostly, in fact) about the person you've become through it all—your personal transformation. What I didn't know is that the transformation doesn't end there; the process of writing a memoir *itself* is transformative, shaping who you're becoming along the way. You're documenting events, but in the background, you're also going on a journey of relentless self-discovery—more intense than any therapy session you've ever encountered. When my book coach warned me about that, I thought she was exaggerating. I quickly found out she wasn't.

Each memory unearthed brought a deeper understanding of myself—the grievances I was holding on to, the patterns that held me back, the glimmers of a bolder future I hadn't allowed myself to see, and the healing I still needed to do. It was at times extremely uncomfortable, always revealing, and ultimately, a profound act of homecoming, a reclamation of the self beneath all these layers.

I was not alone on this path. I am immensely grateful to the incredible humans who supported, challenged, and cheered me on, helping shape not only this book, but the person I became in the process.

To Caroline, my steadfast book coach, thank you for guiding me through every step of the writing process, teaching me the craft, and helping me manage my energy and expectations at each stage. Working with you was such a growth experience.

To Julie, my brilliant editor, your impact extends far beyond words (pun intended!). Thank you for seeing me, for seeing the soul of this book and for helping me give it the voice it deserved, with precision and kindness. I couldn't have done it without you, and I don't say this lightly.

To my wonderful coaches, Amel, Sanae, and Mirjam, I feel so fortunate to have you in my life. Thank you for sharing your gifts, believing in me, and being my champions, especially through challenging times.

To empress Lizi, your wisdom during those fluid moments of transformation remains a guiding light. I cherish your friendship deeply.

To Jess and Naren at Amplify, thank you for seeing the potential in *Uncaged* and for welcoming me to your author family. To Jenna, Sabrina, and the entire Amplify team, it's a joy to work with you and to know my work is in such capable hands.

To my Uncaged Retreat pioneers, thank you for sharing your journeys with me. Your courage, encouragement, and input have been invaluable.

To my clients, you inspired me to write this book, and I hope it fuels your own journeys. It's a privilege to be part of your journeys and witness as you take the leap and reclaim your dreams.

To my mother, thank you for instilling in me the strength and trust in my own abilities, and for tirelessly supporting me, wherever I was in the world.

To my beautiful children, your unconditional love and support fuel my spirit. Thank you for inspiring, challenging, and teaching me every single day. You are the best part of my life's work.

To Michael, my eternal companion, my best friend, my champion. Thank you for seeing me before I could even see myself and embracing and celebrating all parts of me, the light and the shadow. You are my home, always.

And to you, my reader, I hope that, if you're not on your way already, this book will inspire you to embark on your own reinvention journey, questioning your narratives, reclaiming your truest self, and uncovering the truths that might just set you free.

About the Author

KATIA VLACHOS is a reinvention coach, author, and speaker, committed to helping individuals navigate life transitions and break free from social conditioning. With a master's from the Harvard Kennedy School and a PhD from the RAND Graduate School, Katia began her career as a policy analyst. Her own reinvention journey led to the publication of *A Great Move: Surviving and Thriving in Your Expat Assignment*, recognized as a *Financial Times* Business Book of the Month (June 2018). Featured in the *New York Times*, *Harvard Business Review*, and more, Katia's insights on overcoming limitations, embracing bold choices, and reclaiming one's authentic self have resonated on stages and podcasts worldwide. Whether through her writing, transformative retreats, or one-on-one coaching, she empowers women to chart their own ambitious course toward a more fulfilling, uncaged life. Katia lives in Zurich, Switzerland, with her family.